Learn to Write DAX
A Practical Guide to Learning Power Pivot for Excel and Power BI

by
Matt Allington

Holy Macro! Books
PO Box 541731
Merritt Island, FL 32953

Learn to Write DAX

Author: Matt Allington

Layout: Jill Bee

Copyediting: Kitty Wilson

Cover Design: Madeline Allington & Shannon Mattiza

Indexing: Nellie Jay

Published by: Holy Macro! Books, PO Box 541731, Merritt Island FL 32953, USA

Distributed by: Independent Publishers Group, Chicago, IL

First Printing: November, 2015. Printed in USA at Hess Print Solutions

ISBN: 978-1-61547-041-9 Print, 978-1-61547-231-4 PDF, 978-1-61547-354-0 ePub, 978-1-61547-131-7 Mobi

LCCN: 2015940635

Table of Contents

1: Concept: Pivot Tables vs. Power Pivot...3

2: Concept: Loading Data...5

3: Concept: Calculated Fields...24

4: DAX Topic: SUM(), COUNT(), COUNTROWS(), MIN(), MAX(), COUNTBLANK(), and DIVIDE()............34

5: Concept: Filter Propagation...51

6: DAX Topic: The Basic Iterators SUMX() and AVERAGEX()..57

7: DAX Topic: Calculated Columns...66

8: DAX Topic: CALCULATE()...69

9: Concept: Evaluation Context and Context Transition..76

10: DAX Topic: IF(), SWITCH(), and FIND()...80

11: DAX Topic: VALUES() and HASONEVALUE()...83

12: DAX Topic: ALL(), ALLEXCEPT(), and ALLSELECTED()..90

13: DAX Topic: FILTER()...103

14: DAX Topic: Time Intelligence...112

15: DAX Topic: RELATED() and RELATEDTABLE()..135

16: Concept: Disconnected Tables...139

17: Concept: KPIs and Multiple Data Tables...149

18: Concept: Cube Formulas...160

19: Moving from Excel to Power BI..166

20: Next Steps on Your DAX Journey...173

Appendix A: Answers to Practice Exercises...175

Index..182

Acknowledgements

There are a few people I want to thank who have encouraged and helped me in my venture into my own business and helped me to get this book written and released:

Rob Collie: What can I say but thanks! Thanks for trailblazing this Power Pivot thing and making my journey so much easier. And thanks for everything you have personally done to help me succeed.

Scott Senkeresty: Thanks for generously helping me out a lot when I was still learning. (But do we ever really stop learning?!)

Avi Singh: Thanks for generously sharing your knowledge with me.

Bill Jelen: Thanks for backing me with my first book.

Marco Russo and Alberto Ferrari: Thanks for the generous and numerous free resources that you share with everyone across the web. I have learnt a lot from you guys.

John Hackwood and Tina Taylor: Thanks for being my guinea pigs and giving me so much great feedback about how to improve the book so it makes more sense to someone who is learning.

Nick Colebatch: Thanks for the original idea that eventually morphed into this book.

Chandoo: Thanks for your advice and coaching about this book and more.

Kathy, Kaitlin, and Maddie: Thanks for supporting me in my decision to pursue my passion to go it alone. I wouldn't have chanced it without your support.

Introduction

Power Pivot is a revolutionary piece of software that has been around since 2009. Despite it being more than six years old at this writing, most people who could benefit from Power Pivot still don't know it exists. The good news is that you are not one of those people. If you are reading this, then you already know about Power Pivot, and chances are good that you already know enough about it to know that you need to learn to write DAX.

Bill Jelen, aka MrExcel, has said, "Power Pivot is the best thing to happen to Excel in 20 years." I totally agree with Bill: Power Pivot is simply awesome. Power Pivot brings everything that is good about enterprise-strength business intelligence (BI) tools directly to you right inside Excel—and without the negative time and cost impacts you would normally expect from big-scale BI projects. In addition, it is not just the time and money that matter. The fact that you can do everything yourself with Power Pivot is very empowering. Analyses that you would never have considered viable in the past are now "can do" tasks within the current business cycle.

When you learn to write DAX, you will unleash enormous power, and you can use that power to "excel" with your workbooks like never before.

Why You Need This Book

I am a full-time Power Pivot consultant, trainer, and BI practitioner. I have taught many Excel users at live training classes and helped countless more people online at various Power Pivot forums. This teaching experience has given me great insight into how Excel users learn Power Pivot and what resources they need to succeed. Power Pivot is very learnable, but it is also very different from Excel, so you definitely need some structured learning if you want to use the tool. I have learnt that Excel users need two things:

1. They need to read some good books. In my view, Rob Collie's *DAX Formulas for Power Pivot: The Excel Pro's Guide to Mastering DAX* is the best general book for Excel users who are starting out on their Power Pivot journey. If you are an Excel user and don't have any books (other than this one) on how to use Power Pivot, then you should definitely buy that book.

2. They need practice, practice, practice. The book you're reading right now, *Learn to Write DAX: A Practical Guide to Learning Power Pivot for Excel and Power BI*, is designed for exactly that purpose: to give you practice and to teach you how to write DAX. If you can't write DAX, you will never be good at Power Pivot.

I refer above to *Excel users*, and that is quite deliberate. I have observed that Excel professionals learn DAX differently than do IT/SQL Server professionals. People who have a career as an IT/SQL Server professional are simply not the same as Excel business users. SQL Server professionals have a solid knowledge of database design and principles, table relationships, how to efficiently aggregate data, etc. And of course there are some Excel users who also have knowledge about those things. But I believe IT/SQL Server professionals can take a much more technical path to learning DAX than most Excel users because they have technical grounding to build upon. Excel users need a different approach, and this book is written with them in mind. That is not to say that an IT/SQL Server professional would not get any value from this book/approach; it really depends on your learning style. But suffice it to say that if you are an Excel professional who is trying to learn DAX, this book was written with your specific needs in mind.

> **Note** *Learn to Write DAX: A Practical Guide to Learning Power Pivot for Excel and Power BI* has been written using Excel 2013, and all the screen shots in the book are from Excel 2013. There are a few cosmetic differences between Excel 2013 and Excel 2010 but nothing material. So whether you use Excel 2010 or 2013 or are an early adopter of Excel 2016, the book will be a useful tool to teach you the fundamentals of how to write DAX.

Incremental Learning

I am an Excel user from way back—a long way back actually. I'm not the kind of guy who can sit down and read a novel, but I love to buy Excel reference books and read them cover to cover. And I have learnt *A LOT* about Excel over the years by using this approach. When I find some new concept that I love and want to try, most of the time I just remember it. But sometimes I will add a sticky note to the page so I can I find it again in the future when I need it. In a way, I am incrementally learning a small number of new skills on top of the large base of skills I already have. When you incrementally learn like this, it is relatively easy to remember the detail of the new thing you just learnt.

It's a bit like when you work at a company and a new employee starts. You only have to remember the name of that one new person. But the new employee has to remember the name of everyone in the entire company. It is relatively easy for you to remember one new name and a lot harder for the new person to start from scratch and learn everyone's name. It's a bit like that when you're an experienced Excel user reading a regular Excel book. You already know a lot and will need to learn only a few things that are new—and those new bits are likely to be gold. It is easy to remember those few new things because often they strike a chord with you. Even if you don't remember the details, the next time you face this problem, you'll remember that you read something about it once, and you'll be able to go find your book to look it up.

Well, unfortunately for seasoned Excel users, Power Pivot is a completely different piece of software from Excel. It shares some things in common (such as some common formulas), but many of the really useful concepts are very different and completely new. They are not super difficult to learn, but indeed you will need to learn from scratch, just like that new employee has to learn everyone's name. Once you get a critical mass of new Power Pivot knowledge in your head, you will be off and running. At that point, you can incrementally learn all you want, but until then you need to read, learn, and, most importantly, practice, practice, practice.

Passive vs. Active Learning

I think about learning as being either passive or active. An example of passive learning is lying in bed, reading your Power Pivot book, nodding your head to indicate that you understand what is being covered. I have read Rob Collie's *DAX Formulas for Power Pivot* several times this way, and the clarity in the book is amazing. But the first time I sat in front of my computer and wanted to write some DAX, I was totally lost. What I really needed to do was change from a passive learning approach to an active approach, where I was participating in the learning process rather than being a spectator.

Passive learning on its own is more suited to incrementally adding knowledge to a solid base. Passive learning is not a good approach when you are starting something completely new from scratch. I'm not saying that passive learning is bad. It is useful to do some passive learning in addition to active learning, but you shouldn't try to learn a completely new skill from scratch using *only* passive learning.

Reading Two Books at Once

I love Rob's book *DAX Formulas for Power Pivot*, and I recommend that you read it in addition to the one you're reading right now. (See http://xbi.com.au/books for details about Rob's book.) I actually suggest that you read both of these books in parallel. When you have some passive reading time available (at night or when you are sitting on a bus travelling to work), read Rob's book. Then find yourself the same amount of time each day to actively read and work with this book you are reading now. Sit in front of your computer and actively work through the practice exercises yourself. If you read both of these books in parallel in this way, I promise you that you won't be sorry.

How to Get Value from This Book

If you think you can get value from this book by reading it and not doing the practice exercises, let me tell you: You can't. If you already know how to complete a task and you have done it before, then just reading is fine. However, if you don't know how to do a task or an exercise, then you should practice in front of your computer. First try to do an exercise without looking at the answers. If you can't work it out, then reread the worked-through examples (labelled "Here's How") and then try to do the example again. Practice, practice, practice until you have the knowledge committed to memory and you can do it without looking.

There are 30 "Here's How" worked-through examples and more than 70 individual practices exercises in this book. That gives you more than 100 opportunities to learn and practice, so make the most of these opportunities to develop your skills; after all, that is why you purchased this book in the first place.

Don't Treat This Like a Library Book

When we were kids going to school, most of us were taught that you should not write in library books. And I guess that is fair enough. Other people will use the book after you are finished, and they probably don't want to read all your marks and scribbles. Unfortunately, the message that many of us took away from school was "Don't write in *any* book *ever*." I think it is a mistake to think that you can't write in your own books. You bought it, you own it, so why can't you write in it? In fact, I would go one step further and say *you should* write in the reference books you own. You bought them for a reason: to learn. If you are reading the book and want to make some notes to yourself for future reference, then you should definitely do that.

But I guess I am forgetting the eBook revolution. I know you can't write in an eBook, but I know you can highlight passages of text in a Kindle, and I assume you can do something similar in other eBooks. You can also type in your own notes and attach them to passages of text in many eBooks. There are lots of advantages of eBooks, and the one that means the most to me is the fact that I can have a new book in front of me just moments after I decided to buy it.

Personally I find that eBooks are not a great fit as reference books. I prefer to have a tactile object so I can flip through the pages, add sticky notes, and so on. But that is just me, and we are all different. I am sure there are plenty of people in both camps. Whichever camp you are in, I encourage you to write in this book and/or make notes to yourself using the eBook tools at your disposal. Doing so will make this book a more useful, personalized tool well into the future.

Refreshing Your Pivot Table Skills

This is not a book about how to use pivot tables. Pivot tables have been around for more than 20 years and are one of the best summarisation and visualisation tools available for large data sets. This book assumes that you already know how to use a pivot table and are reasonably competent in doing so. The assumed skills include:

- How to create a pivot table from a standard Excel list
- How to add data to rows, columns, and filters to a pivot table

If you don't know how to do these things well, I suggest you brush up on your skills now before you move forward. There are lots of really good tutorial videos available on YouTube.

Setting Up a Pivot Table

One important concept that is repeated throughout this book is that you need to set up a pivot table before you create your DAX formulas. This is especially important for Excel users as it provides context for the formulas you will write (more on that later).

You use five areas of the PivotTable Fields list to create or update a pivot table: Filters (#1 in the figure below), Columns (#2), Rows (#3), Values (#4), and Slicers (#5). Say that the instructions in this book tell you to set up a pivot table with `Product[Category]` on Rows, `Customer[Gender]` on columns, `Calendar[Year]` on Filters, `Customer[Occupation]` on Slicers, and a calculated field such as `[Total Sales Amount]` on Values. In that case, you should then use the PivotTable Fields list (shown on the right below) to build the pivot table (shown on the left below) as instructed. If you are not clear on how to do this, then you should definitely brush up on building pivot tables before proceeding.

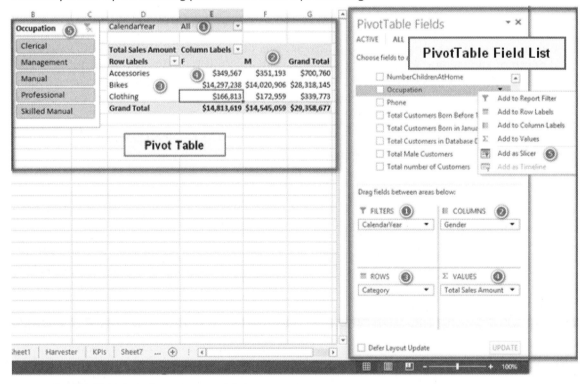

Note There are a few ways to add a slicer to a pivot table. In the PivotTable Fields list (on the right in the image above) you can right-click on any column in any table and then select Add as Slicer (#5 above). You can also navigate to the Excel Insert tab and click the Slicer button there. Just make sure that you first select the pivot table before trying to insert a slicer.

Exercise Data

It is surprisingly difficult to create your own database of meaningful data to use for data analysis practice. Think about the data that exists in a commercial retail business, for example: customer data, finance data, sales data, products, territories, etc. And it is not a simple task to create a meaningful quantity of realistic data from scratch; it is a lot of work. Microsoft has created a number of sample databases that anyone can download and use for free. I use the Microsoft AdventureWorks in Access 2010 database in this book. (Note that you do not need to have Access installed to use this database.) You can download a copy of it by going to http://xbi.com.au/learndax. This is the same sample database that Rob Collie and I use when training people to use DAX.

AdventureWorks contains sample data for a fictitious retail bicycle company that sells bikes and accessories in multiple countries. The data consists of the customers, products, and territories for the AdventureWorks business, along with five years of transactional sales history. The examples I use in this book therefore focus on reporting and analysis that would apply to a retail business, including such things as sales results, profit margins, customer activity, and product performance.

Clearly not everyone who wants to learn to write DAX will operate in a retail environment. However, the retail concepts covered in this book should be familiar to everyone. So it doesn't matter if your specific BI needs are for something other than retail. The scenarios in this book are explained throughout, so you don't need to be a retail expert to complete the exercises.

Getting Help Along the Way

Hopefully you will be able to complete the exercises in this book on your own. But sometimes you might just need to ask someone a question to help you move forward. I encourage you to become a member of http://powerpivotforum.com.au and participate as someone who asks questions and also as someone who helps others when they get stuck. Answering questions for other people is a great way to cement your learning and build depth of knowledge. You will notice from the URL that this is an Aussie forum, but it is open to everyone. At this writing only 15% of all traffic at the forum was from Australia, with the balance coming from more than 70 other countries around the world. I suggest you sign up and get involved; your DAX will be better for it.

You can find a subforum dedicated to this book at http://xbi.com.au/ldf. In the unfortunate event that there are errors in this book, details of these errors will be posted at this subforum.

How This Book Is Organised

I've organised this book to help you learn the material in an order that makes sense to a new Excel user. The general structure of the chapters is as follows:

- Each chapter title begins with either "DAX Topic" or "Concept." The former type covers one or more specific DAX formulas, including the syntax and usage; the latter type covers one or more principles that you need to understand in order to be competent with Power Pivot. I've ordered the chapters so that you can learn incrementally.

- Each "Concept" chapter starts with a description of the concept, and each "DAX Topic" chapter starts with some information about the DAX language to help you understand the topic.

- Almost every chapter provides at least one worked-through example. When you see "Here's How," you know you're reading one of those, and it's time to sit in front of your computer and follow along with me as I explain the concept.

- Almost every chapter includes a number of practice exercises that help you practice what you have learnt.

- DAX is a lot like Excel in that there is often more than one way to do something. If you do an exercise differently than I show how to do it, as long as you get the correct/same answer, all is good. Just realise there are differences in the approaches and move on.

Naming Conventions

This book uses best-practice naming conventions for Power Pivot:

- There are no spaces in table names, like this:

  ```
  TableName
  ```

- Columns in tables *always* include the table name followed by the column name in square brackets, like this:

  ```
  TableName[Column Name]
  ```

- Calculated fields (also called measures) *never* include a table name and are wrapped in square brackets, like this:

  ```
  [Calculated Field Name]
  ```

- Calculated field formulas are written with the calculated field name followed by the formula, like this:

  ```
  [Total Sales] = SUM(Sales[ExtendedAmount])
  ```

Note In addition to the naming conventions in this book, you should note that there is another naming convention used in DAX that is not used in this book.

There are two places you can write DAX formulas: in the Excel window and in the Power Pivot window. When you write a calculated field (aka, a measure) in the Power Pivot window, you are required to provide the calculated field name on the left side of the formula and then use a *colon and equals sign* (: =) between the calculated field name and the actual formula, like this:

```
Total Sales := SUM(Sales[ExtendedAmount])
```

This syntax is not used at all in this book as the book teaches you to write formulas from within the Excel window and not the Power Pivot window. But you should be aware of this difference in syntax for when you are reviewing formulas from within the Power Pivot window.

1: Concept: Pivot Tables vs. Power Pivot

Some people wonder what the difference is between Power Pivot and pivot tables, so I'm going to start by explaining. Read on, and you'll have it sorted out in no time.

What Is a Pivot Table?

A pivot table is a summarisation and visualisation tool. The job of a pivot table is to connect to a data source and create on-the-fly totals and subtotals to help you and others make sense of data. The larger the set of data and the more granular the data, the more useful a pivot table becomes. Because pivot tables are embedded right inside Excel, with them you get all the other benefits of Excel as well.

Data Sources for Pivot Tables

Historically, there have been two main types of data sources that you can connect to with a pivot table: flat tables and data cubes.

Connecting to a Single Flat Table

To connect to a single flat table inside Excel, click in the table, select Insert, Pivot Table, and off you go. There are some limitations with this approach, however:

- It is very common to have to do a lot of `VLOOKUP()`s (or similar operations) to be able to join data from different data sources into a single flat table.
- Excel has a 1 million row limit. In fact, though, if you are using lots of `VLOOKUP()`s in a single flat table, you will reach performance limits well before you ever hit 1 million rows.

These two issues have historically prevented Excel from being a scalable BI tool. But Power Pivot changes that, as you'll see in a few moments.

Connecting to a Data Cube

A less common but very powerful use of pivot tables is to connect directly to a reporting cube such as a SQL Server Analysis Services multidimensional cube directly from Excel. Many large enterprises have multidimensional data cubes available for reporting. Allowing Excel users to connect directly to a cube and use a pivot table for reporting is super easy and convenient. But this is a relatively rare use case compared to the general use of Excel and the more common single-table use of pivot tables.

Enter Power Pivot

Power Pivot doesn't change anything about pivot tables, but it changes everything when it comes to the data that pivot tables connect to. Power Pivot adds a third (and, in my view, the best) method of connecting to source data.

Power Pivot is a *data modelling tool* that is used to structure and extend source data so that it can be analysed using Excel pivot tables (among other tools). *Data modelling* is not a term that is often familiar to Excel users as it is normally the domain of IT BI professionals. But this is no longer the case with Power Pivot for Excel.

What Is Data Modelling?

Data modelling is the process of taking data from various sources; loading, structuring, and relating data logically to other data; and enhancing, embellishing, and generally preparing the data for use.

The data modelling process includes:

- Determining the optimal structure and shape of the source data to analyse (e.g., whether to bring in all the data, full data, or summary data).
- Loading the data from the source into the data model (Power Pivot in this case).
- Defining the logical relationships between the various tables (which is similar to what you do with `VLOOKUP()` inside Excel).

- Defining data types (e.g., specifying whether a column of data is numeric or a column of currency values or a column of text fields).

- Creating new insights from the source data so that you can analyse concepts that don't exist natively in the source data but yet can be calculated or created inside the data model. For example, if you have a table of transactional data with cost price and sell price, you can extend the data model to include a calculation for margin, margin percentage, etc., even though these concepts are not explicitly in the source data. Once you have modelled these new facts in the data model, they can be reused over and over by people using your workbook.

When you learn Power Pivot, you are actually learning data modelling. The term can be a little bit scary, but there is no reason to be concerned. By the time you have finished this book, you will be well on your way to being an accomplished data modeller using Power Pivot. Just use the techniques covered in this book and keep in mind that what you are actually doing is learning to be a data modeller using Power Pivot.

2: Concept: Loading Data

Before you can start to write DAX and use Power Pivot, you need to load some data. Power Pivot always loads a complete copy of the source data into the Data Model as the first step in the process. Once it's loaded, you can share your workbooks with others, and there is no need for anyone else to have direct access to your source data.

When you load data, you have to decide which data to import, including which tables, which columns in each table, and also what "shape" the data should be when imported. In the following section, you will simply load data that has been prepared for you. But you need to be aware that the process of deciding which data to import is an important part of the data modelling process—and it has been done for you in this case.

Here's How: Loading Data from a New Source

You can download a copy of the sample AdventureWorks database used in this book from http://xbi.com.au/learndax. You should download the database now, unzip it, and place it in a location that is easy for you to find.

You are going to start off by loading the following tables from the AdventureWorks Access database:

- Sales
- Products
- Territories
- Calendar
- Customers

Then you will prepare these tables for use in Power Pivot.

Follow these steps to load data into a workbook for use in Power Pivot:

1. Open a new blank Excel workbook. You should see the PowerPivot tab at the top of the sheet.

2. If you don't see the PowerPivot tab, select File, Options, Add-Ins. Then scroll to the bottom of the window and select COM Add-ins from the Manage list. Then click Go.

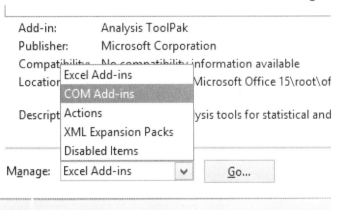

3. In the COM Add-ins dialog that appears, check the Microsoft Office PowerPivot check box and then click OK.

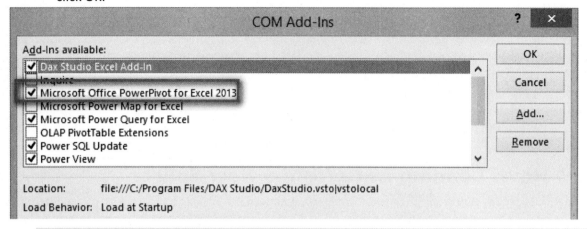

What if I Can't Find the Power Pivot Add-in?

If you are using Excel 2013+ and you can't see the Power Pivot add-in, then I have some bad news for you: Your version of Excel does not include Power Pivot, and you will need to purchase a different version to get it.

If you are using Excel 2010, then all is not lost. You can download the Power Pivot plug-in from the Internet. This option is not available to Excel 2013+ users, though.

For more information about Power Pivot versions, go to http://xbi.com.au/versions.

4. If you haven't already done so, download the sample database from http://xbi.com.au/learndax. Unzip the zip file and place the contents somewhere you can easily find again later.

5. On the PowerPivot tab, click Manage.

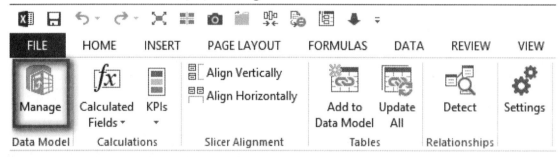

Take a moment to look at the Windows taskbar, shown in the image below. Hover your mouse over Excel in the taskbar and notice that there are now two separate windows: the traditional Excel window (see #1 below) and the Power Pivot window (#2).

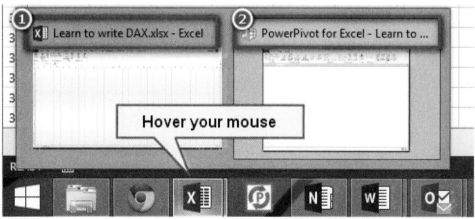

Note Power Pivot is a separate application that is completely embedded inside Excel. Throughout this book I often tell you to switch between Excel and Power Pivot. This is what I mean when I say this: Switch between these two windows. If at any time you can't see the Power Pivot window because it is not open, you can open it by going to the PowerPivot tab in Excel and clicking Manage.

6.   In the Power Pivot window, select Home, From Database (see #1 below), From Access (#2).

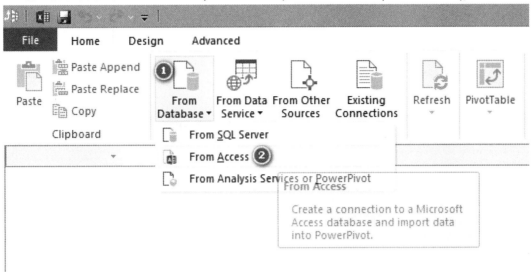

7.   Browse to the location of the sample database you downloaded and unzipped in step 4 and then click Next.

8.   Accept the default option in the Table Import Wizard dialog (as shown below) and then click Next.

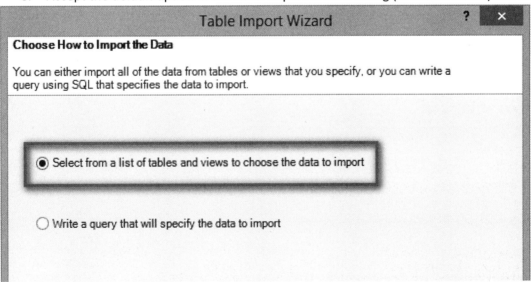

9. Select the five views at the bottom of the list by placing a check mark in the box next to each one. (Note the different icons for queries/views and for tables.)

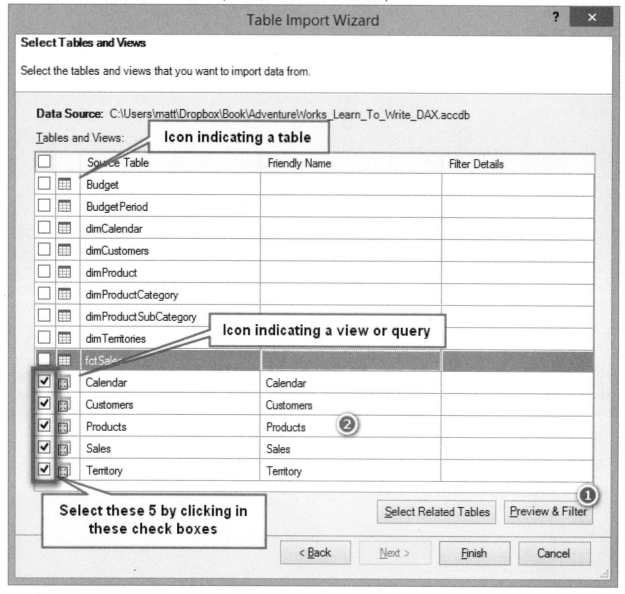

Note If needed, you can filter the rows and columns you bring in from the database in each table by clicking the Preview & Filter button (see #1 above) and also give the views new names in the Friendly Name column (see #2 above).

Also note that the tables have names like `dimProduct` and `fctSales`. It is very common for database tables to have prefixes like this. `dim` indicates *dimension*, and `fct` indicates *fact*. Excel users can think of a dimension table as a lookup table and a fact table as a data (or transactions) table. The fact that there are two different types of tables (lookup tables and data tables) is a very important concept in Power Pivot, and you will learn a lot more about this as you work through this book.

It is best practice for Excel users to remove the `dim` and `fct` prefixes from the table names before importing these tables into Power Pivot. These prefixes have meaning to IT folk and help identify the type of table, but given that these table names will be visible to nontechnical people who use your pivot tables (from the PivotTable Fields list), it is best to remove these prefixes during import. To do so, you just give each table a new friendly name, as shown above. After all, you probably want your Excel users (who are likely business users) to see `Products` rather than `dimProducts` when working on your pivot table.

10. Click Finish, and the wizard imports your data.

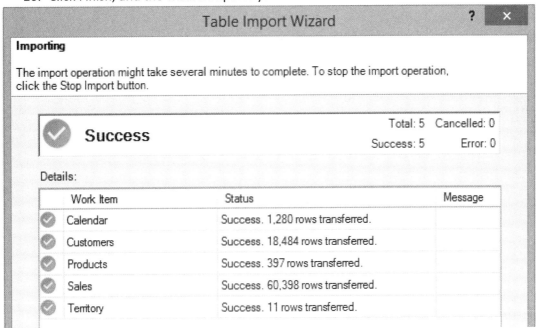

When you close the Table Import Wizard, you see the five tables you have just imported in the Power Pivot window. There should be five new tabs, one for each of the tables you just imported. Each of the tables is a complete copy of the data you imported from the source files (an Access database in this example). You don't need the source files again until you are ready to refresh the data—typically when the data changes at some time in the future. This is one of the many great things about Power Pivot: You can simply refresh the data when the data changes, and your workbooks are updated with the new data.

> **Note** It is important that you make any changes to table and column names early. Power Pivot will not automatically update the references to your tables and columns if you rename them after you have started to write DAX. This renaming of tables is also part of the data modelling process.

11. Ensure that you are in Data view by selecting Data View on the ribbon (see #1 below).

12. In the Data view, double-click on the Territory tab and rename it Territories for consistency.

Note The next stage of the data modelling process is to create the logical relationships between the tables.

13. Switch to Diagram view by clicking the Diagram View button on the ribbon (see #2 above).

14. If you can't see all five tables on the screen, click on the Zoom to Fit button to reveal the hidden tables.

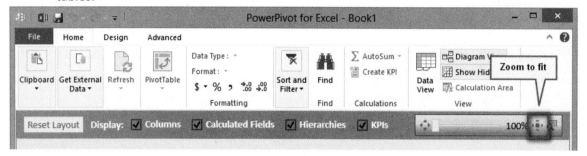

15. Position your tables so that any data table or tables (there is only one in this case) are at the bottom of the screen and the lookup tables are at the top.

Note A data table contains transactional information—in this case sales transactions. Lookup tables contain information about logical groups of objects, like customers, products, time (calendar), etc.

In the old world before Power Pivot, an Excel user needed to create one big flat table in Excel before creating a pivot table. Often that meant writing VLOOKUP() formulas to bring in other data from other tables into the one allowed big flat table. These other tables containing the extra data needed are the lookup tables in Power Pivot. Each of these tables must have a unique ID column, such as ProductNumber, CustomerNumber, etc. These unique columns are sometimes called *keys*.

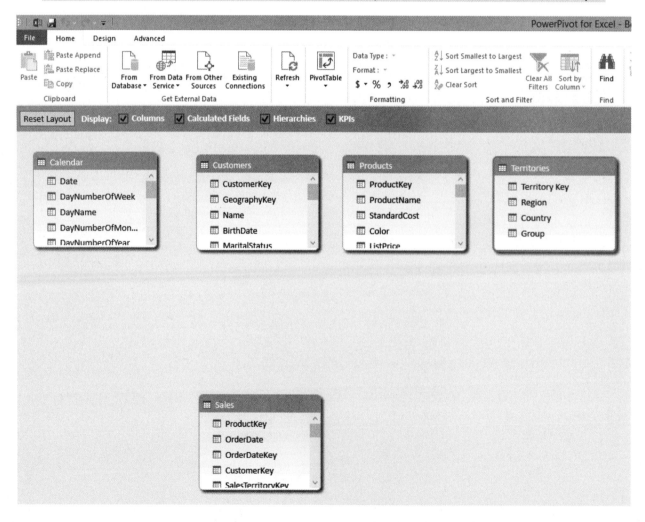

Once you've completed the preceding steps, you need to join the data table(s) to the lookup table(s), as described shortly.

> **Note** The relationship between tables in Power Pivot is always of the type "one to many." Unlike in database programs, there is no other type of table join available in Power Pivot (for versions up through Excel 2013 anyway). The data table may contain none, one, or many rows of data for each row in the lookup table. The following example explains how to join tables.

Relationships Between Tables

A customer table typically has a list of all customers that a business has on file. But some of these customers may have never purchased anything from the company. Some customers may have made only a single purchase, and some customers may have made many purchases. So for each entry in the `Customers` table, there is either none, one, or many records in the `Sales` table.

The `Sales` table can be joined logically to the `Customers` table by using the customer key (customer number or ID). When these tables are joined on the customer key, there will be a one-to-many (`Customers`-to-`Sales`) relationship between these two tables.

Here's How: Joining Tables in Power Pivot

To join a lookup table to a data table in Power Pivot, follow this process:

1. Select a column from the data table (the table down at the bottom of the Power Pivot screen, as shown below). To do this, click the `OrderDate` column in the `Sales` table and hold down the mouse button (see #1 below).

2. Drag the column up and hover over the matching key in the lookup table (in this case, the `Date` column in the `Calendar` table; see #2).

3. Release the mouse button to complete the join.

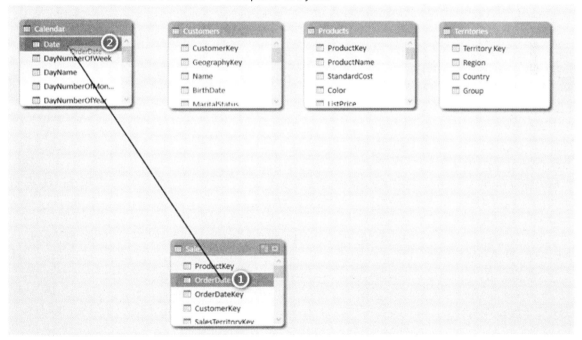

4. Complete the same process for the other three tables. See if you can work out on your own which are the correct columns to join before you look at the answers below:

Data Table	Column	Lookup Table
Sales	ProductKey	Products
Sales	CustomerKey	Customers
Sales	TerritoryKey	Territories

Because the relationships are always one-to-many, the joins are specifically single-directional. Always drag from the data table up to the lookup table, not the other way around. As you can see in the image below, the dot end of the relationship points to the data table, and the arrow points to the lookup table.

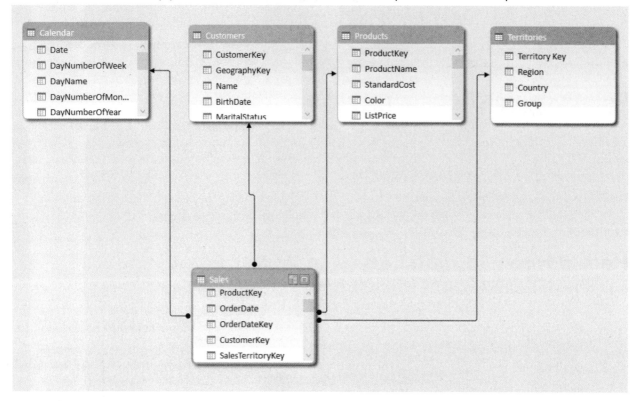

By putting the data table at the bottom, you get a visual clue that the tables at the top of the screen are lookup tables. (Get it? You have to "look up" to see the lookup tables.)

5.   Save the workbook by clicking the Save icon.

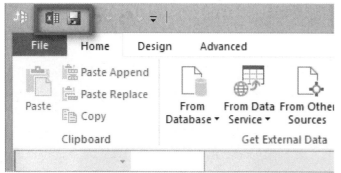

When you click the Save icon, you save both the Excel workbook and the Power Pivot data model at the same time (just as happens when you click the Save button within Excel). The Excel workbook and the Power Pivot data model are always saved together inside the same Excel file (e.g., .xlsx, .xlsb, .xlsm, etc.). If you want to switch you back to the Excel window, click the Excel button.

Shaping the Data

It's time to pause for a minute to discuss the optimal shape of data for Power Pivot. When I say "shape" of data, I am taking about things like how many tables you import, how many columns are in each table, which columns are in each of the tables, etc.

Shaping data is a huge topic, and I don't have room here to discuss it fully. But I do want to give some foundational advice to get you started. One reason this advice is important is because the shape of data in transactional systems (or relational databases) is seldom the ideal shape for Power Pivot. When the IT department executes an enterprise BI project, one of the important first steps is to shape the data so it is optimal for reporting. This step is normally completely transparent to the end user (i.e., you), and hence the end user is shielded from the need to do this. But I am sharing this important information with you here and now because you need to understand data shaping if you want to have efficient and effective Power Pivot data models. Just copying what you have in your source data is unlikely to be optimal.

Choosing a Schema (or Layout)

The generally accepted approach to bringing data into Power Pivot is to bring in your data in as what's known as a *star schema*. This is a technical term that comes from the Kimball methodology (also known as dimensional modelling; Google it) and describes the logical way data should be structured for optimal reporting performance. The visual layout of the tables in the following image (which includes exactly the same data you just imported) shows why it is called a star schema.

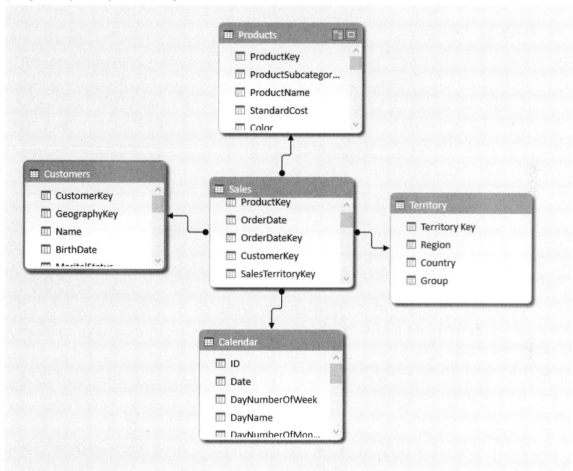

In short, there are data tables (only one, `Sales`, in this example) surrounded by lookup tables (`Customers`, `Products`, `Territory`, and `Calendar` in this example), and together they visually make a star shape.

> **Note** While the optimum data model shape is a star schema, other shapes will work, too. For example, you can use a snowflake schema, where there are secondary lookup tables joined to the primary lookup tables; however, the extra relationships can come at the cost of worse performance and possibly also confusion to users, particularly if they access the PivotTable Fields list.

The Visual Layout of Tables in the Diagram View

When it comes to visually positioning your tables in the Power Pivot Diagram view, I teach Excel users to position the tables in such a way that the lookup tables are located at the top of the window and the data tables are located at the bottom of the window (as shown below).

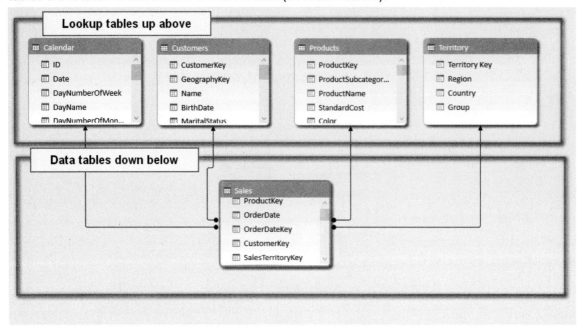

If you compare the last two images, you will see that they both have exactly the same logical relationship (links) between the tables: *They are both star schemas*, but they have different visual layouts.

The visual layout in the second image, the one just above, is the one developed and recommended by Rob Collie, and we can call it the Collie layout methodology. The Collie layout methodology involves placing the lookup tables at the top of the window and the data tables at the bottom. The importance of this for Excel users learning Power Pivot will become evident later in the book. For now, just trust me and do follow the Collie layout methodology.

So in summary, there is no one correct way to shape your data, but the star schema is the best approach where possible. When you import your data in the shape of a star schema, you should use the Collie layout methodology (lookup tables on top, data tables down the bottom) to visually layout your data in the Power Pivot Diagram view.

Understanding the Two Types of Tables: Lookup Tables and Data Tables

In the professional BI world, lookup tables are referred to as *dimension tables*, and data tables are called *fact tables*. For Excel users, though, I suggest using the terminology *lookup tables* and *data tables*.

Lookup Tables

You should have one lookup table for each "object" that you need for reporting purposes. For example, in the data being used here, these objects are customers, products, territories, and time (i.e., calendar). A key feature of a lookup table is that it contains one and only one row for every individual item in the table and as many columns as needed to describe the object.

So there is only one row for each unique customer in the Customers table. The Customers table has lots of columns describing each customer, such as customer number, customer name, customer address, etc., but there is only one row for each customer. Each row is unique based on the customer number, and no duplicates are allowed.

Data Tables

It is possible to have many data tables, but there is only one in this example: the `Sales` table. This data table contains lots of rows (60,000+ in this case) and contains all the transactional records of sales that occurred over several years. Importantly, the data table contains one column key that matches to each of the keys in each lookup table needed for reporting. This example has a date, a customer number, a product number, and a territory key so that the data table can be logically joined to the lookup tables.

Ideally, data tables should have very few columns but as many rows as needed to bring in all the data records. Data tables normally have lots of rows (sometimes in the tens of millions).

The Shaping Bottom Line

When it comes to shaping data, you need to remember the following:

- There are two types of tables: data tables that contain the data that you want to analyse and lookup tables that contain metadata about the objects you are going to analyse, like the name, address, and city of each customer.

- The optimal way to shape your data is to use a star schema, but other schemas such as a snowflake schema can work, too, though such schemas can be less efficient.

- For Excel users, it is best to position your tables in the Power Pivot Diagram view using the Collie layout methodology. (You'll learn more about why you should do this in Chapter 5.)

Here's How: Making Changes to a Table That Is Already Loaded

Say that you want to make changes to the `Calendar` table so that you only bring in dates for the years 2002 and 2003, and you also want to remove the fiscal date columns from the table. The following steps walk you through how to make changes like these to a table that is already loaded:

1. In the Power Pivot window, select the `Calendar` table (in either Data view or Diagram view).

2. Navigate to the Design tab (see #1 below) and click the Table Properties button (#2).

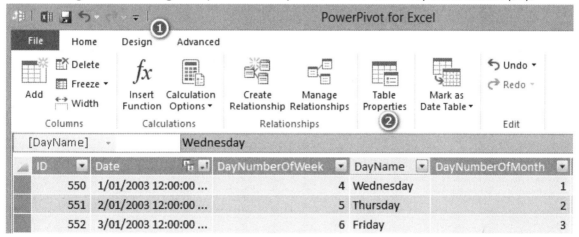

3. In the Edit Table Properties dialog that appears, click the arrow at the right end of the `CalendarYear` column (see #1 below).

4. Deselect years 2001 and 2004 (#2 and #3) and then click OK.

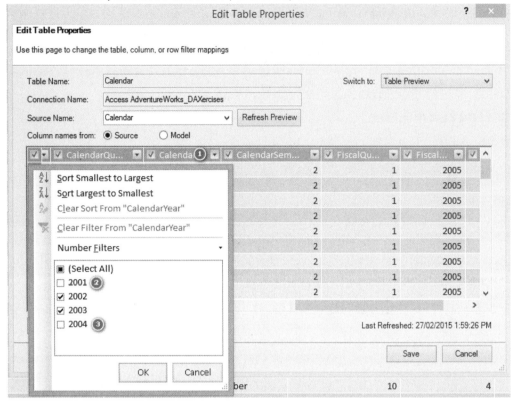

5. Deselect the three fiscal columns on the right side of the table (#1, #2, and #3 below) and click Save.

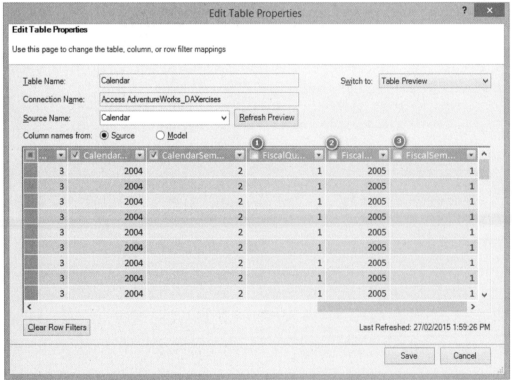

6. Save the workbook.

Now that you've seen how to make changes to a table that you have previously imported to the Power Pivot data model, you should get some practice. Go back and clear the filters you applied on the `CalendarYear` columns because you will need all the rows in the `Calendar` table for the practice exercises in this book.

Here's How: Importing New Tables from an Existing Connection

In this exercise you will open the existing connection to your Access database, bring in the `ProductSubCategory` table, and join it to your data model. Follow these steps:

1. On the Home tab (see #1 below), click the Existing Connections button (#2). (In Excel 2010, this button is on the Design tab.)

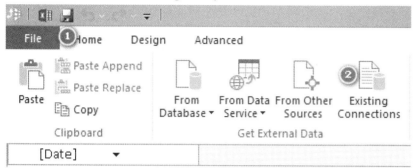

2. Click on the Access connection you created earlier (see #1 below) and then click Open (#2).

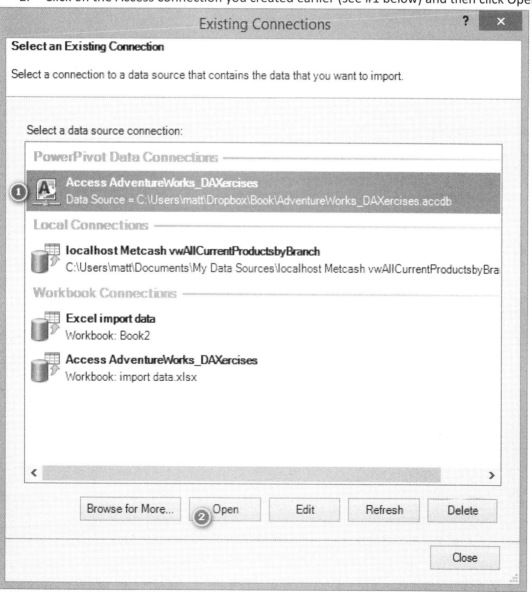

3. Accept the default option, highlighted below, and click Next.

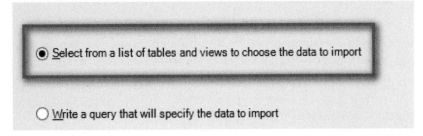

4. Select the `dimProductSubCategory` table, give it the friendly name `SubCategory`, and click Finish.

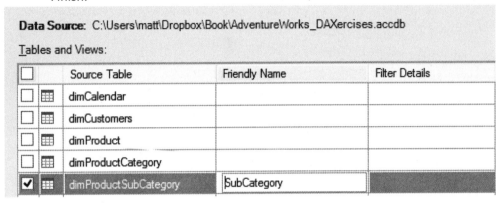

5. Connect the existing `Products` table to the new `SubCategory` table. `SubCategory` is a look-up table of the `Products` table, so if you're using the Collie layout methodology, you should place the `SubCategory` table above the `Products` table, as shown below.

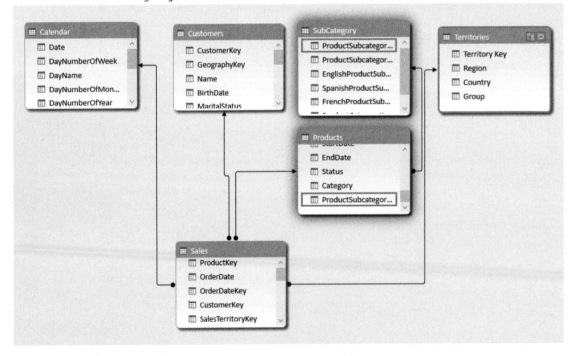

6. Save the workbook.

Note Now that there is a second lookup table (`SubCategory`) connected to another lookup table (`Products`), this is technically now a snowflake schema. It will work, but it can be less efficient than a star schema. You won't need this `SubCategory` table again, so you should now delete it. Just right-click the table and select Delete. The purpose of this exercise was simply to show you how to reopen an existing connection.

Here's How: Changing the File Location of an Existing Connection

It's important to know how to move an Access database to a new location and then point the existing data connection to the new location. You will need to do this if you ever send your Excel workbook as well as the data source to another user or if you need to change your file locations on your own computer.

The data connections you create in Power Pivot are relative to your computer. When you send an Excel workbook and data source to another user, that person will have to edit the data connection so that it will work on his or her own PC.

> **Note** You need to follow the steps in this section only if you send both a workbook and a data source to another user. But that is not normally what you would do. Normally you would just distribute a workbook and not the data source.

Follow these steps to change the file location of an existing connection:

1.   In Windows Explorer, create a new folder.

2.   Navigate to your Access database and move it into the new folder.

3.   On the Home tab (see #1 below), click the Existing Connections button (#2). (In Excel 2010, this button is on the Design tab.)

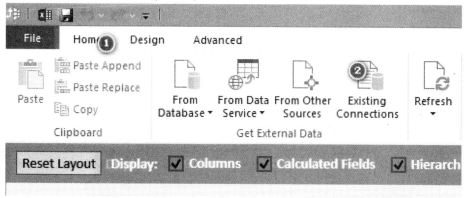

4. Select the existing Access database from the list of connections (see #1 below) and then click Open (#2). Note the error (#3): The data source can't be found. Click the Edit button (#4) to edit the connection.

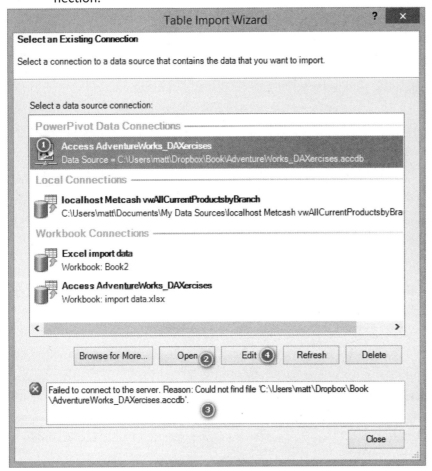

5. Click Browse (see #1 below) and then browse to the new folder you created in step 1.

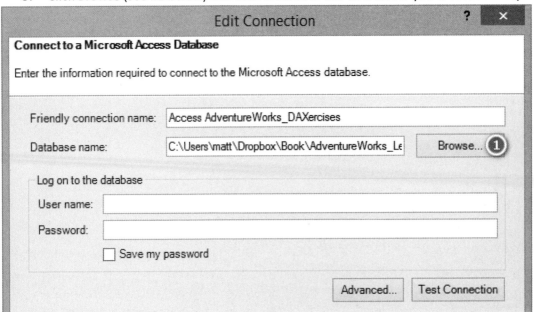

6. Select the Access database and click Open. Note the message saying the connection has been changed.

7. Click Save to finalise the changes.

8. Save the workbook.

Here's How: Inserting a New Pivot Table

There are several ways to insert a new pivot table. Here are the steps for inserting one from the Power Pivot window:

1. On the Home tab of the Power Pivot window (see #1 below), click PivotTable (#2).

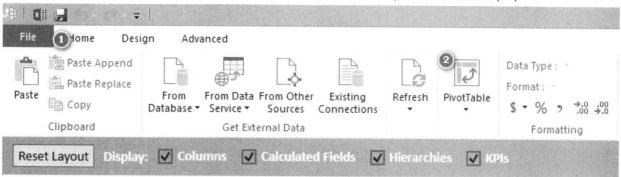

2. Accept the default New Worksheet and click OK.

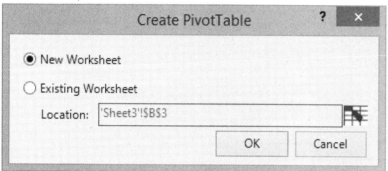

The PivotTable Fields list appears on the right of the Excel worksheet that contains the new pivot table. Note that there are multiple tables visible in the PivotTable Fields list. This is an indication that the pivot table is connected to the data model.

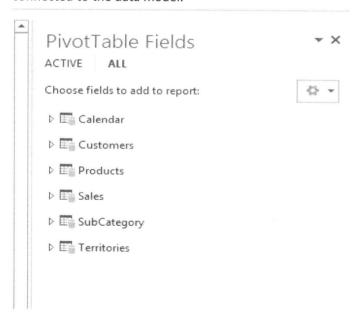

When you add a pivot table from within the Power Pivot window, the new pivot table is automatically connected to your Power Pivot data model (i.e., it is connected to the Power Pivot data you have imported).

Note In Excel 2010, there is a button on the Excel Power Pivot tab that is identical to the one in the Power Pivot window. It inserts a new pivot table connected to the Power Pivot data model. There is no such button available in Excel 2013.

Note It is also possible to create traditional pivot tables that are not connected to the Power Pivot data model, and this can cause confusion, particularly in Excel 2013, given that there is no button to insert a Power Pivot pivot table. Don't get confused with these traditional pivot tables and a pivot table connected to the Power Pivot data model. The pivot table concept is the same, but the data sources are completely different.

Here is another way to insert a pivot table connected to the data model in Excel 2013:

1. Navigate to a new sheet (or simply use an existing sheet).

2. Click Insert, PivotTable (see #1 and #2 below).

3. In the Create PivotTable dialog that appears, select Use an External Data Source (#3) and Choose Connection (#4). Then click OK (#5).

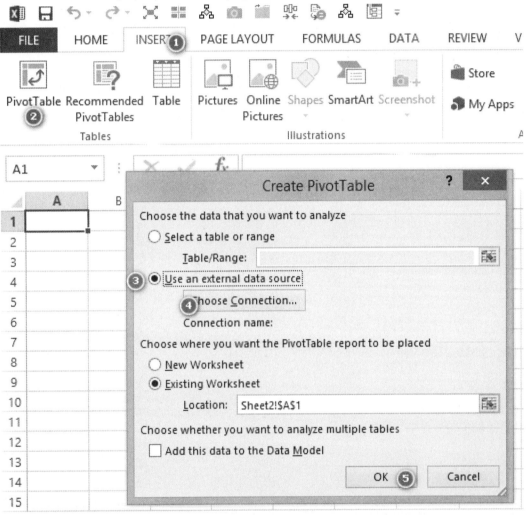

4. In the Existing Connections dialog that appears, on the Tables tab (#6 below) select Tables in Workbook Data Model (#7).

5. Click Open (#8) and then click OK.

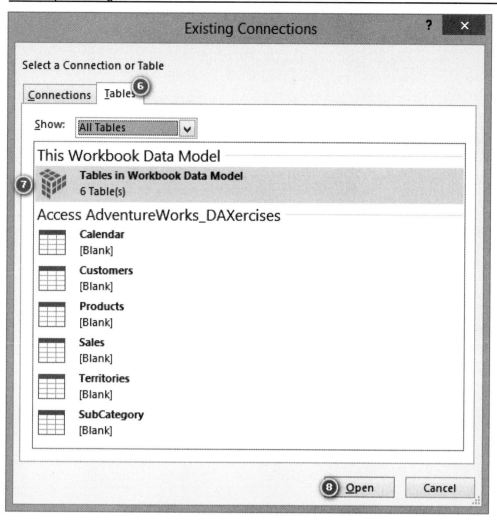

If you use Excel 2013, it is worth practicing inserting a new pivot table a couple times to get practice with this process so it sticks in your memory. But remember that if you use Excel 2010, you don't need to use the above technique; you can easily use the Insert Pivot Table button that appears on the Power Pivot tab.

Other Data Sources

A number of other data sources are available in Power Pivot. You can see these in the Get External Data menu from within Power Pivot, as shown below.

The general principle for importing data is the same regardless of the data source you use. You simply select the appropriate data source and then follow the import wizard just like with the Access database example earlier in this chapter.

3: Concept: Calculated Fields

Calculated fields have been around for many years—maybe as long as pivot tables themselves. But the original calculated fields are not the same thing as the newer Power Pivot calculated fields in Excel 2013.

There are four important things related to calculated fields that you need to know about:

- **Original calculated fields for standard pivot tables**—The original calculated fields are very basic in capability. I have never found the original calculated fields particularly easy to use, and I've never really gotten into them. Thanks to Power Pivot, there is really no reason to use the original calculated fields at all now. If you are able to write calculated fields using the original approach, then you are more than capable of using Power Pivot calculated fields—and you will be a long way in front for doing so. So you can forget about these original calculated fields; you don't need them anymore.

- **Measures in Power Pivot for Excel 2010**—In the first release of Power Pivot (in Excel 2010), Microsoft introduced measures. Measures are kind of like the original calculated fields, but they are significantly more powerful. My guess is that measures are at least 100 times better than the original/old calculated fields from standard pivot tables. Measures allow you to enhance your Power Pivot data model so that the pivot tables you create can give you the calculations you need and want. Most of the rest of this book is dedicated to teaching you how to write measures, so there will be a lot more about measures to follow.

- **Calculated fields in Power Pivot for Excel 2013**—In Excel 2013, Microsoft renamed Power Pivot measures, and it now calls them calculated fields. So Power Pivot calculated fields in Excel 2013 are the same as measures in Power Pivot for Excel 2010. Both of the Power Pivot versions are different from the original calculated fields in standard pivot tables. Personally, I think it was a bad decision to rename measures to calculated fields as it has created confusion between the old calculated fields for standard pivot tables and the new calculated fields for Power Pivot. (And this is on top of the confusion for those migrating from Power Pivot for Excel 2010 to Excel 2013.)

- **Measures in Excel 2016**—Thanks to a lot of lobbying to Microsoft by Rob Collie and others, Microsoft has decided to reverse its decision to rename measures to calculated fields; in Excel 2016, measures will again be called measures. So Excel 2013 is the first and last version to use the term calculated field as it relates to Power Pivot, and soon this term will be relegated to history as a sad and sorry saga. (Microsoft, it takes guts to admit you made a mistake and reverse the decision—so good job!)

Note Even though I prefer to use the term *measures*, in this book I use the term *calculated fields* to refer to the *new capability* that was first created in Power Pivot for Excel 2010 (then called measures) and then became calculated fields in Excel 2013. In this book I use the term *calculated fields* to match what Excel 2013 users see on the ribbon. The old calculated fields that are part of standard pivot tables are completely redundant, I never use them, and I will never refer to them again in this book. Apart from the text in this book, though, I always refer to these things as measures, and I suggest you do, too, since Microsoft is going to join us shortly.

Techniques for Writing DAX Calculated Fields

There are three places you can write DAX calculated fields:

- You can write a calculated field in the formula bar in the Power Pivot window, as shown below. If you use this method, you must specify the calculated field name followed by a colon and then the formula.

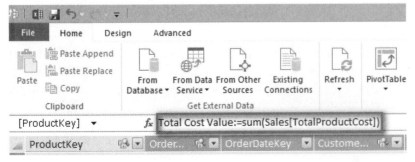

- You can write and edit calculated fields in any empty cell in the calculation area at the bottom of the Power Pivot window, as shown below.

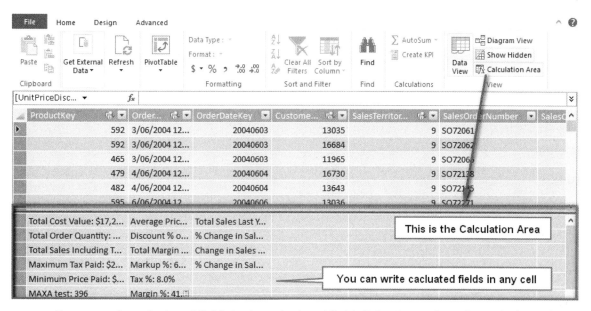

- You can write calculated fields in the calculated field dialog in Excel, as shown below. This calculated field dialog can be opened from within Excel by navigating to the Power Pivot tab and clicking on the Calculated Field button.

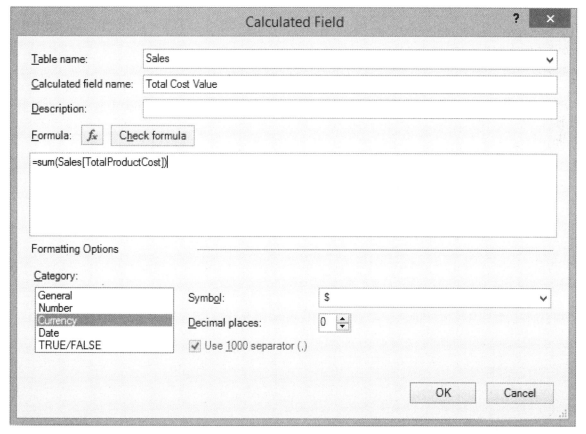

In general, Excel users should write DAX in the Calculated Field dialog box in Excel. And it is normally best to first create a pivot table that provides some context for the calculated field you are about to write. If you do it this way, you will immediately see the calculated field in a pivot table once you click OK, and this will give you immediate feedback about whether the formula looks correct.

Here's How: Writing Calculated Fields

The approach to writing new calculated fields described here is what I recommend for Excel users. Until you get the hang of it, this procedure for creating calculated fields will be foreign, so be sure to practice. Follow these steps:

1. Create a new blank pivot table connected to your data model (or use an existing one if you already have something appropriate).

2. Add some relevant data to the rows in your pivot table. For the sample database used in this book, I suggest that you go to the Products table and place [Category] on Rows in the pivot table (see #1 below).

3. Click inside the pivot table, navigate to the Power Pivot tab, click the Calculated Fields drop-down arrow (#2), and then select New Calculated Field (#3). The Calculated Field dialog appears.

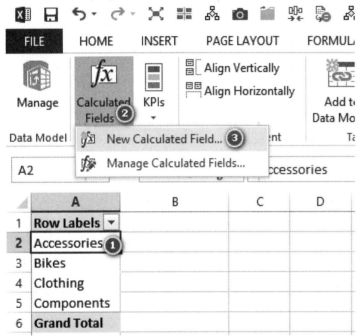

> **Tip** You should use the Calculated Field dialog (shown below) as a process flow/guide. If you don't do this, you risk missing one or more of the steps. Missing a step will end up costing you time and causing rework. Get in the good habit of following the process steps I describe here, using the dialog to remind you of all the steps. Always follow the order outlined here.

4. In the Table Name drop-down (see #1 below), select where your calculated field will be stored. You should place the calculated field in the table where the data comes from, and in this case, the "data" you are using is in the Sales[ExtendedAmount] column, which is in the Sales table, so select Sales in the Table Name drop-down.

5. In the Calculated Field Name text box (#2), give the new calculated field a meaningful, unique name.

> **Note** In the examples in this book, you should use the names I tell you to use. When you are writing your own DAX with your own data in the future, you should use descriptive, meaningful names (including spaces). Don't try to abbreviate a name like Total Sales Value as TSV as this will cause you or others confusion down the track.

6. In the Formula box (#3) write the DAX formula.

7. Click Check Formula (#4) to check whether the formula you wrote is syntactically correct. Fix any errors if you need to.

8. Select an appropriate formatting option from the Category list (#5), including a suitable Symbol and Decimal places in the area to the right of the Category list.

9.   Click OK to save (#6).

Note I generally don't enter anything in the Description box, but it is there for you to use if you like. It's for reference only and doesn't impact the behaviour of the formulas.

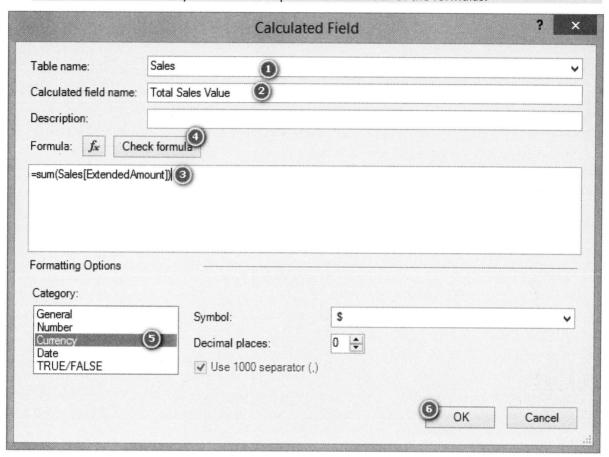

After you click OK, you get immediate feedback about whether everything is working as you expect (as shown below).

	A	B
1	Row Labels ▾	Total Sales Value
2	Accessories	$700,760
3	Bikes	$28,318,145
4	Clothing	$339,773
5	**Grand Total**	**$29,358,677**

Remember that following this procedure will save you time because you will not have to go back and fix things you missed. Practice doing it this way right from the start, and you will develop a good habit that will serve you well in the future.

Avoiding Implicit Calculated Fields

You can create a calculated field by dragging a column from a table and dropping it in the Values section of the PivotTable Fields list, as shown below. When you do this, you create what is called an "implicit calculated field." This is the way you always had to do it with traditional pivot tables; there was no other option. However, I recommend that you avoid doing this when using Power Pivot.

There are several reasons not to create implicit calculated fields:

- The name of the implicit calculated field that Excel generates for you is not very helpful. Compare [Sum of ExtendedAmount] (the name of this implicit calculated field) with [Total Sales Amount] when you explicitly write and name the calculated field yourself.

- No formatting is applied when you drag to create an implicit calculated field.

- Drag and drop works only with SUM and COUNT (i.e., the count is automatically used when you drag and drop a text column into the Values section). If you want anything else (e.g., AVERAGE), you have to edit the DAX code anyway.

- You won't learn how to write good DAX if you let Excel do it for you.

So do yourself a favour and don't drag and drop your table columns when writing DAX. Of course, if you just want a quick look at a field for some testing, then doing this is fine. But undo the change immediately after you have taken a look. If you want to keep a calculated field, then write it from scratch using your DAX skills.

Here's How: Using IntelliSense

When you type in a DAX formula in the Calculated Field dialog, I recommend that you learn to leverage the IntelliSense tooltips that appear. The following steps show how this works:

1. Click in an existing pivot table (the one you created above is fine or create a new one) and then create a new calculated field and name it Test.

2. In the Formula box, click just after the equals sign (which is already there by default).

3. To enter the SUM function, start typing **sum** (lowercase is fine). After you have finished typing these three letters *but before your type a parenthesis*, Excel displays an IntelliSense tooltip that provides a description of the function (see below). These tooltips often contain information that is valuable, particularly while you are learning.

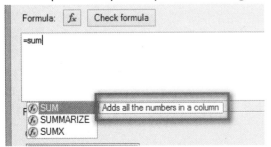

4. After reading the tooltip and making sure this is what you want, type an open parenthesis, **(**. A new tooltip pops up to help you with the correct syntax. As shown below, this function is expecting you to pass it a column name.

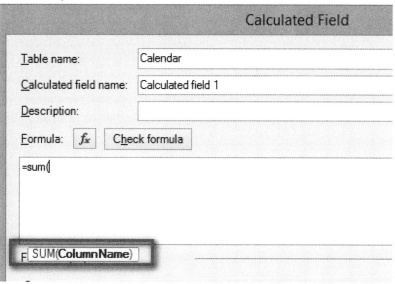

5. It is best practice in DAX to type the table name before every column name, so type **S** for sales. As shown below, a tooltip now shows a list of possible matching values (tables and columns). Use the up and down arrow keys to select the `Sales` table (the one with the *T* in the icon) and then press Tab. (If necessary, you can type more letters of the table name to further refine the search and make it easier to find the table in the list before you select it and press Tab.)

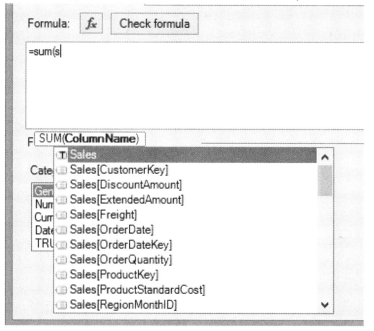

6. Type **[** to start the column name. As shown below, a list of the possible column names appears in a tooltip list. In this example, you use the `Sales[ExtendedAmount]` column, so you can either keep typing the name of the column or navigate up and down the list by using the arrow keys again to select the column. Then press Tab again to select the correct column.

Tip Try to use the keyboard and not the mouse to select from the tooltip, particularly if the list is short. It may be slower for you to start with, but it will be faster in the long run if you learn to do it this way.

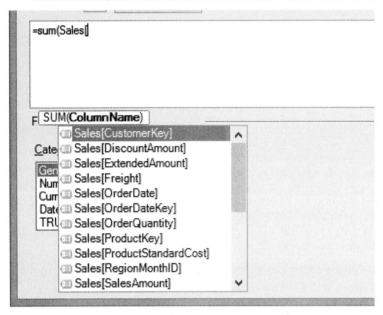

7. Close the formula by typing **)** and then click Check Formula.

If you practice writing your DAX this way, you will become very fast very quickly. Stick with it until you can do this as second nature.

Here's How: Editing Calculated Fields

It is easy to go back and edit (or simply review) calculated fields after you have written them. Follow these steps from within Excel:

1. On the Power Pivot tab, click Calculated Fields (see #1 below) and then Manage Calculated Fields (#2) to see a list of all of the calculated fields you have created.

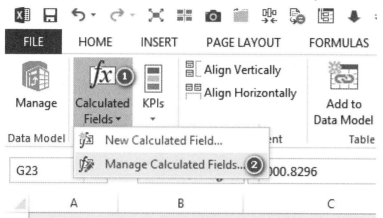

The Manage Calculated Fields dialog appears, as shown below.

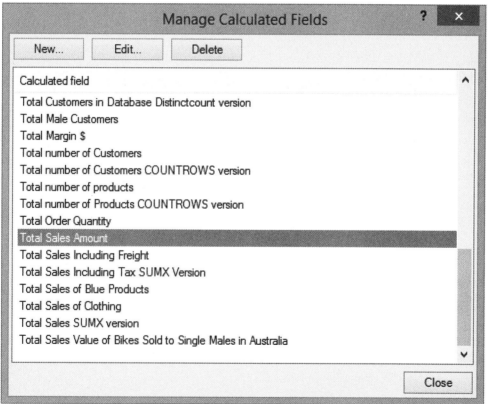

2. Use the Manage Calculated Fields dialog to create, edit, and delete any calculated fields as needed.

Note In Excel 2010, you just need to find the calculated field you want anywhere in the PivotTable Fields list, right-click it, and select Edit.

What to Do When Something Goes Wrong Writing DAX

At some point you will start the process of creating a new calculated field, and something will go wrong. For one reason or another, you will need to stop what you are doing and go back into Excel. This can be a problem for two reasons:

- The Calculated Field dialog box is *modal*, so while it is open, you can't do anything else until you dismiss this box.

- The formula you add must be valid DAX; otherwise, it can create problems. Sometimes you can't even close the dialog if the DAX is not valid.

In such cases, you may lose the work you have already done (e.g., the steps you have already completed, such as selecting the table, typing the name of the formula, selecting the formatting, etc.), and you may even have the DAX formula half written. But because the formula is incorrect, you can't save it! There are two tricks to handling this problem, depending on how deep you are in.

The first trick can be used when you don't have any meaningful DAX that you want to save, but you have already selected the table, typed the name of the formula, etc. In this case, simply enter =1 in the formula section, as shown below.

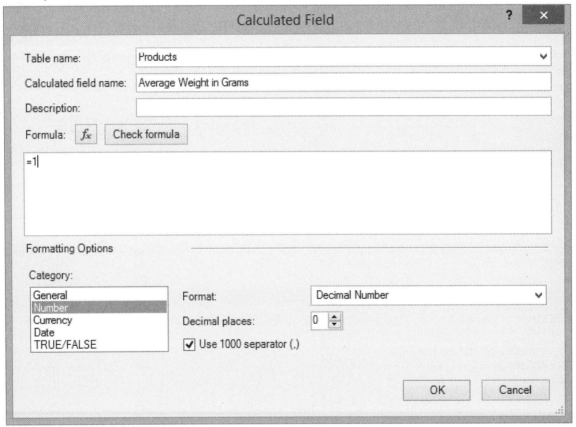

When you do this, the formula is saved with the name, table selection, and formatting. You can come back any time you are ready and edit the formula.

You use the second trick when you are having problems writing your formula, and you want to come back to it later (e.g., maybe you need to do some research on the web). Consider the formula shown in the image below as an example. Once you are this deep into a calculated field, you don't want to start again from scratch, nor do you want to replace the formula with =1 as suggested above.

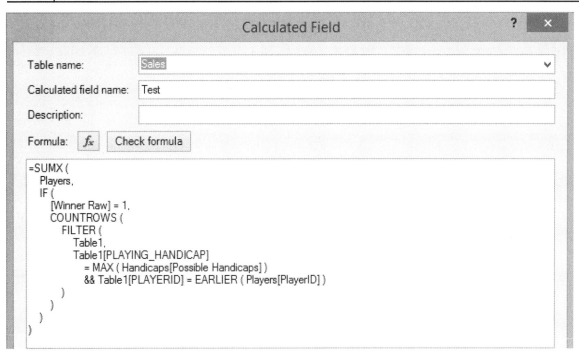

There is a simple solution to this problem, and it leverages the fact that DAX can return text results to a pivot table. If you need to suspend writing this calculated field midstream, simply wrap the formula in double quotes, as shown below.

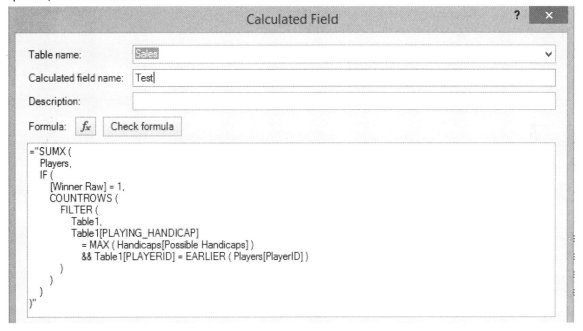

DAX then treats the entire formula as a text constant and allows you to save the formula. You can later come back and change the formula after you have had a chance to do your research.

The only time this doesn't work is when you have a genuine need to use double quotes in the formula, as in this example:

```
=CALCULATE([Total Number of Customers],
        Customers[Gender] = "M")
```

In this case, you can temporarily replace the double quotes in your formula with single quotes and then wrap the whole thing in double quotes, as shown here:

```
="CALCULATE([Total Number of Customers],
        Customers[Gender] = 'M')"
```

You can reverse the process when you are ready to re-edit the calculated field.

4: DAX Topic: SUM(), COUNT(), COUNTROWS(), MIN(), MAX(), COUNTBLANK(), and DIVIDE()

This chapter starts out with some basic DAX formulas to get you started. Most of the DAX functions in this chapter accept a column as the only parameter, like this: =FORMULA (*ColumnName*) . The only exception is =COUNTROWS (*Table*) , which takes a table (not a column) as the parameter.

All the functions in this chapter are *aggregation functions,* or *aggregators*. That is, they take inputs from a column or table and somehow aggregate the contents (differently for each formula).

Think about the column Sales[ExtendedAmount], which has more than 60,000 rows of data. You can't simply put the entire column into a pivot table because the pivot table can't "fit" a column into a single cell on the spreadsheet.

The following example shows a DAX formula that uses a "naked" column without any aggregation function. This will not work when you're writing a calculated field. Note the last sentence in the error message.

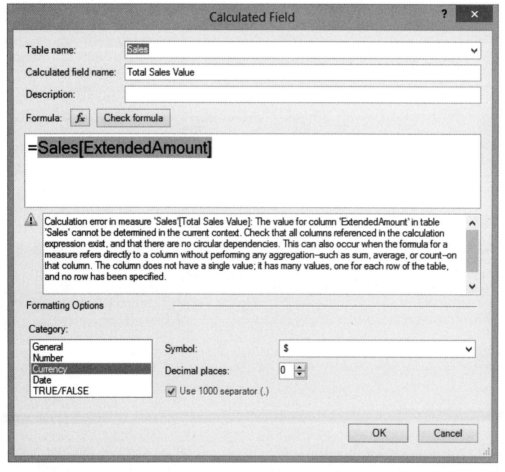

You have to tell Power Pivot how to aggregate the data from this column so that it returns just a single value to each cell in the pivot table. All of these aggregators effectively convert a column of values into a single value.

The next example shows the correct way to write this calculated field. Note how I used the table name and the column name in the formula. This is best practice.

> **Note** Always refer to the table name *and* the column name when writing DAX. Never refer to a column without also specifying the table name first. In future versions of Power Pivot, the table name will be added automatically, but for now you need to manually type both the table name and the column name. It will become clear why this is the case shortly.

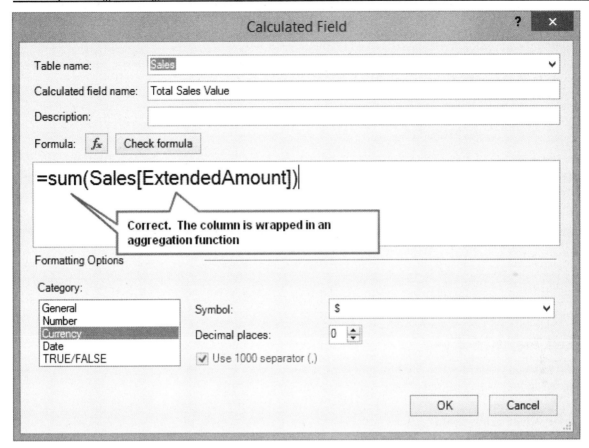

Reusing Calculated Fields

One important capability in DAX is that you can reuse calculated fields when writing other calculated fields. Say that you create a new calculated field called [Total Sales Value]. Once this calculated field exists in the Power Pivot data model, it can be referenced and reused inside other calculated fields. For example, after creating the calculated field [Total Sales Value], you could use the following formula to create a new calculated field for 10% tax on the sale of goods:

```
[Total Tax] = [Total Sales Value] * 0.1
```

Note that the new calculated field [Total Tax] is a calculation based on the original calculated field [Total Sales Value] multiplied by 0.1.

It is good practice to reuse calculated fields inside other calculated fields.

Writing DAX

It's time to start to write some DAX of your own. When I say *write*, I mean sit in front of your PC, open your workbook with the data loaded (from Chapter 1), and really write some DAX. Especially if you have never written formulas using these functions, you should physically do it now, as you read this section. Imagining yourself doing it in your mind is not enough.

If you haven't already done so, go ahead and load the test data, following the steps from Chapter 1. Once it is loaded and prepared, you are ready to create the new calculated fields listed in the following sections.

The first calculated field you will write is the same one from "Here's How: Using IntelliSense" in Chapter 3.

Practice Exercises

Periodically throughout the rest of this book you will find practice exercises that are designed to help you learn. You should complete each exercise as you get to it. The answers to all of these extra practices exercises are provided in "Appendix A: Answers to Practice Exercises" on page 175.

Practice Exercises: SUM()

Try to write the following DAX formulas without looking back at how it was done. If you can't do it, refer to Chapter 3 and then give it another go. Remember that you are here to practice! Find the solutions to these practice exercises in Appendix A.

Write DAX formulas for the following columns using SUM().

1. [Total Sales Amount]

Write a new calculated field that is the total of the sales in the ExtendedAmount column from the Sales table. This new calculated field will be the same formula covered at the start of this chapter, but I have given the calculated field a new name here in this practice exercise in case you already wrote the previous version when reading Chapter 3.

2. [Total Cost Value]

Create a calculated field that is the sum of one of the cost columns in the Sales table. This calculated field uses exactly the same structure as the calculated field above, but it adds the cost of the product instead of the sales amount. You can use any of the product cost columns in the Sales table; all the cost columns are the same in this sample database.

3. [Total Margin $]

Create a new calculated field for the total margin, which is total sales minus total cost. Make sure you reuse the two calculated fields you created above in this new calculated field.

4. [Total Margin %]

Create a new calculated field that takes Total Margin $ from above and express it now as a percentage of total sales. Once again, reuse the calculated fields you created above.

5. [Total Sales Tax Paid]

Create another calculated field for total sales tax paid. Look for a tax column in the Sales table and add up the total for that column.

6. [Total Sales Including Tax]

Note that the total sales amount above excludes tax, so you will need to add two calculated fields together to get this total.

7. [Total Order Quantity]

This is just the same as the others, but this time you add up the quantities purchased. Look for the correct column in the Sales table.

	A	B
1	Row Labels	Total Sales Value
2	Accessories	$700,760
3	Bikes	$28,318,145
4	Clothing	$339,773
5	Grand Total	$29,358,677

Did you do the following?

- Did you create a pivot table first, and put Products[Category] on Rows in your pivot table (or something else on Rows that is appropriate for these calculated fields)? This is best practice for Excel users because you get immediate feedback after you write your calculated field; you can *see* the results.

- Did you reference all columns in your calculated fields in the format *TableName* [*ColumnName*] (i.e., always reference the table name)? ou should never reference a column in DAX without first specifying the table name; always use the table name and the column name.

- Did you use the Calculated Field dialog box as your process flow prompt, filling each step along the way without skipping any steps? Using this dialog box is a great way to make sure you don't miss anything.

- Did you click on the Check Formula button before clicking OK? Power Pivot is a bit clunky and sensitive to incorrect syntax. (Well, the current versions, in Excel 2010 and Excel 2013, are clunky anyway.) Clicking OK when there is an error with the formula can create errors in your workbook, including pivot table errors and even workbook corruption. It's just better to get it right before you click OK, so *always* use the Check Formula button, even for the most basic formulas.

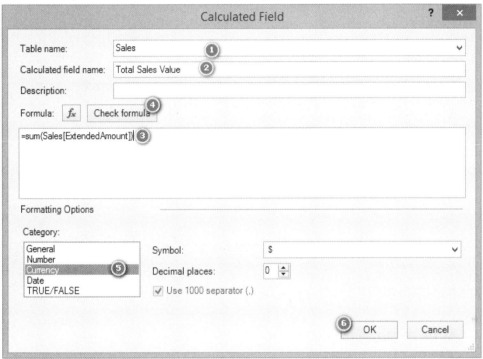

- Did you put the calculated fields in the `Sales` table? The rule is that you should always put a calculated field in the table where the data is stored. As you can see above, `[Total Sales Value]` is a formula that adds up the column `Sales[ExtendedAmount]`. This column of data is in the `Sales` table, so this is where you put the calculated field.

- Did you use the keyboard and look at the IntelliSense when you typed the calculated fields? Try not to use the mouse. It may be faster now (for some people), but relying on the mouse will prevent you from getting faster in the future. Learn to use the keyboard and follow the process covered in the section "Here's How: Using IntelliSense."

Remember that the answers to all the exercises in this book are available in "A. SUM()" on page 175. This is to stop you from peeking when you should be thinking and typing. If you do the thinking now, you will *learn how to do it*, and that will pay you back in spades in the future.

Okay, it's time to move on with a new DAX formula.

The COUNT() Function

As you write this new formula using COUNT(), take the time to look again at how IntelliSense can help you write DAX.

Remember, whenever you type a new formula, you can pause before you type the ((open parenthesis) or press Tab to see a description of the formula appear on the screen. **The description has some very useful information.**

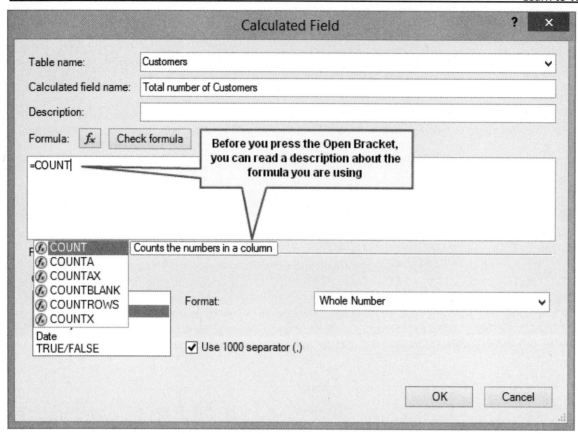

Note above that the tooltip says that this function "counts the numbers in a column." This gives you three very useful pieces of information. You've already worked out the first one: It *counts*. In addition, this tooltip tells you that the function counts *numbers* and also that the numbers need to be in a *column*. This should be enough information about the COUNT() function for you to write some calculated fields using it.

Practice Exercises: COUNT()

Now it is time to write some DAX formulas using the COUNT() function. Find the solutions to these practice exercises in Appendix A.

> **Note** Don't forget to set up a pivot table first. A good approach is to give the sheet in your last exercise a name such as SUM and then create a new sheet for this exercise called COUNT. This way you can easily look back at your work later for a refresher. When you set up a new pivot table, make sure you have something meaningful on Rows in your pivot table, such as Products[Category]. Look at the image below if you are not sure how to set up the pivot table.

8. [Total Number of Products]

Use the Products lookup table when writing this calculated field. Just count how many product numbers there are. Product numbers and product keys are the same thing in this example.

9. [Total Number of Customers]

Use the Customers lookup table. Again, just count the customer numbers. Customer numbers and customer keys are the same thing in this example.

Did you end up with the following pivot table?

Row Labels ▼	Total Number of Customers	Total Number of Products
Accessories	18,484	35
Bikes	18,484	125
Clothing	18,484	48
Components	18,484	189
Grand Total	**18,484**	**397**

If not, check your answers against those in "B. COUNT()" on page 175.

> **Note** The above table is a bit confusing because [Total Number of Customers] doesn't seem to be correct. It is returning the same value for every row in the pivot table, and this is not something you are used to seeing. But if you think about it, it does actually make sense. You are not counting how many customers purchased these product categories; you are just counting the number of customers in the customer master file, and the number of customers doesn't change based on the product categories; the customers are either on file, or they are not. (More on this in the next chapter.)

Did you get any errors that you weren't expecting? Did you use the correct column(s) in your calculated fields? Remember from the tooltip above that the COUNT() function counts numbers. It doesn't count text fields, so if you try to count the names or descriptions, you get an error.

The COUNTROWS() Function

Let's move on to a new function, COUNTROWS(). I personally prefer to use COUNTROWS() instead of COUNT(). It just seems more natural to me. These functions are not exactly the same, even though they can be used interchangeably at times. If you use COUNT() with *TableName*[*ColumnName*] and the column is missing a number in one of the rows (for some reason), then that row won't get counted. COUNTROWS() counts every row in the table, regardless of whether the columns have a value in every row. So be careful and make sure you select the best formula for the task at hand.

Practice Exercises: COUNTROWS()

In these exercises, you need to rewrite the two calculated fields from Practice Exercises 8 and 9 using COUNTROWS() instead of COUNT(). Find the solutions to these practice exercises in "C. COUNTROWS()" on page 175.

10. [Total Number of Products COUNTROWS Version]

Count the number of products in the Products table, using the COUNTROWS() function.

11. [Total Number of Customers COUNTROWS Version]

Count the number of customers in the Customers table, using the COUNTROWS() function.

Not surprisingly, you should get the same answer you got with COUNT(), as shown below.

Row Labels ▼	Total number of Customers COUNTROWS version	Total number of Products COUNTROWS version
Accessories	18,484	35
Bikes	18,484	125
Clothing	18,484	48
Components	18,484	189
Grand Total	**18,484**	**397**

A Word on Naming Calculated Fields

You may have noticed that I sometimes use very long and descriptive names for calculated fields. I encourage you to make calculated field names as long as they need to be to make it clear what the calculated fields actually are. You will be grateful down the track when you are trying to work out the fine difference between two similar-sounding calculated fields.

It is possible to change the "display name" of a calculated field once it is in a pivot table. Just click on the name of the calculated field (see #1 below) and then edit the name in the formula bar in Excel (#2).

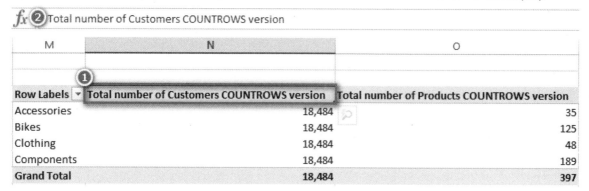

You can edit the display name directly in the pivot table, too, if you prefer. Doing this will not change the name of the actual calculated field, just the name that is displayed in your pivot table (and in the PivotTable Fields list).

Once you have renamed your calculated fields, you get something more like this:

Row Labels ▼	Total Customers	Total Products
Accessories	18,484	35
Bikes	18,484	125
Clothing	18,484	48
Components	18,484	189
Grand Total	**18,484**	**397**

After you have changed the display name, you can change it back by right-clicking on the name (see #1 at right) and selecting Value Field Settings (#2).

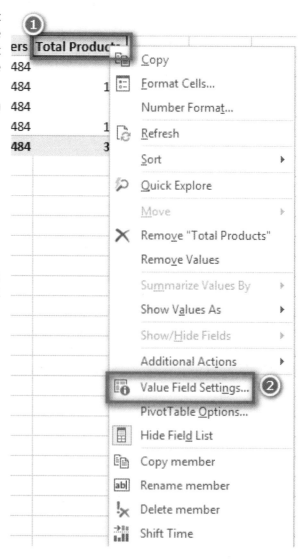

Then, in the Value Field Settings dialog, you can change the custom name back to the original name by setting the Custom Name text box to the same value as the Source Name text box above it—or any other name, for that matter.

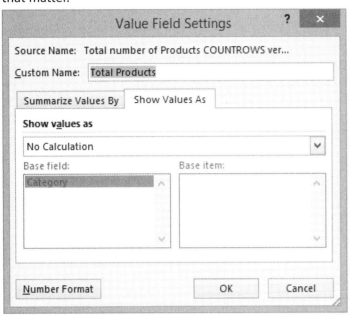

The method you've just seen is useful when you want a shorter name to appear in your pivot table. Sometimes the name of the calculated field will make sense only in certain situations (i.e., in certain pivot table layouts) and not in other pivot tables. However, if you want to keep using a longer descriptive name but just want to make it fit in the pivot table, you need a VBA macro that Rob Collie has shared on his website to automatically wrap the names so they are more readable. Just go to http://powerpivotpro.com and search for "more readable pivots," and you will find it. I have this VBA code on my PC and a button on the Quick Access Toolbar to run the VBA code (see #1 below).

This is a must-have button for serious Power Pivot users. The other button I use a lot is the Insert Power Pivot Table button (see #2 above). You can read about this one on my blog, at http://exceleratorbi.com.au. Just search for "insert Power Pivot table." This is only useful in Excel 2013 due to the missing Insert Power Pivot Table button.

> **Note** If you don't know how to use VBA tools that others make available, take a look at the blog post I wrote on this topic at http://xbi.com.au/vba.

The DISTINCTCOUNT() Function

DISTINCTCOUNT() counts each value in a column once and only once. If the value appears more than once in a column, it is still counted only once. Consider the Customers table: In this case, the customer key is unique, and by definition each customer key appears only once in the table (note that customer key = customer number). So in this case, the DISTINCTCOUNT() of the customer key in the Customers table gives you the same answer as COUNTROWS() of the Customers table. But if you were to do a DISTINCTCOUNT() of the customer key in the Sales table, you would actually be counting the total number of customers that had ever purchased something—which is not the same thing.

Practice Exercises: DISTINCTCOUNT()

To practice using DISTINCTCOUNT(), create a new pivot table and put Customers[Occupation] on Rows in the pivot table and [Total Sales Amount] on Values. Then write the following calculated fields using DISCTINCTCOUNT(). Find the solutions to these practice exercises in "D. DISTINCTCOUNT()" on page 175.

12. [Total Customers in Database Distinctcount Version]

You need to count a column of unique values in the Customers table. Go ahead and write the calculated field now. Once you are done, add the [Total Number of Customers] calculated field you created earlier to the pivot table as well. You should end up with a pivot table like the one below.

Row Labels ▼	Total Sales Amount	Total Customers in Database Distinctcount version	Total number of Customers
Clerical	$4,684,787	2,928	2,928
Management	$5,467,862	3,075	3,075
Manual	$2,857,971	2,384	2,384
Professional	$9,907,977	5,520	5,520
Skilled Manual	$6,440,081	4,577	4,577
Grand Total	$29,358,677	18,484	18,484

Did you get the same answer as above in the new calculated field? Did you remember to format the calculated field to something practical (like a whole number with thousands separators)?

13. [Count of Occupation]

Create a new pivot table and put Customers[YearlyIncome] on Rows in the pivot table. Then create the calculated field [Count of Occupation].

Use DISTINCTCOUNT() to count the values in the Occupation column in the Customers table. You end up with a pivot table like the one shown below left. The way to read this table is that there are customers in three different occupations that have incomes of 10,000, there are customers across four occupations that have incomes of 30,000, etc.

Row Labels ▼	Count of Occupation	Row Labels ▼	Count of Occupation
10000	3	10000	3
20000	3	20000	3
30000	4	30000	4
40000	4	40000	4
50000	3	50000	3
60000	3	60000	3
70000	3	70000	3
80000	3	80000	3
90000	3	90000	3
100000	2	100000	2
110000	2	110000	2
120000	2	120000	2
130000	2	130000	2
150000	2	150000	2
160000	2	160000	2
170000	2	170000	2
Grand Total	5	Grand Total	5

Using Conditional Formatting to Make Pivots More Readable

It is much easier to read the pivot table if you apply some of the "out of the box" visualisations from standard Excel; for example, compare the pivot table above left with the conditionally formatted version above right. I am sure you agree that it is much easier to read the insights from the table on the right.

Next I show you how to apply conditional formatting in a pivot table, step by step. If you do it the way I describe here, the formatting will be applied to the entire pivot table, and the formatting will update when the pivot table grows and shrinks. If you just select the cells and apply formatting directly to individual cells or groups of cells, the formatting will not update when the pivot table changes shape.

Here's How: Applying Conditional Formatting to a Pivot Table

Here is the step-by-step process for applying conditional formatting to a pivot table:

1. Highlight one cell you want to receive the formatting (see #1 below).

2. On the Home tab in Excel, click Conditional Formatting (#2), Data Bars (#3) and select the visualisation effect you want to use (#4).

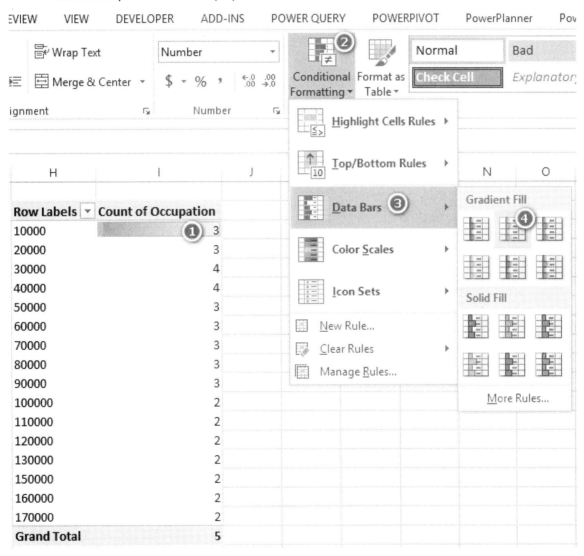

3. Click the formatting popup box that appears.

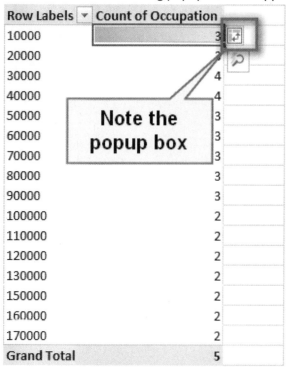

You are presented with three options on how to apply the formatting:

- The first option is just for the current cell (see #1 below).

- The second option allows you to apply the formatting to every row in the table and the grand total (see #2 below). You should use this option only if the data in the rows and the grand total are similar in size and scale. For example, if your grand total has a value of 10,000 and the individual rows in the pivot table have a maximum value of 500, then this second option will not give you very useful results. A good example of when to use this second option is for "percentage change" calculated fields.

- The third option is the one you should use most often (#3). It applies the formatting to the rows only and not to the grand total. Why the third option is the best choice will make more sense when you get to some of the other examples later in the book.

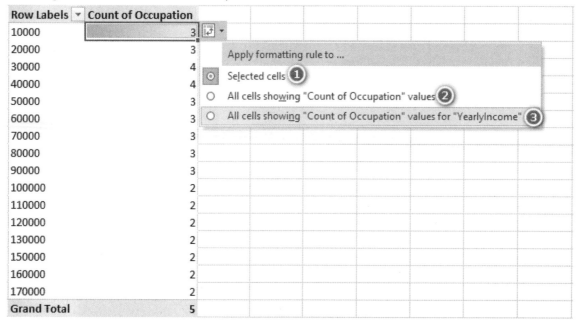

Using well-placed conditional formatting is a great way to make your pivot tables easier to read and make the insights jump out, as shown below.

Row Labels ▼	Count of Occupation
10000	3
20000	3
30000	4
40000	4
50000	3
60000	3
70000	3
80000	3
90000	3
100000	2
110000	2
120000	2
130000	2
150000	2
160000	2
170000	2
Grand Total	**5**

Practice Exercises: DISTINCTCOUNT(), Cont.

The following exercises give you more practice DISTINCTCOUNT(). Find the solutions to these practice exercises in "D. DISTINCTCOUNT()" on page 175.

14. [Count of Country]

Create a new pivot table and put Territories[Group] on Rows. Write a new calculated field called [Count of Country], using DISTINCTCOUNT() over the Country column in the Territories table.

Row Labels ▼	Count of Country
Europe	3
NA	1
North America	2
Pacific	1
Grand Total	**7**

This pivot table shows you how many countries exist in each sales group.

15. [Customers That Have Purchased]

Create a new pivot table and put `Products[SubCategory]` on Rows. Then, using `DISTINCTCOUNT()` on data from the `Sales` table, create the new calculated field `[Total Customers That Have Purchased]`.

If you haven't already done so, apply some conditional formatting to the pivot table using the technique you learnt in the previous section and then sort the column from largest to smallest. You can see below that Tires and Tubes has the highest number of customers that have purchased at least once.

Row Labels	Customers Purchasing
Tires and Tubes	8,490
Road Bikes	6,397
Helmets	5,960
Bottles and Cages	4,548
Mountain Bikes	4,089
Jerseys	3,192
Touring Bikes	2,143
Caps	2,132
Fenders	2,110
Gloves	1,376
Shorts	1,019
Cleaners	875
Hydration Packs	719
Socks	559
Vests	557
Bike Racks	325
Bike Stands	243
Grand Total	18,484

Earlier in the chapter I explained the options to apply conditional formatting to just the rows in the pivot table or the rows and grand total. The conditional formatting in the above pivot table has been applied to the rows only. If I applied the conditional formatting to the grand total as well, then the bar in the grand total would be significantly longer than all of the other bars in the pivot table, as you can see in the pivot table below.

Row Labels	Customers That Have Purchased
Tires and Tubes	8,490
Road Bikes	6,397
Helmets	5,960
Bottles and Cages	4,548
Mountain Bikes	4,089
Jerseys	3,192
Touring Bikes	2,143
Caps	2,132
Fenders	2,110
Gloves	1,376
Shorts	1,019
Cleaners	875
Hydration Packs	719
Socks	559
Vests	557
Bike Racks	325
Bike Stands	243
Grand Total	18,484

When you apply this formatting to the grand total, it often makes the conditional formatting harder to read. This is why you normally select the third option for applying conditional formatting (#3 below), particularly in the case where the grand total is an aggregation of the row items above.

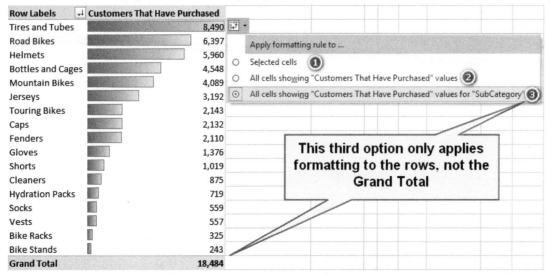

Now put `Calendar[CalendarYear]` on Columns in your pivot table and notice how the pivot table changes. If you applied the conditional formatting as described in this section, the conditional formatting will "stick" to the pivot table, and it will automatically update as the shape of the pivot table changes.

Customers Purchasing	Column Lab ▼				
Row Labels ↓	2001	2002	2003	2004	Grand Total
Tires and Tubes			3,766	5,147	8,490
Road Bikes	840	2,062	2,558	2,369	6,397
Helmets			2,541	3,617	5,960
Bottles and Cages			1,903	2,744	4,548
Mountain Bikes	173	615	1,961	2,094	4,089
Jerseys			1,316	1,922	3,192
Touring Bikes			824	1,332	2,143
Caps			874	1,280	2,132
Fenders			879	1,236	2,110
Gloves			567	829	1,376
Shorts			435	584	1,019
Cleaners			376	509	875
Hydration Packs			300	425	719
Socks			246	317	559
Vests			205	354	557
Bike Racks			136	191	325
Bike Stands			117	129	243
Grand Total	1,013	2,677	9,309	11,377	18,484

When you wrote this calculated field, did you remember to select the `Sales` table as the location to store it? Best practice says to put the calculated field in the table where the data comes from.

Practice Exercises: MAX(), MIN(), and AVERAGE()

`MAX()`, `MIN()`, and `AVERAGE()` are aggregators as they take multiple values as input and return a single value to the pivot table. Create the following new calculated fields. Find the solutions to these practice exercises in "E. MAX(), MIN(), and AVERAGE()" on page 176.

You should use the columns of data in the `Sales` table for these exercises. There are some additional pricing columns in the `Products` table, but these prices are only theoretical prices, or "list prices." In this sample data, the actual price information related to the transaction is stored in the `Sales` table.

16. [Maximum Tax Paid on a Product]

Remember to use a suitable column from the `Sales` table and use the `MAX()` function.

17. [Minimum Price Paid for a Product]

Again, use a suitable column from the `Sales` table but this time use the `MIN()` function.

18. [Average Price Paid for a Product]

Again, use a suitable column from the `Sales` table but this time use the `AVERAGE()` function.

You should end up with a pivot table like the one shown below.

Row Labels ▼	Maximum Tax Paid on a Product	Minimum Price Paid for a Product	Average Price Paid for a Product
Accessories	$12.72	$2.29	$19.42
Bikes	$286.26	$539.99	$1,862.42
Clothing	$5.60	$8.99	$37.33
Grand Total	$286.26	$2.29	$486.09

Notice that when you write these calculated fields from within a pivot table, you get positive immediate feedback about whether your calculated fields look correct.

Understanding When Calculated Fields Are Added to a Pivot Table Automatically

By now you have probably seen that new calculated fields you write automatically appear in your pivot table. For this to happen, two things must be true. First, you must select the pivot table before you start to write your calculated field. Second, you must save the calculated field without creating an error on save. If you forget to click the Check Formula button and save your calculated field *and* it creates an error, the calculated field will not be automatically added to your pivot table when you go back and fix the error. If this happens, you need to manually add the calculated field later, as described next.

Here's How: Manually Adding a Calculated Field to a Pivot Table

Follow these steps to add a calculated field to a pivot table:

1.   Click anywhere inside the pivot table.
2.   In the PivotTable Fields list, locate and select the calculated field you want to add to the pivot table then click in the check box next to the calculated field to add it to the pivot table.

If you can't find the calculated field, it is most likely that you forgot to select the correct table for storing your calculated field when you wrote the calculated field. Check in the other tables in the PivotTable Fields list to see if you can find it. If you have put the field in the wrong table, you just need to move the calculated field to the correct table, as described next.

Here's How: Moving an Existing Calculated Field to a Different Table

Follow these steps to move a calculated field to a different table:

1.   In the Excel window, navigate to the Power Pivot tab.
2.   Click Calculated Fields, Manage Calculated Fields.
3.   Select the calculated field in the list and then click Edit.
4.   Select the Table Name drop-down at the top of the Calculated Field dialog and then select the correct table from the list.
5.   Click OK to save your changes.

Practice Exercises: COUNTBLANK()

It's time for a new function: COUNTBLANK(). In this exercise, you'll use it to create a calculated field to check how complete the master data is.

Start a new pivot table and put Customers[Occupation] on Rows. Then click in your pivot table and start to write a new calculated field. In these exercises, you want to find out two things:

•   How many customers are missing Address Line 2 from the master data?

•   How many products in the Products table do not have a weight value stored in the master data?

Next, you'll write calculated fields to find this information. Find the solutions to these practice exercises in "F. COUNTBLANK()" on page 176.

19. [Customers Without Address Line 2]

The Address Line 2 column is in the Customers table. As you write the calculated field [Customers Without Address Line 2], be sure you do the following:

1.   Select the right table to store the calculated field.
2.   Give the calculated field a name.

3. Start typing your calculated field. Pause after you have the formula selected in IntelliSense and read what the formula does (if you don't already know). As shown below, it does exactly what you want it to do: count how many blanks are in this column.

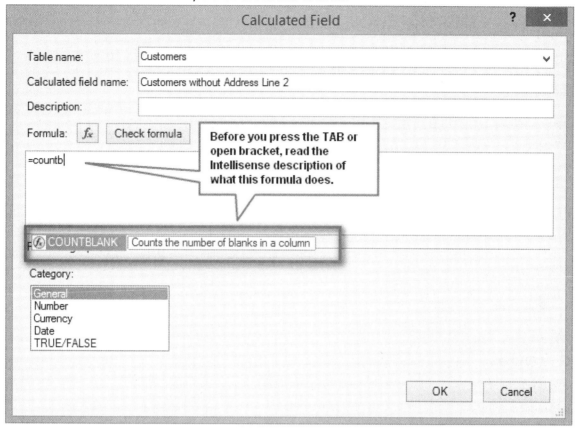

4. Complete the formula, apply the formatting, check the formula, and then save.

20. [Products Without Weight Values]

The column you need to use is in the `Products` table. You should end up with a table like the one shown below.

Row Labels	Customers without Address Line 2	Products without weight values
Clerical	2,878	122
Management	3,007	122
Manual	2,350	122
Professional	5,440	122
Skilled Manual	4,497	122
Grand Total	18,172	122

Note that the first calculated field, [Customers Without Address Line 2], is being filtered by the pivot table (i.e., Customers[Occupation] on Rows), and the values in the pivot table change with each row. But the second calculated field, [Products Without Weight Values], is not filtered; the values don't change for each row in the pivot table. You have seen this earlier in this book, and the technical term for it is *filter context*. Chapter 5 provides a detailed explanation of what filter context is, and that will help you understand what is happening and why.

The DIVIDE() Function

DIVIDE() is a simple yet powerful function; it is also known as "safe divide." DIVIDE() protects you against divide-by-zero errors in a pivot table. In an Excel spreadsheet, when you divide by a zero value, you get an error message. The same is true in a pivot table, but it can be worse in a pivot table as the entire pivot table may stop working as desired.

A pivot table, by design, hides any rows or columns that have no data. If you get an error in a calculated field inside a pivot table, it is possible that you will see lots of rows that you would otherwise not see, along with the unsightly error message. The DIVIDE() function is specifically designed to solve this problem. If you use DIVIDE() instead of the slash operator (/) for division, DAX returns a blank where you would otherwise get a divide-by-zero error. Given that pivot tables filter out blank rows by default, a blank row is a much better option than an error.

The syntax is DIVIDE(*numerator, denominator, optional-alternate-result*). If you don't specify the alternate result, a blank value is returned when there is a divide-by-zero error.

Practice Exercises: DIVIDE()

Create a new pivot table and put Products[Category] on Rows. Then add [Total Sales Amount] and [Total Margin $] to the pivot so you have some data to look at. This helps set the context for the new calculated fields you will write next.

Write the following calculated fields using DIVIDE(). Find the solutions to these practice exercises in "G. DIVIDE()" on page 176.

21. [Margin %]

Write a calculated field that calculates the percentage margin on sales (Margin $ divided by Total Sales). Reuse calculated fields that you have already written.

> **Note** This is a duplicate of a calculated field, called [Total Margin %], that you already wrote at the start of this chapter. This time write the formula using the DIVIDE() function but give it the name [Margin %]. The result will be the same, of course.

22. [Markup %]

Find Margin $ divided by Cost Price.

23. [Tax %]

Divide the total tax by the total sales amount.

Row Labels ▼	Total Sales Amount	Total Margin $	Margin %	Markup %	Tax %
Accessories	$700,760	$438,675	62.6%	167.4%	8.0%
Bikes	$28,318,145	$11,505,797	40.6%	68.4%	8.0%
Clothing	$339,773	$136,413	40.1%	67.1%	8.0%
Grand Total	**$29,358,677**	**$12,080,884**	**41.1%**	**69.9%**	**8.0%**

Did you format the results as Number and Percentage? These formatting options are a bit hard to find. The dialog below shows how you set these options.

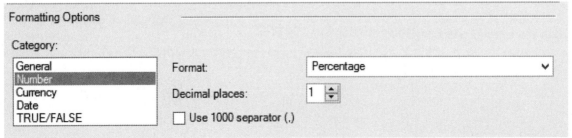

5: Concept: Filter Propagation

It's time to talk about filter propagation. In Chapter 4 we looked at the COUNT() function and saw some strange behaviour with the [Total Number of Customers] calculated field. You need to understand the process of filter propagation before you can truly understand what is happening here.

Consider the following pivot table.

Row Labels ▾	Total Number of Customers	Total Number of Products
Accessories ①	18,484	35
Bikes	18,484	125
Clothing	18,484	48
Components	18,484	189
Grand Total	**18,484**	**397**

The result [Total Number of Products] in this pivot table is displaying a different value for each product category (i.e., each row in the pivot table has a different number of products), but the value for [Total Number of Customers] is the same for each product category in the pivot table. The technical reason this happens is because the row labels in the pivot table (see #1 above) are "filtering" the products in the Products table in the data model *before this calculated field is evaluated.* But these same rows (product categories) are *not filtering the* Customers *table at all*.

Pivot tables, by their very nature, "filter" data. The filtering applied to a pivot table is called the *initial filter context—initial* because it is possible to change the filter context coming from a pivot table by using the CALCULATE() function. (This is covered in Chapter 8.) So the initial filter context is the standard filtering coming from a pivot table before any possible modifications from DAX formulas using CALCULATE().

The initial filter context comes from four areas of a pivot table:

- Rows (see #1 below)
- Columns (#2)
- Filters (#3)
- Slicers (#4)

Reading the Initial Filter Context

The following pivot table, repeated here from Chapter 4, shows [Total Number of Customers] and [Total Number of Products]:

Row Labels ▼	Total Number of Customers	Total Number of Products
Accessories	18,484	35
Bikes	18,484	125
Clothing	18,484	48
Components	18,484	189
Grand Total	18,484	397

In Chapter 4 this pivot table was a bit confusing because it had the same value for [Total Number of Customers] on every row in the pivot. Once you learn to read the initial filter context in a pivot table, you will be able to make more sense of what is going on here.

Let's step through the process of reading the initial filter context from this pivot table. Before we do that, though, you should add the [Total Sales Amount] calculated field to the pivot table so it looks like the one below.

Row Labels ▼	Total Number of Customers	Total Number of Products	Total Sales Amount
Accessories	18,484	35	$700,760
Bikes	18,484	125	$28,318,145
Clothing	18,484	48	$339,773
Components	18,484	189	
Grand Total	18,484	397	$29,358,677

Then point to the cell that's highlighted in red below and say this out loud (really): *"The initial filter context for this cell is* Products[Category] = Accessories.*"* Then point to the cell underneath the red-highlighted cell; this cell has an initial filter context of Products[Category] = Bikes. You can figure out the rest based on this pattern. It is important that you learn to "read" the initial filter context from your pivot tables because it will help you understand how the value for each cell in a pivot table is calculated. And it is important to refer to the *full table name and column name* because that forces you to look, check, and confirm exactly which tables you are using in your pivots.

Understanding the Flow of the Initial Filter Context

Now that you know what the initial filter context is, you can mentally apply the following steps to your data model and track how the filters flow through relationships (technically the filters propagate from one table to another):

1. The initial filter context coming from the pivot table is applied to the underlying table(s) in the data model. In this example, there is just one table, the Products table (see #1 below), where Products[Category] = "Accessories". The Products table is filtered so that only rows in the table that are equal to Accessories remain; all other rows are filtered so that they are not in play. (Note that the initial filter context can impact more than one table, but in this example, it is just the one table.)

2. The filter applied to the Products table then automatically propagates through the relationship(s) between the tables, flowing *downhill* to the connected table(s) (see #2 below). The filters only ever automatically flow from the "one" side of the relationship to the "many" side of the relationship; from the "arrow" side to the "dot" side; from the lookup table to the data table—whatever terms you use, it's always downhill. This is one of the reasons it is good for Excel users to lay out the tables using the Collie layout methodology: with the lookup tables above and the data tables below. This is a mental cue for you, to help you instantly visualise how automatic filter propagation works. (See "Shaping the Data" in Chapter 2.)

3. The connected table, the `Sales` table, is then also filtered (see #3 below). (Remember that there can be more than one connected table.) Only the products that are of the type `Products[Category]` = `"Accessories"` remain in play in the `Sales` table, too, and all the other products are filtered away. This is just temporary—just for this calculation of *this one single cell in the pivot.*

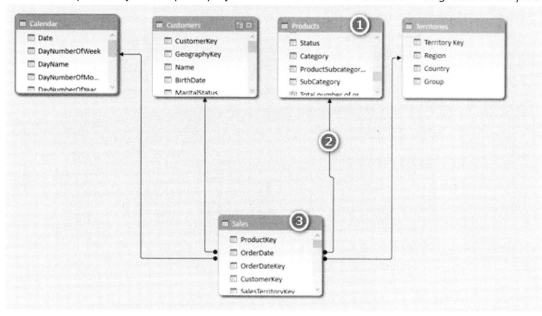

After all the automatic filter propagation has been completed, then and only then does the calculated field get evaluated. In this case, the calculated field is `[Total Sales Amount]` = `SUM(Sales[ExtendedAmount])`. It returns the value $700,760 to the single pivot table cell we started to look at in this example. This process is repeated for every single cell in the pivot table, including subtotal and grand total cells.

Simulating What Has Happened Here

Allow me to belabour the point here to ensure that this is clear. A useful simulation is to go to the Power Pivot window, click on the drop-down filter on the `Products[Category]` column (see #1 below) and select the Accessories filter (#2).

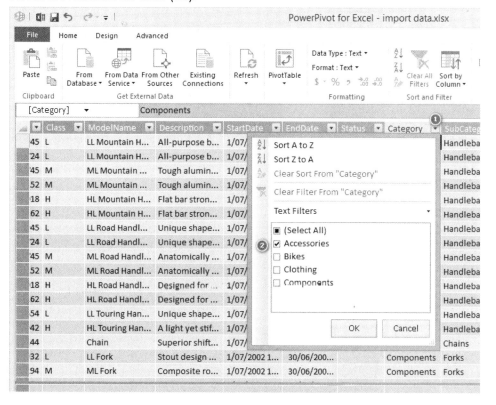

After you do this, you can see how many rows in your table are left after the filter in the record locator in the bottom-left corner of the Power Pivot window. In this case, the list of products gets filtered from 397 down to just the 35 accessories.

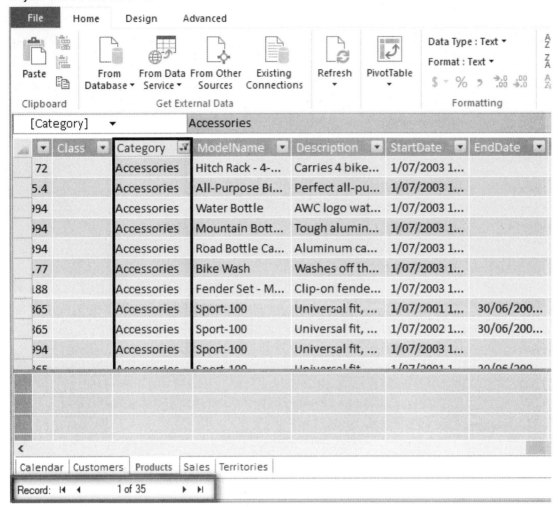

Understanding Filter Propagation

Let's look at another cell in the pivot table. You always evaluate each cell one at a time, without regard for any other cell in the pivot table, even if the cell is a subtotal or grand total cell. All cells are evaluated using the same process, without regard for any other cell in the pivot table.

Look at the pivot table below and read the initial filter context for the highlighted cell out loud: *"The initial filter context for this cell is* `Products[Category] = Clothing.`*"*

Row Labels	Total Number of Customers	Total Number of Products	Total Sales Amount
Accessories	18,484	35	$700,760
Bikes	18,484	125	$28,318,145
Clothing	18,484	48	$339,773
Components	18,484	189	
Grand Total	**18,484**	**397**	**$29,358,677**

The initial filter context filters the tables in your data model as follows:

1. The initial filter context is applied to the table(s). In this example `Products[Category]` = "Clothing". The `Products` table (see #1 below) is then filtered so that only rows in the table that are equal to `Clothing` remain.

2. This filter automatically propagates through the relationships that exist between the tables, flowing *downhill only* to the connected table(s) (see #2 below).

3. The connected table (`Sales` in this example) is then also filtered so that the same products in the `Products` table will remain in the `Sales` table (i.e., only clothing products will be visible in the `Sales` table) (see #3 below).

4. The filter applied to the `Sales` table *does not* automatically flow back uphill to the `Customers` table (or to the other two tables, for that matter) (see #4 below). Filters *only* automatically propagate through the relationships *downhill* from the "one" side of the relationship to the "many" side.

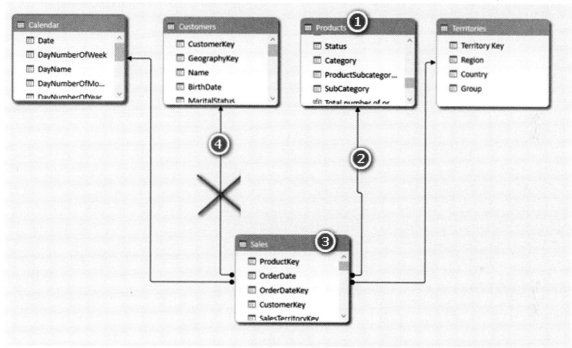

So the net result is that the `Customers` table is completely *unfiltered* by the initial filter context. Because the `Customers` table is unfiltered, the total 18,484 is returned to the pivot table in this cell (and the same is true for every other cell for this calculated field in the current pivot).

Even if this doesn't seem right to you yet, realise that it is working as designed. Understanding gives you power, so stick with it until you are clear about how it works. Read this section a few times if you need to. You will learn to love the way it is designed and will learn to make it work for you.

Adding Relationships Where Needed

It is quite likely that you will now have a warning message from Excel, suggesting that a relationship may be needed. This warning may pop up above the PivotTable Fields list whenever Excel detects that the filter context in your pivot table is not filtering your calculated fields. In the example above, the initial filter context from the `Products` table (`Products[Category]` on Rows) is not filtering the `[Total Number of Customers]` calculated field. Power Pivot realises that this might be a mistake and sends you a warning message.

If you can't see the message at this point, try removing the `[Total Number of Customers]` calculated field and then adding it back again, and you should get the warning shown below.

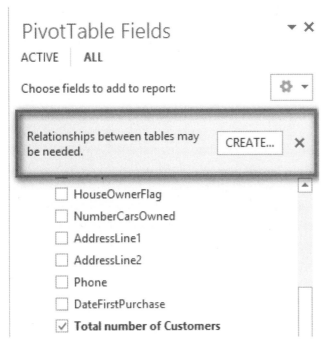

Now sometimes this warning is valid, but in my experience, there are as many false warnings as there are valid warnings, particularly as you write more complex DAX. If you see this message, take a look at your pivot table and data model and decide whether the warning is valid. If you are missing a relationship between tables, then you can go ahead and create that relationship in the Power Pivot window. If you are not missing a relationship, then you can just close this warning by clicking the X. In Excel 2010 you can turn off this warning message prompt, but unfortunately that is not possible in Excel 2013.

Tip Never click the Create button in this warning box. If you do click it, Power Pivot tries to work out what is wrong, and it may even automagically fix it. But if that happens, you will have no idea what Power Pivot is doing, and it may or may not be the correct fix for the problem. Either way, it is much better to investigate yourself because you will improve your understanding of how filter propagation works, and this will make you more confident about ignoring false warnings in the future.

Note You simply *must* understand how filter propagation works in Power Pivot, or you will never be really good at writing DAX. I suggest that you read this chapter multiple times if necessary to make sure you are clear about it.

6: DAX Topic: The Basic Iterators SUMX() and AVERAGEX()

The formulas we covered in Chapter 4 are all aggregation formulas. Those aggregation formulas act on an entire column or table and use a specific aggregating technique to return a single value to a cell in the pivot table.

There is a second class of formulas that can return the same answers as these aggregation functions—but using a different approach. These "X-functions" (i.e., any function that has an X on the end of the name) are part of the family called *iterators*.

Iterator Functions and Row Context

The main difference between iterator functions and the other functions we have looked at so far is that the iterators have what is called a "row context." *Row context* means that the function is "aware" of *which row* it is referencing at any point in time. Rather than getting into a theoretical explanation, let's move on to the first iterator, SUMX(), and talk about row context as you learn how to use this function.

Using SUMX(*table, expression*)

SUMX() takes two parameters: a table name and an expression to evaluate. SUMX() creates a row context in the specified table and then iterates through each row of the table, one row at a time, and evaluates the expression for each row as it gets to it. A row context is a concept in DAX that creates "awareness" of the existence of the rows in the table so it can iterate through them one at a time until it has touched every single row once and only once. You can think of a row context as a *numbered check list* of all rows that SUMX() can use to keep track of where it is up to. SUMX() can then work through the rows one at a time, "ticking off" each row to make sure none has been missed. This row context only exists in certain DAX formulas including the X-functions (Chapter 6), in calculated columns (Chapter 7 on page 66), and Filter() (Chapter 13 on page 103).

To demonstrate the point, let's write a new version of the [Total Sales Including Sales Tax] calculated field. First, create a new pivot table, put Products[Category] on Rows, and then write out this calculated field:

```
[Total Sales Including Tax SUMX Version]
    = SUMX(Sales, Sales[ExtendedAmount] + Sales[TaxAmt])
```

Notice that in this calculated field, you are not wrapping the columns in an aggregation function. In this case, you *are* referring to "naked columns," and that is perfectly okay inside an iterator. There is no need to wrap the columns in an aggregation function when using an X-function (or any other function that creates a row context). The way an X-function works is that it goes to the table specified (in this case, Sales), creates a row context for it to use as a reference, and then takes each single row in the table one at a time and evaluates the expression for that single row.

As you can see at right, when there is only one single row from the table in play, DAX is able to refer to the exact intersection of each column and the specific row it is currently iterating over. Therefore, during each step of the iteration process, the column names in the expression are actually only referring to a single value—the value that is the intersection of the column and the current row in the row context.

ExtendedAmount	TaxAmt
564.99	45.1992
564.99	45.1992
24.49	1.9592
8.99	0.7192
8.99	0.7192
564.99	45.1992
53.99	4.3192
53.99	4.3192
120	9.6

So one row at a time, the single value in the Sales[ExtendedAmount] column is added to the single value of the Sales[TaxAmt] column. After the first row is evaluated (and the result is stored temporarily in memory for later), SUMX() then selects a second row and does the same thing, then a third row and does the same thing, and so on until it has iterated through every single row in the table, missing none. It iterates through every single row once and only once (not necessarily in the order you see on the screen). Once it has completed this calculation for every single row in the specified table, it sums all the results together and returns a single value to the pivot table cell.

Practice Exercises: SUMX()

Write the following calculated fields for practice. Find the solutions to these practice exercises in "H. SUMX()" on page 176.

24. [Total Sales SUMX Version]

Use `Quantity` times `UnitPrice` from the appropriate columns in the `Sales` table

25. [Total Sales Including Tax SUMX Version]

Add the `ExtendedSales` column to the appropriate tax column in the `Sales` table.

26. [Total Sales Including Freight]

Add the `ExtendedSales` amount to the `Freight` cost.

Did you get the following pivot table?

Row Labels ▾	Total Sales SUMX version	Total Sales Including Tax SUMX Version	Total Sales Including Freight
Accessories	$700,760	$756,821	$718,281
Bikes	$28,318,145	$30,583,596	$29,026,099
Clothing	$339,773	$366,954	$348,267
Grand Total	**$29,358,677**	**$31,707,371**	**$30,092,647**

When you use the Calculated Field Wizard to step you through the process, you can make sure you do the following (without missing any steps):

1. Put the calculated fields in the correct tables.
2. Give the calculated field a meaningful name.
3. Write the formula and then check to ensure that it was written correctly.
4. Apply suitable formatting.

27. [Dealer Margin]

Create a new pivot table. Put `Product Category` on Filters and select Accessories from this filter. Then put `ProductName` on Rows. You should have something like this table (though what is shown here is truncated):

Category	Accessories ▾T
Row Labels ▾	
All-Purpose Bike Stand	
Bike Wash - Dissolver	
Cable Lock	
Fender Set - Mountain	
Headlights - Dual-Beam	
Headlights - Weatherproof	
Hitch Rack - 4-Bike	

Write a calculated field that shows the theoretical margin the dealer gets (i.e., the difference between the product list price and the product dealer price). Both columns you need for this calculated field are in the `Products` table.

Did you get the answers shown below? (Once again, my pivot table in the image below is truncated; it shows only the first nine rows, but yours should be longer.)

Category	Accessories ▼T
Row Labels ▼	**Dealer Margin**
All-Purpose Bike Stand	$63.60
Bike Wash - Dissolver	$3.18
Cable Lock	$10.00
Fender Set - Mountain	$8.79
Headlights - Dual-Beam	$14.00
Headlights - Weatherproof	$18.00
Hitch Rack - 4-Bike	$48.00
HL Mountain Tire	$14.00
HL Road Tire	$13.04

When to Use X-Functions vs. Aggregators

Now you know that you can use X-functions such as `SUMX()`, and you can also use aggregators such as `SUM()`, and they do similar things but using different approaches. Which should you use? The following examples will help you figure this out.

Example 1: When the Data Doesn't Contain the Line Total

If your `Sales` table contains a column for quantity (Qty in the image below) and another column for price per unit, then you will necessarily need to multiply the quantity by the price per unit to calculate total sales (because the actual total doesn't exist at the line level).

Date ▼	Product ▼	Qty ▼	Price Per Unit ▼
1/01/2003	A	3	2.5
1/01/2003	B	1	6.8
2/01/2003	A	5	2.5
2/01/2003	C	3	3.5

If this is the structure of your data, then you simply must use `SUMX()`, like this:

```
[Total Sales 1] = SUMX(Sales,Sales[Qty] * Sales[Price Per Unit])
```

In this example, you have to calculate the totals for each row first, one row at a time. This is what the iterator functions are designed to do.

Example 2: When the Data Does Contain a Line Total

If your data contains a single column with the extended total sales for that line item, then you can use `SUM()` to add up the values:

```
[Total Sales 2] = SUM(Sales[Total Sales])
```

Date ▼	Produc ▼	Total Sales ▼
1/01/2003	A	7.5
1/01/2003	B	6.8
2/01/2003	A	12.5
2/01/2003	C	10.5

There is no need for an iterator in this example. Note, however, that you *could* still use `SUMX()` like this to get the same answer:

```
[Total Sales 2 alternate] = SUMX(Sales, Sales[Total Sales])
```

So Which Should You Use, SUM() or SUMX()?

Whether you use SUM() or SUMX() comes down to personal preference, the structure of your data, and the size of your data model.

If your workbooks are small and performance is good, then it doesn't really matter which you use. However, in very large data models, performance is likely to be an issue. There is no single right way to design a solution. As Marco Russo and Alberto Ferrari always say, "It depends."

Generally, if the data in a table supports an aggregator, then you should use the aggregator and not the iterator. So in Example 2 above, you technically can use either SUM() or SUMX(). But because the data supports SUM(), you should use SUM(). Iterations tend to be heavy on processing power, so you shouldn't use them if you don't have to.

But it may be possible for you to change your data at the source, and, for example, import quantity (Qty) and price per unit *instead of Total Sales*. If you changed your data at the source like this, then you could use SUMX() if you wanted to. Why would you do this? Well, Power Pivot compresses the data you load into the data model. The more unique values that exist in each column, the less compressed the data will be. The less compressed the data, the more memory that is required and potentially the slower the calculations will be.

Take another look at the table from Example 2:

Date	Produc	Total Sales
1/01/2003	A	7.5
1/01/2003	B	6.8
2/01/2003	A	12.5
2/01/2003	C	10.5

The column of data Sales[Total Sales] contains all unique values. This column would not compress well.

Compare it to the Example 1 table again:

Date	Product	Qty	Price Per Unit
1/01/2003	A	3	2.5
1/01/2003	B	1	6.8
2/01/2003	A	5	2.5
2/01/2003	C	3	3.5

In this table, there are duplicate values in the Qty column and also the Price per Unit column. It is likely that the data in Example 1 will be more compressed than the data in Example 2 because of these duplicate values in each column (but it does depend on your data).

If Example 1 ends up compressing materially smaller than Example 2, then it is possible that Example 1 with SUMX() may be more efficient than Example 2 with SUM(). But again, it depends.

When Totals Don't Add Up

There is another use case when you need to use SUMX() that is less obvious. However, when you encounter this problem, you need to use an iterator to solve it.

In the example below, I have simulated 10 customers shopping over a 14-day period. Each customer shops on a different number of days (anywhere from 5 days to 9 days in this example).

Customer Number ▼	Visits	Count of days	Average Visits Per Day 1	Average Visits Per Day 2
10001	12	9	1.3	1.3
10002	8	8	1.0	1.0
10003	8	7	1.1	1.1
10004	11	7	1.6	1.6
10005	8	7	1.1	1.1
10006	9	5	1.8	1.8
10007	11	6	1.8	1.8
10008	7	5	1.4	1.4
10009	10	8	1.3	1.3
10010	11	8	1.4	1.4
Grand Total	**95**	**14**	**6.8**	**1.4**

The column Average Visits per Day 1 is calculating how many times each customer shopped, on average (for the days he or she actually shopped). Customer 10001 shopped, on average, 1.3 times each day, and customer 10002 came in only once for each day shopped. But do you spot the problem here? The grand total of 6.8 doesn't make any sense. The average across all customers is not 6.8 (it is actually 1.4). The problem is that the grand total above is calculated as 95 total visits divided by 14 total days. But aggregating Visits and Count of Days *before* calculating the average means that you end up losing the uniqueness in the customer-level detail.

This problem would not occur if you used an iterator because an iterator calculates each line one at a time. An aggregator, on the other hand, adds up all the numbers *before* the calculation, effectively losing the line-level detail required to do the correct calculation.

So why not just use the iterator? Well, as I mentioned above, an iterator is *normally* a slower formula to execute. Also, in this case, it is only the grand total that is not working as expected; the rows of the pivot are fine, and they are using an aggregator. So the generally excepted approach in this case is to use a compound formula that checks to see if the calculation is being done for an individual customer or for many customers by using the HASONEVALUE test.

The first two calculated fields below are using aggregators (COUNTROWS and DISTINCTCOUNT in this case). Both of these aggregator functions use the storage engine to do the calculation, so they are lightning fast:

```
[Visits] = COUNTROWS ( Sales )
[Count of days] = DISTINCTCOUNT ( Sales[Date] )
```

When these two formulas are placed inside the following calculated field, it works only when a single customer is selected:

```
[Average Visits Per Day 1] = DIVIDE ( [Visits], [Count of days] )
```

In this case, we are using the rows in the pivot table to filter for the single customer (i.e., the initial filter context from the pivot table filters a single customer before the calculation). This calculated field gives the correct answer at the row level, but it gives the wrong answer at the grand total level.

The formula below first checks whether there is a single customer, and if so, it just uses the formula above (which is fast and efficient):

```
[Average Visits Per Day 2] =
IF (
    HASONEVALUE ( Sales[Cust Number] ),
    DIVIDE ( [Visits], [Count of days] ),
    DIVIDE (
        SUMX ( VALUES ( Sales[Cust Number] ), [visits] ),
        SUMX ( VALUES ( Sales[Cust Number] ), [Count of days] )
    )
)
```

But if there are multiple customers in the filter context (e.g., at the grand total level), then it uses SUMX () to calculate the values for each customer, one customer at a time, before it does the final division.

Avoiding Data You Don't Need

I mentioned earlier that if you had Total Sales in a table, you might be able to go back to the source data and import Qty and Price per Unit instead of Total Sales. One important point to note here is that you should *definitely not* have all three columns. It should be obvious that if you have Qty and Price per Unit in a table, you can "calculate" the value of Total Sales any time you need it. Similarly, if you have Total Sales and Qty in a table, you can calculate Price per Unit any time you like.

You should never bring in columns of redundant data that can be calculated on-the-fly inside your data model. Doing so just increases your file size and makes everything refresh more slowly. The general rule is to bring in the minimum number of columns you need to do the job, and it is best to bring in the columns with the lowest numbers of unique values where possible.

A Final Word on X-Functions

Things are not always as they seem in the complex world of DAX. One of the many things I have learnt from Alberto Ferrari at SQLBI.com is that Power Pivot is very smart. It's so smart, in fact, that it can change the way it executes a query from what you have asked it to do in your DAX if there is a more efficient way to do it. So it seems that in some cases, if you write a SUMX() function, Power Pivot may actually execute the query like an aggregator with the storage engine rather than like an iterator with the formula engine.

For a more in-depth look at this phenomenon, take a look at page 10 of this excellent (but advanced) paper from SQLBL.COM: http://www.sqlbi.com/wp-content/uploads/DAX-Query-Plans.pdf. You might not want to actually go down the path of trying to understand this at such an early stage of your DAX journey, but it is interesting to get an idea of how complex DAX can get. The last half of page 10 in this paper seems to suggest that using the following DAX is the most efficient way to write the DAX in the original exercise at the start of this section:

```
[Total Sales 1] = SUMX(Sales, Sales[Qty] * Sales[Price Per Unit])
```

This formula will work in the rows in the pivot table as well as the grand total, and because Power Pivot is smart enough to leverage the storage engine for the calculation, it is going to be fast. But beware: This smart override will not work in all situations, so you should not rely on this feature unless you are sure what is happening.

Avoiding Too Many Calculated Columns

Now is a good time to talk about the most common mistake I see Excel users make when learning Power Pivot. The formulas we have been writing using SUMX() can also be written directly into a custom calculated column in a table. But this *normally* is the *wrong* way to do it. Let me explain why.

To write a calculated column, go to the Power Pivot tab in Excel and click on the Manage button.

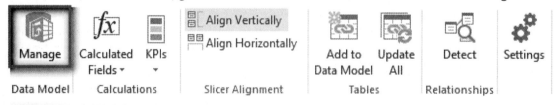

Once you are in the Power Pivot window, you can select Design, Add Columns.

You could rewrite the [Total Sales Plus Tax] calculated field as a calculated column, as shown here:

```
fx  =Sales[ExtendedAmount] + Sales[TaxAmt]
```

A calculated column has a row context—just like SUMX() —and as a result, it is fine to refer to naked columns. Just like with SUMX(), though, DAX creates a row context and then iterates over the rows in the calculated column one at a time. At each step in the process, there is only one row in play, and hence each column only has one possible value for each row iteration step. So you end up with a column of data like the one below, with the calculate total for each row stored in the column.

ExtendedAmount	TaxAmt	Sales Plus Tax Column
564.99	45.1992	$610.19
564.99	45.1992	$610.19
24.49	1.9592	$26.45
8.99	0.7192	$9.71
8.99	0.7192	$9.71
564.99	45.1992	$610.19
53.99	4.3192	$58.31
53.99	4.3192	$58.31
120	9.6	$129.60
7.95	0.636	$8.59
24.49	1.9592	$26.45
28.99	2.3192	$31.31
1214.85	97.188	$1,312.04
53.99	4.3192	$58.31

But there is one *big* problem with this approach—and I do mean *BIG*. The problem is that a calculated column always evaluates every row and stores the answer in the workbook as a value in the table. This takes up space in the workbook. What's more, the compression applied to calculated columns is reportedly not as good as for imported columns, and hence the data could be stored inefficiently in the workbook. Now compare that to the SUMX() calculated field created earlier. The calculated field [Total Sales Including Tax SUMX Version] does not store any values in your workbook other than any values needed to display in any pivot tables in your worksheets. If your Sales table has 60,000 rows of data, it probably doesn't matter. But if your Sales table has 50 million rows of data, it definitely will matter.

Excel users tend to gravitate to writing calculated columns rather than writing calculated fields because it seems more "natural" to do so. We are used to living in a spreadsheet world, where we have lots of rows and columns and can refer to them in our calculations. Writing calculated fields is a different experience because we don't get to "see" the data table in front of us when writing the DAX code. Instead, we have to visualise in our minds what we are doing. This is also why creating a pivot table to get immediate feedback after you write your formulas is a good practice for Excel users.

My number-one piece of advice for now is that you shouldn't write calculated columns unless there is no other option. You'll learn more about calculated columns and when to use them in Chapter 7. Until then, you should assume that using a calculated column is not a good approach unless you know from experience what the exceptions are.

Are You Writing Your Formulas Correctly?

It's time to practice some new formulas. Remember that all the formulas that end with an X (referred to as the X-functions) are iterators.

This is the process used so far to write X-function formulas:

1.   Create a new pivot table on a new sheet.
2.   Put Products on Rows.
3.   Click in the pivot table and then create a new calculated field.
4.   Select the table where the calculated field will be stored.

5. Give the calculated field a descriptive name.

6. Start typing the formula and stop once the formula is highlighted in IntelliSense (before you press Tab or type () so you can read the description of the formula, as shown below.

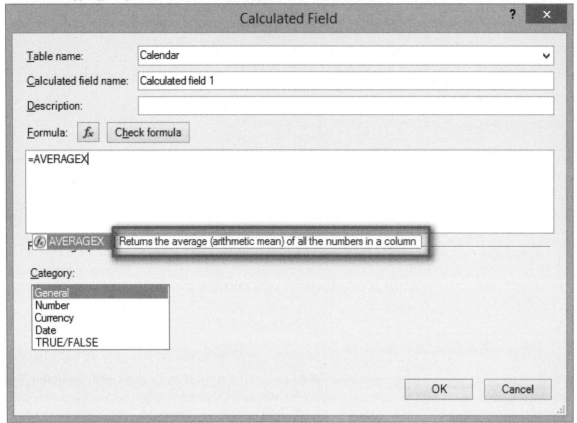

7. Pause after you press Tab or type (to get the syntax, as shown below.

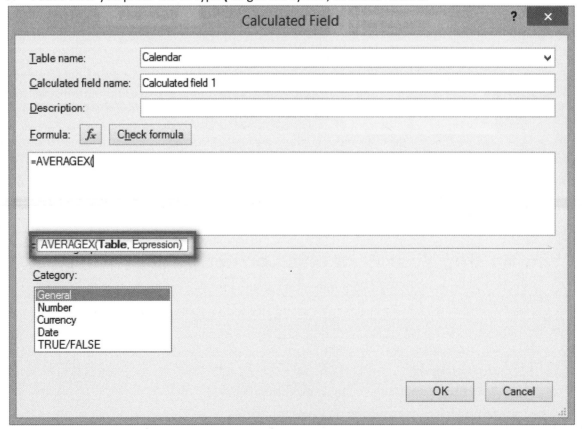

Practice Exercises: AVERAGEX()

Set up a new pivot table and put `Products[Category]` on Rows. Then write the following calculated fields using `AVERAGEX()`. Find the solutions to these practice exercises in "I. AVERAGEX()" on page 177.

28. [Average Sell Price per Item]

Find the column in the `Sales` table that gives the sell price per unit and use `AVERAGEX()` to find the average of this column.

29. [Average Tax Paid]

You need to find the tax column in the `Sales` table.

30. [Average Safety Stock]

There is a safety stock column in the `Products` table, as shown below.

Row Labels ▼	Average Sell Price per Item	Average Tax Paid	Average Safety Stock
Accessories	$19	$2	146
Bikes	$1,862	$149	100
Clothing	$37	$3	4
Components			500
Grand Total	**$486**	**$39**	**283**

> **Note** There are other X-functions that are not included in this book, such as `MAXX()`, `MINX()`, `COUNTAX()`, and `COUNTX()`. You can find out how these are used by typing a formula into the Calculated Field Wizard and reading the IntelliSense.

7: DAX Topic: Calculated Columns

Okay, it's time for a change of pace. I have deliberately left calculated columns until now to allow you to get accustomed to the power of calculated fields first. As mentioned in Chapter 6, the most common mistake I see Excel users make is to use too many calculated columns. And when you think about it, a calculated column is a very comfortable place for an Excel user to hang out, because a table in the Power Pivot window looks and feels a lot like Excel. But as I warned previously, you should avoid using calculated columns until you know when and why to use them. Consciously avoiding calculated columns and trying to find a calculated field solution will make you a stronger DAX user—trust me.

In general, you should not use a calculated column if:

- You can use a calculated field instead.
- You can bring the data into your table directly from your source data.

However, you can and should use calculated columns when you need them. You should definitely use a calculated column when both of the following two conditions are satisfied at the same time:

- You need to filter a pivot table based on the results of a column (i.e., you want to use the column on Filter, Slicer, Rows, or Columns).
- You can't bring the column of data you need in from your source data itself (for whatever reason).

The most common reasons you can't get the column you need from your source data is that it doesn't exist and/or possibly also you can't arrange to get it added (e.g., you don't have access to the source system) or can't get it added in a timely manner.

If possible, you should try to get the column you need added to the source data. If you get it added, you then get the full benefit of compression on data import, and also the column is available for reuse in all your future workbooks. But sometimes this simply isn't possible, and other times it is possible but you can't wait two weeks (or two years!) to get it done. Calculated columns are there for you to use when this happens. And if a new column becomes available in the future, you can simply delete your calculated column and replace it with the new column coming in from the source.

Let's look at an example of where you should use calculated columns.

Example: Is This a Weekend?

Let's say that you extract the `Calendar` table from your enterprise database, and you want a new column that shows whether each date is a weekend or not, but you can't arrange to have this column added for now.

Here's How: Creating an Is Weekend? Calculated Column

Follow these steps to create an *Is Weekend* calculated column in Power Pivot:

1. In the Power Pivot window, navigate to the `Calendar` table and make sure you have the Data view selected.

2. Scroll all the way to the right side of the table, and you see Add Column at the top of the next available column in the table (as shown below).

3. Click anywhere in the column to select a blank field (see #1 below).

4. Click in the formula bar at the top of the window (#2).

5. Type your calculated column formula, as described next.

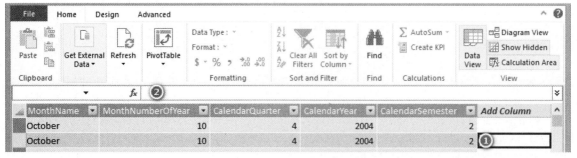

You are going to write this formula in stages. This is a good way to write formulas as it allows you to solve one part of a problem at a time and make sure it works before you proceed to the next step. The end state is to have a column that returns TRUE if the date is a weekend and FALSE if the date is a weekday.

First, you need to determine whether this date is a Sunday. In the formula bar, type the following formula:

```
=Calendar[DayNumberOfWeek]=1
```

The same best-practice rules apply with calculated columns that apply with calculated fields. You should always specify the table name before the column name. This makes it easy for the reader to quickly tell if the reference is to a column in a table or if it is a calculated field.

Calculated columns in Power Pivot are very similar to tables in Excel. You write a formula once in the column, and the formula is copied to each row in the column. The formula for this calculated column has two equals signs. The first is required for all calculated columns, and the second equals sign in this case is used to test if the left side of the formula is equal to the right side (i.e., it is testing for equivalence). This formula returns TRUE if the left side is equivalent to the right side and FALSE if they are not equivalent.

Below you can see the results you end up with in your calculated column. Most of the results are FALSE because there is only one day each week when the formula evaluates to TRUE.

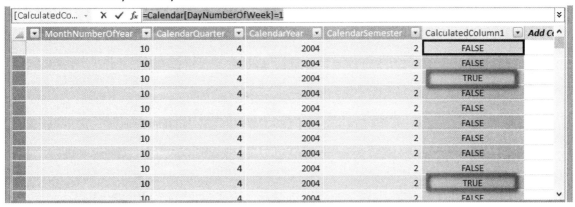

Just as with Excel tables, it is not possible to have more than one formula in a calculated column. You therefore have to write the formula so that it evaluates and handles all the possible scenarios you need. In the example here, you need to test for Sunday *and Saturday*, so you now need to modify the formula you just created so it covers both scenarios.

Click inside the formula in the formula bar and edit the formula so that it tests for two scenarios, as follows:

```
=OR(Calendar[DayNumberOfWeek]=1,Calendar[DayNumberOfWeek]=7)
```

Once you press Enter, the formula is updated, and you have the calculated column you need. The last thing to do is rename the column so that it has a meaningful name. Double-click on the default heading, CalculatedColumn1, and rename it Is Weekend?.

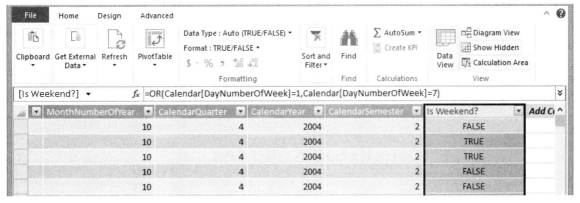

Note It is good practice to write your DAX formulas like this, one piece of the puzzle at a time. In the above example you first wrote a formula to identify Sundays and then extended the formula to identify Saturdays and Sundays. Breaking a problem into pieces like this can really help you get to the right answer quickly, without making lots of mistakes.

Now that you have the new calculated column, it is time to use it in your pivot table. Go to a new worksheet in your workbook and create a new pivot table. Place `Products[Category]` on Rows, place your new column `Calendar[Is Weekend?]` on Columns, and then add `[Total Sales Amount]` to the Values section. You end up with the pivot table shown below.

Total Sales Amount	Column Labels		
Row Labels	FALSE	TRUE	Grand Total
Accessories	$495,995	$204,764	$700,760
Bikes	$20,047,702	$8,270,442	$28,318,145
Clothing	$240,664	$99,109	$339,773
Grand Total	$20,784,362	$8,574,316	$29,358,677

You have successfully gotten some new insights into the data that didn't exist before. You have used data modelling techniques to enhance the data.

Many of the formulas used to write calculated columns use syntax that is similar to that used in standard Excel formulas. Just as when you are writing calculated fields, you can pause your cursor on a function, and IntelliSense will kick in with help on the syntax. Note that the formula below accepts only two parameters (`Logical1` and `Logical2`). This is different from Excel: Whereas Excel allows you to add as many OR conditions as you want in a formula, DAX allows you to have only two in total. Just watch out for these small differences between DAX and Excel.

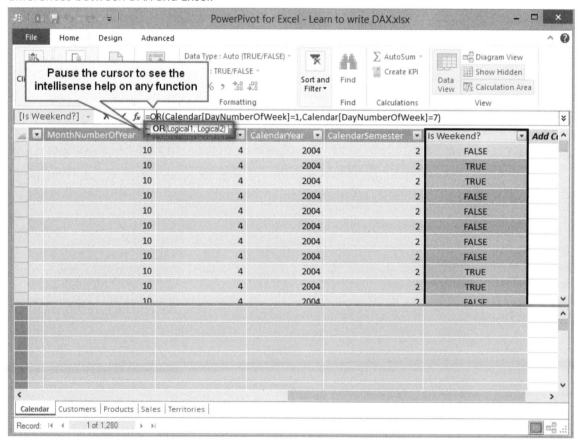

Practice Exercise: Calculated Columns

Write the following calculated column in the `Calendar` table. Find the solution to this practice exercise in "J. Calculated Columns" on page 177.

31. Creating a Half Year Column

Write a calculated column in the `Calendar` table that returns the value `H1` for the first half of each year (January through June) and `H2` for the second half of each year (July through December). *Hint:* You may want to use an `IF` statement.

8: DAX Topic: CALCULATE()

Rob Collie describes CALCULATE() as "your new favourite function" in his book *DAX Formulas for Power Pivot*. I am not going to go deeply into CALCULATE() in this book. Both Rob's book and Marco Russo and Alberto Ferrari's book *Microsoft Excel 2013: Building Data Models with PowerPivot* have excellent chapters on this topic (both also Chapter 8 coincidentally!), and I don't want to cover the same ground here again. I do, however, want to give you enough information so you can understand what CALCULATE() does so that you can start using it competently. If you want to be an expert, then you need to read lots of other books and blogs to build on what you learn here.

> **Note** You can find an up-to-date curated list of the best Power Pivot and Power Query books (including the two mentioned above) at the links provided in Chapter 20 (page 173) of this book.

Ordering Off the Menu

Have you ever gone into a restaurant and looked at the menu only to discover that the standard offering is not quite what you are after? Lots of people love Caesar salad, but many people do not like anchovies. Say that you're one of them, and you read the following on the menu:

Caesar Salad: Romaine lettuce, croutons, parmesan cheese, anchovies, and egg tossed in a creamy Caesar dressing.

When you order the salad, you alter the standard menu option and instead say, "I'll have the Caesar salad, no anchovies." CALCULATE() is a lot like that: It allows you to alter the standard offering (that you get from a pivot table) so you can get some variation that ends up being exactly what you want.

Technically speaking, CALCULATE() alters filter context. It takes an expression (which can be a calculated field or another DAX formula) and modifies that expression by applying new filters. The syntax of CALCULATE() is:

```
=CALCULATE(expression, filter 1, filter 2, filter n...)
```

CALCULATE() alters the filter context coming from the pivot table by using none, one, or more filters prior to evaluating the expression. CALCULATE() "reruns" the built-in filter engine in Power Pivot—the one that makes the filters automatically propagate from the lookup tables and flow downhill to the data tables. When the filter engine is rerun by CALCULATE(), if there are any filters inside the CALCULATE() function, these filters become part of the filter context before the filter engine kicks in. I like to think of Power Pivot "pulling the handle" to rerun the filtering "machine" to make the filter engine work. (You'll find more about how this works in Chapter 9.)

> **Note** I mentioned above that you can use none, one, or more filters inside CALCULATE(). It may seem strange that you can use none at all. Why would you want to do this? Using no filters at all is a special use case that is covered in Chapter 9.

Simple Filters

CALCULATE() can use two types of filters. A simple filter (or raw filter) has a column name on the left and a value on the right, as in these examples:

```
Customers[Gender] = "F"
Products[Color] = "Blue"
Calendar[Date] = "1/1/2002"
Calendar[Calendar Year] = 2003
```

You can use these simple filters as the second and subsequent parameters to CALCULATE() to alter the original meaning of an expression (which is the first parameter). Simple filters are really important in Power Pivot because Power Pivot was designed to be super-fast and efficient when using simple filters. This is "bread and butter" stuff for Power Pivot. Taking a filter from a lookup table and propagating it to the data tables is what Power Pivot was built and optimised to do. Whenever possible, you should use these simple filters in your formulas.

Let's look at an example. First set up a new pivot table. Put `Products[Category]` on Rows and `[Total Sales Amount]` on Values. You should have the pivot table shown below. (You should be getting used to this by now!)

Row Labels ▾	Total Sales Amount
Accessories	$700,760
Bikes	$28,318,145
Clothing	$339,773
Grand Total	**$29,358,677**

Then write the following calculated field:

```
[Total Sales of Blue Products]
    = CALCULATE([Total Sales Amount], Products[Color]="Blue")
```

See how the simple filter used here, `Products[Color]="Blue"`, has altered the initial filter context coming from the pivot table and given a variation to the regular calculated field `[Total Sales Amount]`. It is as if you have changed the recipe for the standard product on the menu and instead received a variation of that regular menu item. Think Caesar salad without anchovies.

Row Labels ▾	Total Sales Amount	Total Sales of Blue Products
Accessories	$700,760	$74,354
Bikes	$28,318,145	$2,169,056
Clothing	$339,773	$35,687
Grand Total	**$29,358,677**	**$2,279,096**

Practice Exercises: CALCULATE() with a Single Table

It's time for you to write some simple `CALCULATE()` examples that filter a single table. Set up a new pivot table with `Customers[Occupation]` on Rows and `[Total Number of Customers]` on Values. You should have the pivot table shown below as your starting point.

Row Labels ▾	Total number of Customers
Clerical	2,928
Management	3,075
Manual	2,384
Professional	5,520
Skilled Manual	4,577
Grand Total	**18,484**

Then write the following calculated fields, using `CALCULATE()`. Find the solutions to these practice exercises in "K. CALCULATE() with a Single Table" on page 177.

32. [Total Male Customers]

Write a new calculated field that modifies the `[Total Number of Customers]` calculated field you wrote previously so that it gives you a total for male customers only. You need to look for a suitable column to use in your filter from the `Customers` table.

33. [Total Customers Born Before 1950]

In this case, you need to enter the date January 1, 1950, into the formula as the filter parameter. You need to use the `DATE()` function to do this. Remember that you can use the tooltips Power Pivot provides in the Calculated Field dialog box. Just start typing `=DATE` inside the Calculated Field dialog, and before you type `(`, a tooltip pops up, explaining the purpose of the function.

As soon as you type **(**, the tooltip changes and gives you the syntax you need to use the function.

Now that you know how to write a date inside a formula, you can go ahead and write the calculated field `[Total Customers Born Before 1950]`.

34. [Total Customers Born in January]

As in Exercise 33, you need to use the `MONTH()` function to turn the information in the `Customers[BirthDate]` column into a month.

35. [Customer Earning at Least $100,000 per Year]

Write a calculated field that counts the number of customers that earn more than $100,000 per year. The following pivot table shows what you should end up with. Look for a suitable column to use for the filter in the `Customers` table.

Row Labels ▼	Total number of Customers	Total Male Customers	Total Customers Born Before 1950	Total Customers Born in January	Customers Earning at least $100,000 per year
Clerical	2,928	1,488	433	132	
Management	3,075	1,592	1,543	136	1,406
Manual	2,384	1,251	134	128	
Professional	5,520	2,727	609	254	792
Skilled Manual	4,577	2,293	234	192	
Grand Total	**18,484**	**9,351**	**2,953**	**842**	**2,198**

Using CALCULATE() over Multiple Tables

In Practice Exercises 32–35 above, the CALCULATE() function touches only ,a single table; the filtering is applied to a table, and the expression is evaluated on the same table. However CALCULATE() can work over multiple tables, too. When you use the CALCULATE() function, CALCULATE() first applies the filters to the relevant tables, and it then reruns the filter propagation engine and makes sure that any new filters inside your CALCULATE() function automatically propagate from the "one" side of the relationship to the "many" side (i.e., the filters flow downhill) before the expression is evaluated. So you can apply a filter to one or more of the lookup tables, these filters will propagate to the data tables, and any expression that evaluates over the connected data tables will reflect the filters from the lookup tables.

Practice Exercises: CALCULATE() with Multiple Tables

Set up a new pivot table. Put Territories[Region] on Rows and [Total Sales Amount] on

Row Labels	Total Sales Amount
Australia ①	② $9,061,001
Canada	$1,977,845
Central	$3,001
France	$2,644,018
Germany	$2,894,312
Northeast	$6,532
Northwest	$3,649,867
Southeast	$12,239
Southwest	$5,718,151
United Kingdom	$3,391,712
Grand Total	$29,358,677

Values. Note that there are now two tables involved. The initial filter context is coming from the Territories table (see #1 below), and the calculation [Total Sales Amount] is operating over the Sales table (#2).

With your pivot table set up as described above, write the following new calculated fields. Find the solutions to these practice exercises in "L. CALCULATE() with Multiple Tables" on page 177.

36. [Total Sales of Clothing]

Use the Products[Category] column in your simple filter. The filter gets applied to the lookup table, but then the calculated field [Total Sales Amount] is modified by the filter. [Total Sales Amount] operates over the Sales table—hence you use CALCULATE() with multiple tables.

37. [Sales to Female Customers]

As the name of this calculated field suggests, you use CALCULATE() to modify the standard calculated field [Total Sales Amount] and create a new calculated field that is for sales to female customers.

38. [Sales of Bikes to Married Men]

You need to use multiple filters on two tables for this one. CALCULATE() can accept as many filters as you pass to it. Just separate the filters with commas.

When you have finished these three practice exercises, you should end up with a pivot table something like the following.

Row Labels	Total Sales Amount	Total Sales of Clothing	Sales to Female Customers	Sales of Bikes to Married Men
Australia	$9,061,001	$70,260	$4,634,993	$4,102,687
Canada	$1,977,845	$53,165	$1,011,320	$983,419
Central	$3,001	$157	$124	
France	$2,644,018	$27,035	$1,271,964	$1,363,434
Germany	$2,894,312	$23,565	$1,539,713	$1,545,459
Northeast	$6,532	$106	$3,836	$2,295
Northwest	$3,649,867	$58,230	$1,843,586	$1,714,218
Southeast	$12,239	$301	$11,938	$1,552
Southwest	$5,718,151	$74,714	$2,881,098	$2,920,039
United Kingdom	$3,391,712	$32,240	$1,615,046	$1,969,411
Grand Total	$29,358,677	$339,773	$14,813,619	$14,602,515

Advanced Filters

So far you have used only simple filters inside `CALCULATE()`, in this format:

```
Table[ColumnName] = some value
```

You can also use a more advanced filter that is passed in the form of a table containing the values required for the filter. This table can be:

- A physical table
- A function that returns a table (e.g., `ALL()`, `VALUES()`, `FILTER()`)

Importantly, both types of tables used as advanced filter parameters *retain all relationships that exist in the data model*. Advanced filters and the way the tables retain their relationships in the data model is a complex topic that is covered in more detail in the coming chapters. For now, it is enough to know that so far you have only learnt about simple filters for `CALCUATE()`, and the advanced table filters are coming later.

Making DAX Easy to Read

Now is a good time to pause and talk about how to lay out your DAX so it is easy to read. Consider this example:

```
[Total Sales Value of Bikes Sold to Single Males in Australia]
= CALCULATE([Total Sales Amount], Customers[MaritalStatus]="S",
Customers[Gender]="M",Territories[Country]="Australia")
```

When you get formulas that are very long like this, they can be very hard to read. The generally accepted approach is to lay out a formula using line breaks and spaces so it is easier to see which parts of the formula belong together. There is no single right way to do this. Here is one way that I find useful:

```
[Total Sales Value of Bikes Sold to Single Males in Australia]
= CALCULATE( [Total Sales Amount],
    Customers[MaritalStatus] = "S",
    Customers[Gender] = "M",
    Territories[Country] = "Australia"
  )
```

To create a new line in the Calculated Field dialog box, you need to press Shift+Enter on the keyboard.

In the example above, I put the first parameter in `CALCULATE()` (which is the expression) on the first line, followed by a comma. Then I placed each filter on a new line and indented them so it is easy to see that they belong to the `CALCULATE()` function.

The final closing parenthesis for the `CALCULATE()` function is on a new line of its own, aligned with the C in `CALCULATE()` so that I know that this bracket closes the `CALCULATE()` function.

> **Note** To create indents from the left, simply press the spacebar four or five times for each line. It is fine to use as many spaces as you like in your DAX formulas: Spaces and line breaks have no impact on the evaluation of the formulas.

Using DAX Formatter

DAX Formatter is a very useful (and free) tool that you can use to help format your DAX. http://daxformatter.com is a free website developed by Marco Russo and Alberto Ferrari from SQLBI. You simply paste your DAX code into the website, and DAX Formatter formats the code for you. You can then cut and paste it back into the Calculated Field dialog box. But before you actually do that, read the following warning.

Warning: Switching Windows with the Calculated Field Dialog Open If you have the Calculated Field dialog box open, cut and paste a formula, and then switch to a browser so you can use DAX Formatter, you may experience a problem when you switch back to Excel. The problem is that the Calculated Field dialog is a modal window.

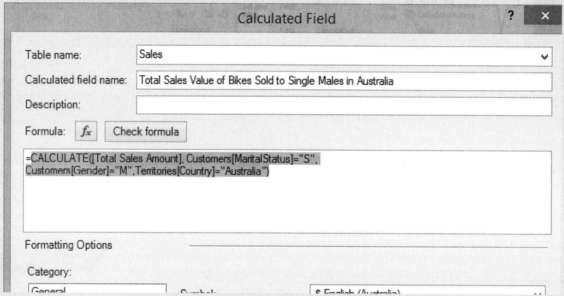

If this window is open, it can sometimes "hide" behind the regular Excel window when you switch back to Excel from another window. When this happens, you can see the regular Excel window, but when you try to click in Excel, you get an annoying "bing, bing" sound that tells you something is wrong. The likely issue is that the Calculated Field dialog box is open and hiding behind the Excel window. To fix this, press and hold the Alt key and then press Tab. Task Manager shows all the windows that are currently open in the background. Look for the Calculated Field dialog and, while still holding down Alt, select it by pressing Tab multiple times until it is in focus. When you release the Alt key, Windows brings the modal window into focus and allows you to finish the task.

When you use DAX Formatter, you have a choice about whether to include the calculated field name. If you include it, you have to add the name and a colon before the equals sign.

Here is the [Total Sales Value of Bikes Sold to Single Males in Australia] formula from DAX Formatter with the calculated field name:

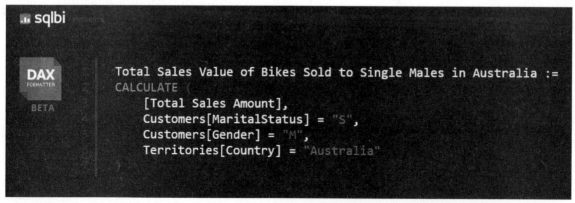

And here it is without the calculated field name:

Error Checking

DAX Formatter does another important job for you: It checks whether your DAX code is legal and written correctly. If it is not, then DAX Formatter does its best to show you where the error is located. To see this in action, try removing one of the commas from the DAX code above (such as the one after Gender = M):

```
[Total Sales Value of Bikes Sold to Single Males in Australia]
= CALCULATE( [Total Sales Amount],
    Customers[MaritalStatus] = "S",
    Customers[Gender] = "M"
    Territories[Country] = "Australia"
  )
```

When you put this erroneous code into DAX Formatter, note that there is a triangle that points to the part of the code where an unexpected value is found:

In this case, DAX Formatter is expecting a comma but instead finds the letter T—the start of the column name. DAX Formatter is a great tool for helping you debug your DAX code when you can't work out what is wrong. I use DAX Formatter all the time to help me with my DAX. I suggest you do, too.

9: Concept: Evaluation Context and Context Transition

This chapter covers one of the hardest topics to understand and master in DAX. As you saw in Chapter 5, some DAX functions have what is called a *filter context*. As you saw in Chapter 6, DAX also has a *row context*. Filter context and row context are the two different types of *evaluation context*.

A Refresher on Filter Context

In Chapter 5 I introduced a number of concepts, including *filter context* and *initial filter context*. Here is a quick refresher.

Filter context refers to any filtering that is applied to the data model in DAX. Filter context is created by a pivot table and also by the CALCULATE() function. The *initial filter context* is the natural filtering that is applied by a pivot table. The initial filter context comes from the following four areas of a pivot table:

- Rows (see #1 below)
- Columns (#2)
- Filters (#3)
- Slicers (#4)

Class	All ③				Size ④	
Total Sales Amount	**Column Labels**				38	
Row Labels	**Accessories** ②	**Bikes**	**Clothing**	**Grand Total**	40	
Black ①	$72,954	$8,659,117	$106,341	$8,838,412	42	
Blue	$74,354	$2,169,056	$35,687	$2,279,096	44	
Multi			$106,471	$106,471		
NA	$435,117			$435,117	46	
Red	$78,028	$7,646,303		$7,724,331		
Silver	$40,308	$5,073,081		$5,113,389	48	
White			$5,106	$5,106	50	
Yellow		$4,770,588	$86,168	$4,856,756		
Grand Total	**$700,760**	**$28,318,145**	**$339,773**	**$29,358,677**	52	

Don't confuse the filter context coming from Rows in a pivot table with row context. These are two completely different things. Filter context is the natural "slicing" that comes from the coordinates of a pivot table. The Row section in a pivot table is one of the four locations that can slice your data, and all four locations are part of the initial filter context.

The filter context created by a pivot table filters the underlying tables in the data model. If the tables are joined, the filters propagate from the "one" side of the relationship (the side with the arrow pointing to it) to the "many" side of the relationship (the side with the dot). But the filter does not propagate from the "many" side of the relationship to the "one" side. This is why it is important (for Excel users anyway) to lay out the data model as shown below (which I've called the Collie layout methodology).

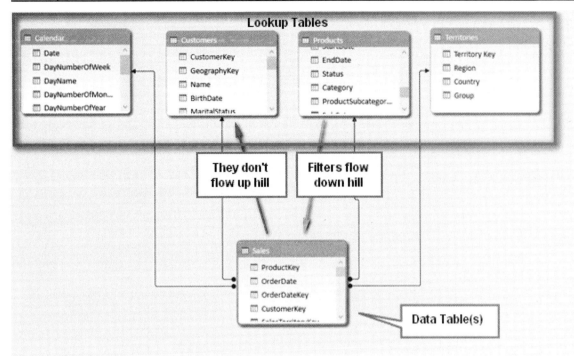

This setup provides a visual clue that the filters flow downhill through the relationships but do not flow uphill through the relationships.

> **Note** It is possible to filter a lookup table (sitting above) based on the results in a data table (sitting below) using DAX instead of filter propagation. But filters only ever automatically propagate through the relationships downhill.

A Refresher on Row Context

Row context refers to the ability of a function or calculated column to be "aware" of which row it is acting on at each stage of formula evaluation. Some functions (e.g., the X-functions, FILTER()) and all calculated columns have a row context. When you think about row context, think of the function (or calculated column) iterating through the table one row at a time and *selecting* the single value (the intersection between the column and row) and then acting on that single value. Regular calculated fields can't do this; only formulas that have a row context and calculated columns can perform this trick.

Let's look again at the SUMX() calculated field from Chapter 6, shown below.

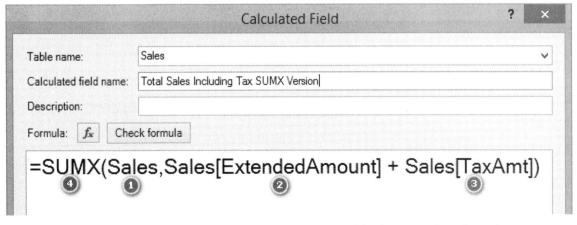

SUMX() first creates a row context over the Sales table (see #1 above). It then iterates through this table one row at a time. At each row, it takes the single value (#2) (which is the intersection of the Sales[ExtendedAmount] column and the current row) and then adds it to the single value (#3) (which is the intersection of the Sales[TaxAmt] column and the current row). It does this for every row in the table and then adds up all the values (#4).

Row Context in Calculated Columns

So now you know that iterator functions and also calculated columns all have a row context. The main difference between an iterator function (like `SUMX()`) and a calculated column is that the calculated column stores the value calculated at each row of the iteration process in the column itself. Calculated fields do not do this. In the `SUMX()` example, the function returns the final result to the pivot table without storing all the intermediate values (beyond the need to keep track of them during the calculation process). This is the main reason you should avoid using calculated columns, if possible: They take up storage space in your data model and hence make your files larger and generally slower.

Understanding That Row Context Does Not Automatically Create a Filter Context

This is a very important point that you must understand clearly: A row context does not automatically create a filter context. The best way to explain this is to use an example.

Go to the Power Pivot data model and jump to the `Products` table. Then go all the way to the right and insert a new calculated column, as shown below.

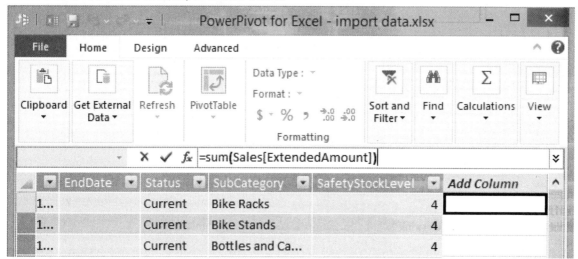

You should recognise this formula because it is exactly the same as the first formula in this book:

```
=SUM(Sales[ExtendedAmount])
```

What value will appear in every row of this new column? Do you expect it to be the total for the product in the row? Do you expect it to be the total for all products? Well, the answers may surprise you, and they are directly related to the point that a row context does not automatically create a filter context.

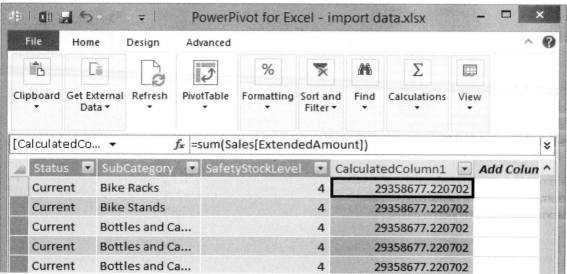

As you can see in the figure above, the value is the same for every single row in the table. There is no filtering on the `Sales` table (or any other table, for that matter) as a result of this formula, and hence the answer is always the same for every row. There is a row context in this formula: The rows are evaluated one at a time. But that row context does not create a filter context, and so the result is completely unfiltered.

It is, however, possible to turn the row context from this calculated column into a filter context through a process called *context transition*. To do this, simply wrap the above formula in a `CALCULATE()` function, as shown below.

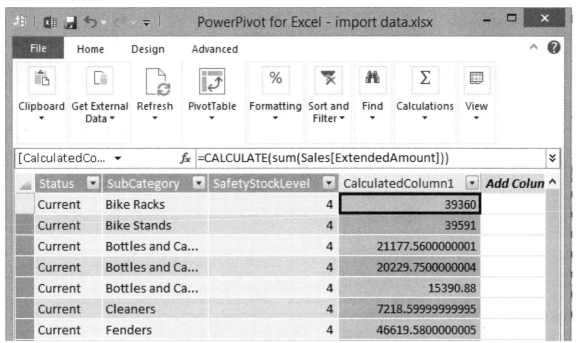

When you do this, the row context that exists in the calculated column is transformed into an equivalent filter context. The `CALCULATE()` function then "pulls the handle" on the filter engine so the filter on the `Products` table propagates through the relationship to the `Sales` table *before* the calculation is completed, and you end up with a different value in each row of the column. The value is actually the total sales for that product.

You can think of the formula working like this:

```
= CALCULATE(SUM(Sales[ExtendedAmount]),
        Products[ProductKey] = the product represented by this row in
    the table
    )
```

The concept of context transition works anywhere that a row context exists—that is, in calculated columns as well as iterators like `FILTER()` and `SUMX()`. This is the special use case mentioned in Chapter 8, where there are no filters at all needed inside `CALCULATE()` but instead `CALCULATE()` creates a new filter from the row context by using context transition. You can add additional filters inside `CALCULATE()`, too, if you want or need to, but none are required.

> **Note** There is a lot to learn about context transition that is beyond the scope of this book. In my view, there is no better reference on this topic than Marco Russo and Alberto Ferrari's book *Microsoft Excel 2013: Building Data Models with PowerPivot*. Chapter 7 focuses on context transition and is a great read for anyone who wants to build a deep understanding on evaluation context. There are also some great videos on the SQLBI.COM website. I provide links to these resources in Chapter 19.

10: DAX Topic: IF(), SWITCH(), and FIND()

DAX has a number of useful functions that allow you to apply a test and then branch the formula based on the results from that test. You will most likely be familiar with this concept from the IF() statement in Excel.

The IF() Function

The IF() function in DAX is almost identical to IF() in Excel:

```
IF(Logical Test, Result if True, [Result if False])
```

Note that the last parameter, [Result if False], is optional. If you omit this parameter and the result is FALSE, the IF() formula return BLANK(). This is very useful because pivot tables do not show row or column values if the result in the values section is BLANK().

The SWITCH() Function

The SWITCH() function is a lot like Select Case in VBA programming. The structure of a SWITCH() formula is as follows:

```
SWITCH(expression, value, result[, value, result]...[, else])
```

This syntax is a little confusing, so let's go through a simple example with another calculated column.

Navigate to the Power Pivot window, go the Customers table diagram view, and move to the right, ready to add this new calculated column:

```
= SWITCH(Customers[HouseOwnerFlag],1,"Owns their house",0,"Doesn't own
their house","Unknown")
```

It is much easier to understand SWITCH() if you use http://daxformatter.com, to improve the layout, as shown here:

```
=
SWITCH (
    Customers[HouseOwnerFlag],
    1, "Owns their house",
    0, "Doesn't own their house",
    "Unknown"
)
```

You can see in the figure above that line 3 is the branching point. The possible values in the HouseOwnerFlag column are 0 and 1 in this instance. Lines 4 and 5 offer up pairs of input and output values. So if the value of HouseOwnerFlag is 1, then the result "Owns their house" is returned. If the value of HouseOwnerFlag is 0, then the result "Doesn't own their house" is returned.

Line 6 is a single value, and it applies to all other possible values of HouseOwnerFlag (of which there are none in this example).

The FIND() Function

The FIND() function is almost identical to the FIND() statement in Excel. In DAX it has this format:

```
=FIND (FindText, WithinText,[StartPos],[NotFoundValue])
```

Even though this syntax suggests that StartPos and NotFoundValue are optional, in my experience in Excel 2013, you actually do need to provide values for these parameters

An Example Using IF() and FIND()

In this example, you will create a calculated column on one of your lookup tables. As I have said previously, it is perfectly valid to create calculated columns in lookup tables, but wherever possible, it is better practice to create these columns back in your source data. Remember why this is important:

- Calculated columns take up more space than imported columns (but this is generally not a major issue for lookup tables).

- If you are manually creating a calculated column, it exists only in that single workbook, and you will need to re-create it over and over for every other workbook where you need the column.

If it is not possible to create the calculated column back in your source data for some reason, then creating a calculated column instead is a great solution, particularly for lookup tables.

In this example, you are going to create a column for Mountain Products that doesn't exist in your lookup table. Any product with the word *mountain* in the description will be flagged as a mountain product.

In Power Pivot, navigate to the `Products` table and switch to Grid view if needed. Scroll all the way to the right of the table until you see the Add Column heading. Click just below Add Column (see #1 below) and then click in the formula bar (#2).

Then type the following formula:

```
=FIND("Mountain", Products[ModelName] ,1,0)
```

This formula will search for the word *mountain* within the `ModelName` column. Remember that because a calculated column has a row context, it is possible to refer to the column in this way, and it will calculate a result for every row in the `Products` table and store it in the column.

The result is an integer representing the starting position where the word *mountain* is found. If the word *mountain* is not found, then the value 0 (the last parameter in the formula) will be returned.

So you get something like the table shown below.

		[CalculatedCo... ▼	*ƒx* =FIND("Mountain", Products[ModelName] ,1,0)		
EndDate ▼	Status ▼	SubCategory ▼	SafetyStockLevel ▼	CalculatedColumn1 ▼
30/06/200...		Handlebars	500	4
	Current	Handlebars	500	4
30/06/200...		Handlebars	500	4
	Current	Handlebars	500	4
30/06/200...		Handlebars	500	4
	Current	Handlebars	500	4
30/06/200...		Handlebars	500	0
	Current	Handlebars	500	0
30/06/200...		Handlebars	500	0

This table is not overly useful as is, but you can wrap an `IF()` statement around this formula to make it more useful. You can use the `IF()` statement to return `TRUE` if the number is greater than zero (i.e., it is a mountain product) and return `FALSE` if it is equal to zero (i.e., it is not a mountain product). You should also rename the column heading to be `Is Mountain Product` (by double-clicking the heading and typing the new name).

[Is Mountain... ▼	f_x	=if(FIND("Mountain", Products[ModelName] ,1,0)>0,"True","False")

EndDate ▼	Status ▼	SubCategory ▼	SafetyStockLevel ▼	Is Mountain Product ▼	Add
30/06/200...		Handlebars	500	True	
	Current	Handlebars	500	True	
30/06/200...		Handlebars	500	True	
	Current	Handlebars	500	True	
30/06/200...		Handlebars	500	True	
	Current	Handlebars	500	True	
30/06/200...		Handlebars	500	False	
	Current	Handlebars	500	False	
30/06/200...		Handlebars	500	False	

Now you have a new calculated column, and you have further enhanced your data model to be more useful. Remember that this calculated column will take up space in your file and disk. However, given the small number of unique values (only `True` and `False` in this case), this column won't take up much space. The greater the number of unique values in a column, the more disk space and memory the column will consume.

You can now use this new column in a pivot table to produce new insights that weren't previously visible in the data. As this formula is a column in the data model, it can be used to filter the pivot table. In the example below, this new column is placed on Columns in a pivot table.

Drag fields between areas below:

▼ FILTERS

▥ COLUMNS

Is Mountain Product ▼

≣ ROWS

Occupation ▼

Σ VALUES

Total Sales Amount ▼

Total Sales Amount	Column Labels ▼		
Row Labels ▼	False	True	Grand Total
Clerical	$3,283,754	$1,401,033	$4,684,787
Management	$3,431,066	$2,036,795	$5,467,862
Manual	$1,964,880	$893,091	$2,857,971
Professional	$6,088,790	$3,819,187	$9,907,977
Skilled Manual	$4,378,594	$2,061,487	$6,440,081
Grand Total	$19,147,085	$10,211,593	$29,358,677

11: DAX Topic: VALUES() and HASONEVALUE()

In Chapter 8 I introduced the idea that CALCULATE() can use two types of filters: simple filters and advanced filters. Simple filters are in this form:

    Table[ColumnName] = some value

On the other hand, an advanced filter takes a table as a filter input. In other words, you use an existing table (or create a virtual table on-the-fly) that contains the rows you want included in the filter, and CALCULATE() applies that filter to the data model before completing the evaluation of the main expression.

Creating Virtual Tables

The tables you create using functions can be thought of as being "virtual" because they are not physically stored as part of the data model. They are created on-the-fly inside your DAX formulas and can be used during the evaluation of just the specific formulas containing the virtual table. Importantly, when you create a virtual table using a formula, the new virtual table will have a virtual relationship to the data model, and that virtual relationship will propagate the filter context in exactly the same way that the permanent relationships do. (More on this later in this chapter.)

Revisiting the VALUES() Function

VALUES() is the first function you have come to in this book that returns a (virtual) table. If you type the word VALUES into the Calculated Field dialog and read the tooltip before typing (, you can see that this function returns a table, as shown below.

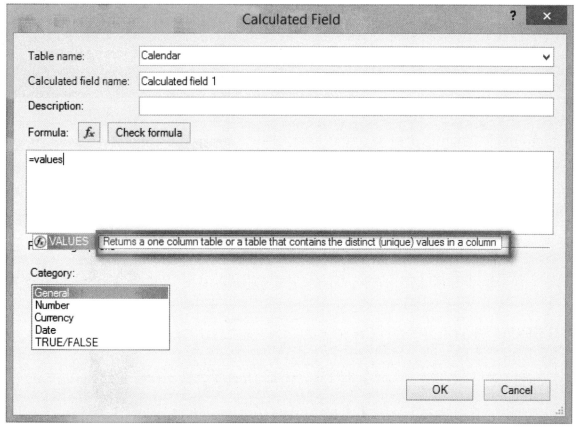

One important thing to note about VALUES() is that it respects the initial filter context coming from your pivot table. So if you combine this fact that VALUES() respects the current filter context with the information in the red box in the image above, you will see that VALUES() returns a single-column table that contains the list of all possible values in the current filter context.

It's time to work through some examples to demonstrate the point.

A Calendar Example

Set up a new pivot table and put Calendar Year on Rows as follows:

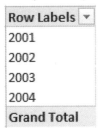

Row Labels ▼
2001
2002
2003
2004
Grand Total

Then write the following formula in the Calculated Field dialog box:

```
[Total Months in Calendar]
    = COUNTROWS (
        VALUES (Calendar[MonthName])
    )
```

> **Note** The following formula will not work here:
>
> ```
> [Total Months in Calendar wrong]
>     = COUNTROWS (Calendar[MonthName])
> ```
>
> This formula doesn't work because COUNTROWS () expects a table as the input, but Calendar[MonthName] is not a table; rather, it is a column that is part of a bigger table (the Calendar table, in this case).

When you wrap Calendar[MonthName] inside the VALUES () function, this single column that is part of the Calendar table is converted into a table in its own right, and it retains a relationship to the original Calendar table. This new table returned by VALUES () is still a single column, but now it technically is a table *and* a column instead of simply being a column inside of some other table (Calendar, in this case).

So VALUES (Calendar[MonthName]) returns a single-column table of possible values that respects the initial filter context coming from the pivot table. It is not possible to put this new table created by VALUES () into a calculated field unless you wrap it inside some other formula (e.g., an aggregator). In the example above, you first create the table (the VALUES part of the formula) and then count how many rows there are in the table with the COUNTROWS () function:

```
[Total Months in Calendar]
    = COUNTROWS (
        VALUES (Calendar[MonthName])
    )
```

Row Labels ▼	Total Months in Calendar
2001	6
2002	12
2003	12
2004	12
Grand Total	12

Notice how the year 2001 has only 6 months, and the other years all have 12. This is proof that the VALUES () function respects the initial filter context from the pivot table. The initial filter context for the first row in the pivot table is Calendar[Year] = 2001. That filter is applied before the formula [Total Months in Calendar] is calculated. VALUES () takes this "prefiltered" table (only dates where the year = 2001 are left unfiltered) and returns a single-column table that contains a distinct list of the possible values.

Simulating the Result from the Pivot Table in the Power Pivot Window

You can simulate what is happening here by going into the Power Pivot window, browsing to the `Calendar` table, and applying a filter on the `Calendar` table to show only Calendar Year = 2001 (see below).

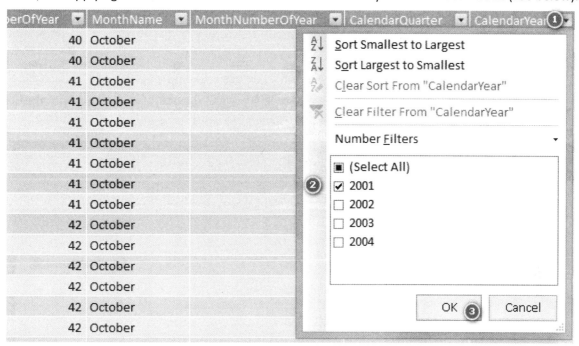

If you then go to the `MonthName` column and select the filter, you will see that only months in the second half of the calendar year exist.

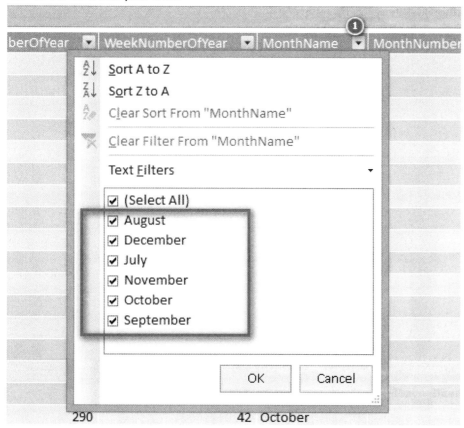

Returning a Single Value

VALUES() returns a single-column table of unique values from another column in another table, and this new table of values respects the current filter context coming from the pivot table. There is another very cool feature of VALUES() that is very powerful: In the special case where VALUES() returns just a single row (i.e., one value), you can refer to this value directly in your formulas.

If you take the example created above, remove CalendarYear from Rows, and put Month-Name on Rows instead, you should get the following.

Row Labels ▼	Total Months in Calendar
April	1
August	1
December	1
February	1
January	1
July	1
June	1
March	1
May	1
November	1
October	1
September	1
Grand Total	**12**

Now you can see that with the exception of the grand total, each row in the pivot table has only a single value for [Total Months in Calendar]. So as long as you write the formula in a way that it only operates over a single row of the table, you can create a calculated field that returns the name of the month into the actual pivot table Values section (i.e., not Rows or Columns).

Row Labels ▼	Total Months in Calendar	Month Name (Values)
April	1	April
August	1	August
December	1	December
February	1	February
January	1	January
July	1	July
June	1	June
March	1	March
May	1	May
November	1	November
October	1	October
September	1	September
Grand Total	**12**	

To write this formula, you need to provide protection for the other possible scenario where the code VALUES(Calendar[MonthName]) has more than one row in the table. This is done using the formula HASONEVALUE(), like so:

```
[Month Name (Values)]
    = IF(HASONEVALUE ( Calendar[MonthName] ),
       VALUES ( Calendar[MonthName] )
    )
```

Remember that the structure of an IF() statement is as follows:

```
= IF(Logical Test, Result if True, [Result if False])
```

The last parameter is optional. If you leave it out, then you are accepting the default value of BLANK().

If you write the above formula without the HASONEVALUE() function, it will throw an error. Even if you remove the grand total from the pivot table, it will still throw an error. DAX will only allow you to use the single value returned in a single row of the single-column table if you protect the formula with HASONEVALUE().

> **Note** In Excel 2016 there is a new DAX function called CONCATENATEX() that iterates over a list of values in a table and concatenates them together into a single value. Using this new function therefore allows you to write a formula that returns the single value when there is just one value and then concatenate all the values into a single value when there are multiple values. Such a formula might look like this:
>
> ```
> [Month Name (Values)]
>     = IF(HASONEVALUE ( Calendar[MonthName] ),
>        VALUES ( Calendar[MonthName] ),
>        CONCATENATEX(VALUES (   Calendar[MonthName]),
>        [MonthName],", ")
>     )
> ```

A Word on Table Sorting

In the example above, you can see that the month names in the pivot table are sorting in alphabetical order rather than in the logical month order of a calendar year. All columns in all tables sort by default in alphanumeric order. It is, however, possible to change the sort order.

Here's How: Changing the MonthName Sort Order

Follow these steps to change the sort order in a table:

1. Go to the Power Pivot window and navigate to the `Calendar` table in the Data view.

2. Click in the `MonthName` column (see #1 below), and then click the Sort by Column button (#2) and then Sort by Column (#3).

3. In the Sort by Column dialog box that appears, set the By Column value to `MonthNumberOfYear`.

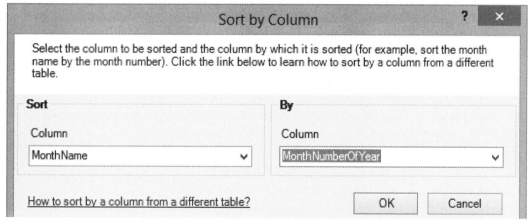

When you return to your pivot table, the rows are sorted in logical month order, as shown below.

Row Labels	Total Months in Calendar	Month Name (Values)
January	1	January
February	1	February
March	1	March
April	1	April
May	1	May
June	1	June

It is best practice to always load a numeric column in your lookup tables for every alpha column that needs to be sorted in a different order. You should therefore always include a numeric column in your `Calendar` table for days of week as well as months of year.

> **Note** When you create a numeric sort column in a table, there must be a one-to-one match between the values in the numeric sort order and the values in the column to be sorted.

Practice Exercises: VALUES()

Create a new pivot table and put `Products[Category]` on Rows and the calculated field `[Total Number of Products]` on Values. Then write the following calculated fields by the first creating a `VALUES()` table and then wrapping this table inside a `COUNTROWS()` function, as in the example earlier in this chapter. Find the solutions to these practice exercises in "M. VALUES()" on page 178.

39. [Number of Color Variants]

40. [Number of Sub Categories]

41. [Number of Size Ranges]

Use the column `Products[SizeRange]` for this one.

You should end up with a pivot table that looks like the one below.

Row Labels ▼	Total number of products	Number of Color Varieties	Number of Sub Categories	Number of Size Ranges
Accessories	35	6	12	2
Bikes	125	5	3	5
Clothing	48	5	8	5
Components	189	7	14	6
Grand Total	397	10	37	11

> **Note** Each of these calculated fields is the equivalent of dragging the column name and dropping it into the Values section for the pivot table. When you drop a text field into the Values section of a pivot table, the pivot table creates an implicit calculated field and uses `COUNT()` as the aggregating method. But recall that I recommended that you never do this. The names created by implicit calculated fields are ugly, and you need the DAX practice, so you should always write explicit DAX calculated fields.

Next, you should use the same pivot table from above but remove the calculated field `[Number of Size Ranges]` from the pivot table. Then write the following calculated fields that each return a single value into the pivot table. Each formula has the word `(Values)` in the name so it is clear that the formulas are returning the actual value to the pivot; this is just a "note to self." In each example, make sure you wrap your `VALUES()` function in an `IF()` or `HASONEVALUE()` function as in the example earlier in the chapter.

42. [Product Category (Values)]

43. [Product Subcategory (Values)]

44. [Product Color (Values)]

When you have finished, your pivot table should look as shown below. Notice that two of these calculated fields are blank. This is because the `VALUES` formula has more than one value, and hence the `IF HASONEVALUE` part of the formula returns a `BLANK()`; this is the default if you omit the last parameter.

Row Labels ▼	Total number of products	Number of Color Varieties	Number of Sub Categories	Product Category (Values)	Product Sub Category (Values)	Product Color (Values)
Accessories	35	6	12	Accessories		
Bikes	125	5	3	Bikes		
Clothing	48	5	8	Clothing		
Components	189	7	14	Components		
Grand Total	397	10	37			

45. Modifying Practice Exercise 43

Try editing the `IF()` statement for `[Product Sub Category (Values)]` so that it returns the value `More than 1` instead of `BLANK()`. The syntax for `IF` is `IF(Logical Test, Result if True, Result if False)`.

46. Modifying Practice Exercise 44

Now do the same with `[Product Color (Values)]`. You should end up with something like this (showing answers for Practice Exercises 45 and 46):

Row Labels	Total number of products	Number of Color Varieties	Number of Sub Categories	Product Category (Values)	Product Sub Category (Values)	Product Color (Values)
Accessories	35	6	12	Accessories	More than 1 Sub Cat	More than 1 Color
Bikes	125	5	3	Bikes	More than 1 Sub Cat	More than 1 Color
Clothing	48	5	8	Clothing	More than 1 Sub Cat	More than 1 Color
Components	189	7	14	Components	More than 1 Sub Cat	More than 1 Color
Grand Total	**397**	**10**	**37**		**More than 1 Sub Cat**	**More than 1 Color**

Finally, add a couple slicers to your pivot table and watch what happens when you use them. Click inside your pivot table and then select Insert, Slicer from the main ribbon. From the `Products` table, add slicers for color and subcategory.

When you click on these slicers, the values in the pivot table update to reflect the filtering in the slicer(s).

Row Labels	Total number of products	Number of Color Varieties	Number of Sub Categories	Product Category (Values)	Product Sub Category (Values)	Product Color (Values)
Accessories	3	1	1	Accessories	Helmets	Blue
Bikes	13	1	1	Bikes	Touring Bikes	Blue
Clothing	3	1	1	Clothing	Vests	Blue
Components	9	1	1	Components	Touring Frames	Blue
Grand Total	**28**	**1**	**4**		**More than 1 Sub Cat**	**Blue**

SubCategory		Color	
Helmets	⌃	Black	⌃
Touring Bikes		Blue	
Touring Frames		Grey	
Vests		Multi	

12: DAX Topic: ALL(), ALLEXCEPT(), and ALLSELECTED()

The DAX functions ALL(), ALLEXCEPT(), and ALLSELECTED() are all very similar in what they do. Let's start off with ALL() and then look at the other two variants.

The ALL() Function

The ALL() function removes all current filters from the current filter context, and for this reason it can be considered the "remove filters" function. The easiest way to understand this is with an example.

Go ahead and create a new pivot table and put Products[Category] on Rows and put the [Total Number of Products] calculated field you created earlier on Values.

Row Labels ▾	Total number of products
Accessories	35
Bikes	125
Clothing	48
Components	189
Grand Total	**397**

Technically what is happening above is that the first row in the pivot table (highlighted in red) is filtering the Products table so that only products that are of type Products[Category]="Accessories" are left visible in the underlying table; the others are all filtered out. They are not really visible, but you can imagine what the underlying table in your data model would look like after a filter was applied to Accessories behind the scenes. You can simulate this in the Power Pivot window like this:

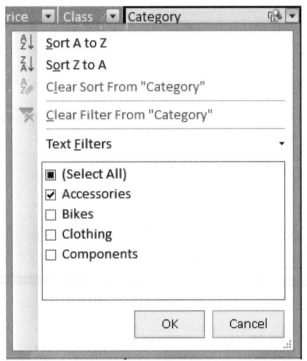

Back to the pivot table. After the pivot table applies a filter to the underlying tables, the calculated field [Total Number of Products] counts the rows that survive the filter. It does this for every cell in the pivot table one at a time, including the grand total cell. In the case of the grand total cell, there is no filter applied at all, so the calculated field counts all rows in the table—completely unfiltered.

Now go ahead and create a new calculated field that uses the ALL() function:

```
[Total All Products] = COUNTROWS(ALL(Products))
```

As you type this formula, if you pause typing while you are inside the ALL() function (as shown below), you see the syntax for ALL() displayed in IntelliSense.

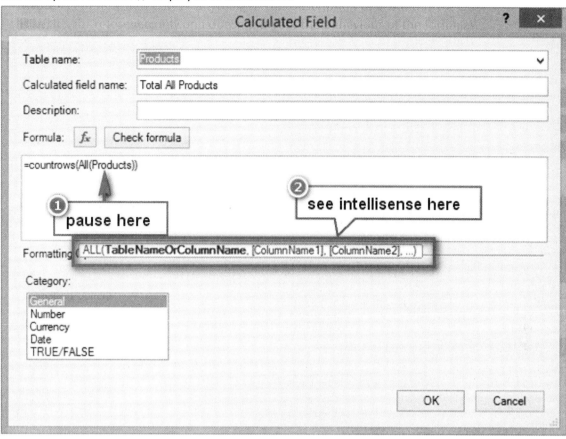

Note that IntelliSense is telling you that you can pass either a table or a single column as the first parameter for ALL(). In this example, you are passing the entire table.

When you have finished typing this formula, you should get this:

Row Labels ▼	Total number of products	Total All Products
Accessories	35	397
Bikes	125	397
Clothing	48	397
Components	189	397
Grand Total	**397**	**397**

You can see from the pivot table that the new calculated formula is ignoring the initial filter context coming from the rows in the pivot. What is happening here is that first of all, the initial filter context is set by the row Products[Category]="Accessories", but then the ALL() function kicks in from the new formula and alters this initial filter context and returns the entire Products table instead of the filtered Products table. So COUNTROWS() returns 397 for every row in the pivot table—including the grand total, as before.

Using ALL() as an Advanced Filter Input

The most common use of ALL() is as an advanced filter table input to a CALCULATE() function. Let's look at an example using ALL() as a table input to CALCULATE().

A good use for ALL() inside CALCULATE() is to remove the filters that are naturally applied to a pivot so that you can access the number that is normally in the grand total line of the pivot table. Once you can access the equivalent grand total in a pivot table from any row in the pivot itself, you can then easily create a "% of total" calculated field, which would be very useful indeed. The concept will make more sense with the following example.

Calculating the Country Percentage of Total Sales

Say that you want to calculate the country percentage of global sales. First of all, set up a pivot table with `Territories[Country]` on Rows and `[Total Sales Amount]` on Values, as shown below.

Row Labels ▼	Total Sales Amount
Australia	$9,061,001
Canada	$1,977,845
France	$2,644,018
Germany	$2,894,312
United Kingdom	$3,391,712
United States	$9,389,790
Grand Total	**$29,358,677**

It is then possible to go to the PivotTable Fields list, right-click on the calculated field `[Total Sales Amount]`, and select Value Field Settings.

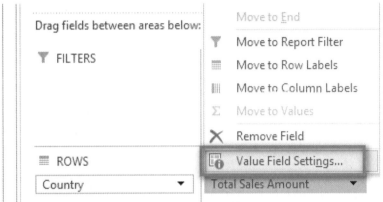

Then you can change the values and force them to display as % of Grand Total.

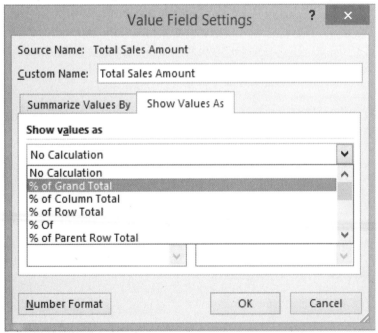

But if you do this, you are only changing the display format of the result and not actually calculating the percentage as part of your data model. This means that you can't use these percentages inside other calculated fields, and you also can't reference the percentages from cube formulas (discussed in Chapter 18). For these reasons, it is much better practice to create a new calculated field that will return the actual value as a reusable asset in your data model. You can do this in two steps. (Remember that it is good practice to break the problem you are solving into pieces and solve one piece of the puzzle at a time.)

Step 1: Create a Grand Total Calculated Field

Click inside your pivot table and create the following new calculated field:

```
[Total Global Sales]
    = CALCULATE([Total Sales Amount] , All(Territories) )
```

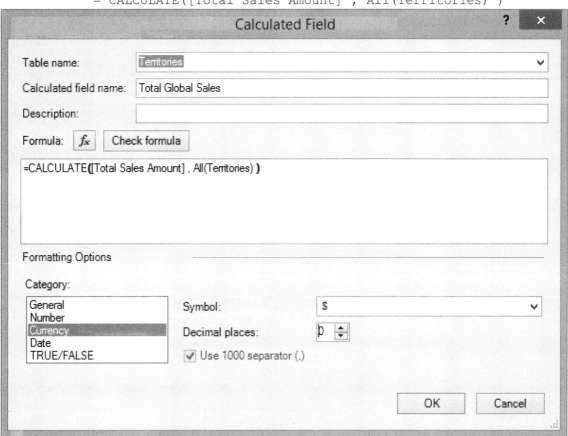

As you know, the first parameter of CALCULATE() is an expression, and the subsequent parameters are filters that modify the filter context. In this case, you are passing a table as the filter context. This table is ALL(Territories), which is actually the entire Territories table with *all filters removed*.

You now see the new calculated field in the pivot table (as shown below).

Row Labels ▼	Total Sales Amount	Total Global Sales
Australia	$9,061,001	$29,358,677
Canada	$1,977,845	$29,358,677
France	$2,644,018	$29,358,677
Germany	$2,894,312	$29,358,677
NA		$29,358,677
United Kingdom	$3,391,712	$29,358,677
United States	$9,389,790	$29,358,677
Grand Total	**$29,358,677**	**$29,358,677**

Step 2: Create the Percentage of Total

After that you have created the calculated field [Total Global Sales], it is easy to create a new calculated field to calculate the country percentage of global sales, as follows:

```
[% of Global Sales]
    = DIVIDE([Total Sales Amount] , [Total Global Sales])
```

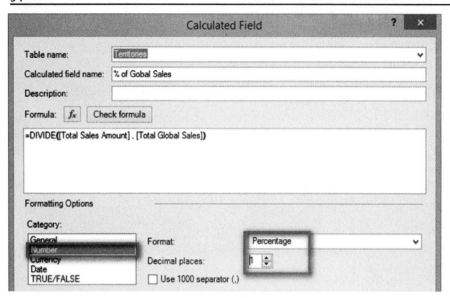

Make sure you format this calculated field so that Category is set to Number, Format is set to Percentage, and Decimal Places is set to 1, as shown above.

You end up with the following:

Row Labels	Total Sales Amount	Total Global Sales	% of Gobal Sales
Australia	$9,061,001	$29,358,677	30.9%
Canada	$1,977,845	$29,358,677	6.7%
Central	$3,001	$29,358,677	0.0%
France	$2,644,018	$29,358,677	9.0%
Germany	$2,894,312	$29,358,677	9.9%
NA		$29,358,677	
Northeast	$6,532	$29,358,677	0.0%
Northwest	$3,649,867	$29,358,677	12.4%
Southeast	$12,239	$29,358,677	0.0%
Southwest	$5,718,151	$29,358,677	19.5%
United Kingdom	$3,391,712	$29,358,677	11.6%
Grand Total	$29,358,677	$29,358,677	100.0%

The final step is to remove the [Total Global Sales] calculated field from the pivot.

> **Note** You don't actually need the interim calculated fields you write to be placed in the pivot in order for the [% of Global Sales] calculated field to work. But you should notice how much easier it is to visualise what is happening when you write these calculated fields in the context of a pivot table. When you do it this way, you can easily see how the [Total Global Sales] value is the same, regardless of the country in the pivot, and hence you can immediately see that you just need to divide the actually country sales by this total global sales amount, and it is going to work.

Here is the final pivot, with some conditional formatting applied to make it easier to read:

Row Labels	Total Sales Amount	% of Gobal Sales
Australia	$9,061,001	30.9%
Canada	$1,977,845	6.7%
Central	$3,001	0.0%
France	$2,644,018	9.0%
Germany	$2,894,312	9.9%
Northeast	$6,532	0.0%
Northwest	$3,649,867	12.4%
Southeast	$12,239	0.0%
Southwest	$5,718,151	19.5%
United Kingdom	$3,391,712	11.6%
Grand Total	$29,358,677	100.0%

Passing a Table or a Column to ALL()

Before finishing with `ALL()`, it is worth pointing out that this next calculated field would return exactly the same result as `[Total Global Sales]` in the pivot table example in step 1 above:

```
[Total All Country Sales]
    = CALCULATE([Total Sales Amount] ,
    ALL ( Territories[Country] ) )
```

Notice that this calculated field passes a single *column* instead of the entire table to the `ALL()` function. So in this specific pivot table, the values for `[Total Global Sales]` and `[Total All Country Sales]` are identical (see below).

Row Labels	Total Sales Amount	Total Global Sales	Total All Country Sales
Australia	$9,061,001	$29,358,677	$29,358,677
Canada	$1,977,845	$29,358,677	$29,358,677
France	$2,644,018	$29,358,677	$29,358,677
Germany	$2,894,312	$29,358,677	$29,358,677
NA		$29,358,677	$29,358,677
United Kingdom	$3,391,712	$29,358,677	$29,358,677
United States	$9,389,790	$29,358,677	$29,358,677
Grand Total	**$29,358,677**	**$29,358,677**	**$29,358,677**

However, the calculated field `[Total All Country Sales]` would not work (i.e., it would not remove the filter) if there were some other column on Rows in the pivot table (something other than `Country`).

To test this out, remove `Territories[Country]` from Rows in the pivot table and replace it with `Territories[Region]`.

Row Labels	Total Sales Amount	Total Global Sales	Total All Country Sales
Australia	$9,061,001	$29,358,677	$9,061,001
Canada	$1,977,845	$29,358,677	$1,977,845
Central	$3,001	$29,358,677	$3,001
France	$2,644,018	$29,358,677	$2,644,018
Germany	$2,894,312	$29,358,677	$2,894,312
NA		$29,358,677	
Northeast	$6,532	$29,358,677	$6,532
Northwest	$3,649,867	$29,358,677	$3,649,867
Southeast	$12,239	$29,358,677	$12,239
Southwest	$5,718,151	$29,358,677	$5,718,151
United Kingdom	$3,391,712	$29,358,677	$3,391,712
Grand Total	**$29,358,677**	**$29,358,677**	**$29,358,677**

Notice the difference between passing the entire table name to the `ALL()` function and passing a single column. `[Total Global Sales]` removes the filter from the entire `Territories` table, but `[Total All Country Sales]` removes filters only from the `Territories[Country]` column of the table.

Remove `[Total All Country Sales]` from the pivot before proceeding.

The ALLEXCEPT() Function

`ALLEXCEPT()` allows you to remove filters from all columns in a table except the ones that you explicitly specify. Consider the following example:

```
[Total Sales to Region or Country]
    = CALCULATE([Total Sales Amount],
        All(Territories[Region]),
        All(Territories[Country])
    )
```

`ALLEXCEPT()` solves the problem implied above where you need to specify many columns individually in the case that you want most (but not all) columns in your formula. The above formula will work when you have `Territories[Country]` on Rows and also when you have `Territories[Region]` on Rows, but it will not work with `Territories[Group]` on Rows. If you have a lot of columns in your table, you would have to write a lot of DAX code to make such a formula work for all but a few of the columns.

This is where `ALLEXCEPT()` comes into play. The above formula can be rewritten as follows:

```
[Total Sales to Region or Country 2]
    = CALCULATE([Total Sales Amount],
      ALLEXCEPT(Territories, Territories[Group]))
```

Note that you must first specify the table that is to be included and then specify the exception columns.

The ALLSELECTED() Function

The last function in this family is `ALLSELECTED()`. It is useful when you want to calculate percentages as shown above and you have a filter applied (say, via a slicer) but you want the total in your pivot table to add up to 100%.

Say that you're working with the same pivot table as above but now with a slicer that filters on `Territories[Group]`. Notice how `[% of Global Sales]` adds up to 38.7%; this is correct because the other countries that make up the remaining 61.3% have been filtered out by the slicer.

Group		Row Labels ▾	Total Sales Amount	% of Gobal Sales
Europe		Canada	$1,977,845	6.7%
North America		Central	$3,001	0.0%
Pacific		Northeast	$6,532	0.0%
NA		Northwest	$3,649,867	12.4%
		Southeast	$12,239	0.0%
		Southwest	$5,718,151	19.5%
		Grand Total	**$11,367,634**	**38.7%**

But say that you want to see what percentage each region is of all the values in the pivot (in this example, just the regions in the group North America). This is where `ALLSELECTED()` comes in. Add the following calculated field to the above pivot:

```
[Total Selected Groups]
    = CALCULATE([Total Sales Amount], ALLSELECTED(Territories))
```

Group		Row Labels ▾	Total Sales Amount	% of Gobal Sales	Total Selected Territories
Europe		Canada	$1,977,845	6.7%	$11,367,634
NA		Central	$3,001	0.0%	$11,367,634
North America		Northeast	$6,532	0.0%	$11,367,634
Pacific		Northwest	$3,649,867	12.4%	$11,367,634
		Southeast	$12,239	0.0%	$11,367,634
		Southwest	$5,718,151	19.5%	$11,367,634
		Grand Total	**$11,367,634**	**38.7%**	**$11,367,634**

Notice how the interim calculated field `[Total Selected Territories]` is returning the same value as the grand total of the items in the pivot table. Using the same steps as before, you can now write a new calculated field `[% of Selected Territories]` and then remove the interim calculated field `[Total Selected Territories]` from the pivot.

Go ahead and write the following calculated field:

```
[% of Selected Territories]
    = DIVIDE([Total Sales Amount] , [Total Selected Territories])
```

Group ▼	Row Labels ▼	Total Sales Amount	% of Gobal Sales	% of Selected Territories
Europe	Canada	$1,977,845	6.7%	17.4%
North America	Central	$3,001	0.0%	0.0%
	Northeast	$6,532	0.0%	0.1%
Pacific	Northwest	$3,649,867	12.4%	32.1%
	Southeast	$12,239	0.0%	0.1%
NA	Southwest	$5,718,151	19.5%	50.3%
	Grand Total	$11,367,634	38.7%	100.0%

Did you remember to format this new calculated field using the settings Number, Percentage, and 1 decimal?

Using Interim Calculated Fields

Remember that it is good practice to split a problem into pieces and solve one piece of the puzzle at a time. My advice is to get used to creating interim calculated fields first and then writing the final calculated field that you actually need. Doing this helps you visualise each step of the process and makes it easier to get each part of the end-state formula correct before you proceed to the next step.

It is, of course, possible to write one single calculated field that does all the steps you just went through:

```
[% of Selected Territories ONE STEP]
   = DIVIDE([Total Sales Amount] ,
      CALCULATE([Total Sales Amount],
      ALLSELECTED(Territories)
      )
   )
```

But this all-in-one formula is much harder to write, read, and debug—particularly when you are learning to write DAX.

Practice Exercises: ALL(), ALLEXCEPT(), and ALLSELECTED()

It's time for some practice. Create a new pivot table and put Customers[Occupation] on Rows and the calculated field [Total Sales Amount] on Values.

Row Labels ▼	Total Sales Amount
Clerical	$4,684,787
Management	$5,467,862
Manual	$2,857,971
Professional	$9,907,977
Skilled Manual	$6,440,081
Grand Total	$29,358,677

Then, using the principles covered in this chapter, create the following calculated fields by first creating the interim calculated field you need and then creating the final calculated field. Find the solutions to these practice exercises in "N. ALL(), ALLEXCEPT(), and ALLSELECTED()" on page 178.

47. [Total Sales to All Customers]

48. [% of All Customer Sales]

Now add a slicer for Customers[Gender] to the pivot table you have just created and filter by Gender = M.

Gender		Row Labels	Total Sales Amount	Total Sales to All Customers	% of All Customer Sales
F		Clerical	$2,421,327	$29,358,677	8.2%
M		Management	$2,793,527	$29,358,677	9.5%
		Manual	$1,463,060	$29,358,677	5.0%
		Professional	$4,773,493	$29,358,677	16.3%
		Skilled Manual	$3,093,651	$29,358,677	10.5%
		Grand Total	**$14,545,059**	**$29,358,677**	**49.5%**

Note how [% of All Customer Sales] doesn't add to 100%. This is correct because the other 50.5% of customers are filtered out with the slicer.

Set up another pivot table as follows, with Customers[NumberCarsOwned] on Rows, Customers[Occupation] on Slicer, and [Total Sales Amount] on Values. Your job is to create the other calculated field in this pivot: [% of Sales to Selected Customers].

Occupation		Row Labels	Total Sales Amount	% of Sales to Selected Customers
Clerical		0	$2,660,886	56.8%
Management		1	$1,204,496	25.7%
Manual		2	$790,154	16.9%
Professional		3	$28,141	0.6%
		4	$1,109	0.0%
Skilled Manual		**Grand Total**	**$4,684,787**	**100.0%**

Remember to create an interim calculated field first, so you actually need to create the following two calculated fields and then remove the first one from the pivot table.

49. [Total Sales to Selected Customers]

50. [% of Sales to Selected Customers]

Inserting Slicers

It's time to revisit slicers. Create a new pivot table and place DayName on Rows and place Calendar Year and MonthName as slicers (by clicking in the pivot table, navigating to the Insert tab, and selecting Slicer).

Create this pivot table now and then read on to learn about the slicers:

MonthName			
April	August	December	February
January	July	June	March
May	November	October	September

CalendarYear		Row Labels	
2001		Friday	
2002		Monday	
		Saturday	
2003		Sunday	
		Thursday	
2004		Tuesday	
		Wednesday	
		Grand Total	

There are two things to notice here. First, the day names and month names are not sorted correctly (as discussed in Chapter 11), and also the month name is set up to display in a grid four wide by three high instead of the default one column wide.

> **Note** Chapter 11 provides instruction on how to change column sort order. The sort order of the table columns affects the sort order in pivot tables and also in slicers. You only need to set the sort order once in your data model (for each column), and the new sort order will change the sorting of both pivot tables and slicers. You should have already changed the sort order for the `MonthName` column in Chapter 11. If you haven't done this already, though, go back and do it now.

There are two ways to insert a slicer with Excel 2013. First, you can click in the pivot table and then click Insert, Slicer and select the column you need (in this case, `MonthName`). But there is an easier way, as shown below.

Here's How: Inserting a Slicer

Follow these steps to insert a slicer:

1. Click inside the pivot table.
2. Go to the PivotTable Fields list and right-click the column you need (shown as #1 below).
3. Select Add as Slicer (#2).

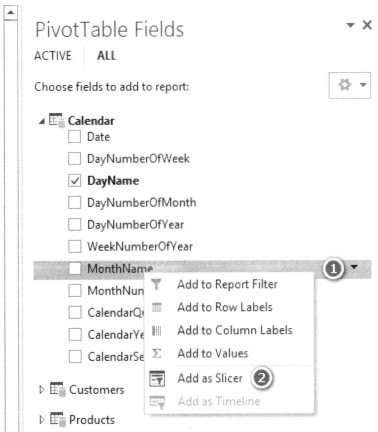

4. Select the slicer, click Slicer Tools, Options (see #1 below), and then change the number of columns to 4 (#2).

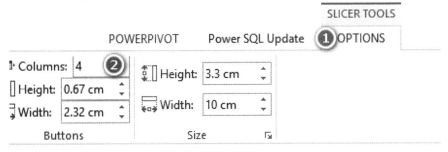

Now is a good time to add [Total Sales Amount] to the pivot as it will help you visualise the interim steps in producing this calculated field.

Practice Exercises: ALL(), ALLEXCEPT(), and ALLSELECTED(), Cont.

Okay, it's time for some more practice exercises. Write the following two formulas. The first one is an interim formula and can be removed from the pivot once you have finished the second formula. Find the solutions to these practice exercises in "N. ALL(), ALLEXCEPT(), and ALLSELECTED()" on page 178.

51. [Total Sales for All Days Selected Dates]

52. [% Sales for All Days Selected Dates]

Here's How: Using ALLEXCEPT()

I don't use ALLEXCEPT() much, and you may not either, but it is still good to work through an example of how it can be used. This will give you some practice while also demonstrating one possible use case.

Say that you want to compare the percentage of sales across all occupations and see how it changes depending on the other customer filters. Follow these steps:

1. Set up a new pivot table and place Customers[Occupation] on Rows.

2. Add slicers for Gender and NumberCarsOwned.

3. Put Total Order Quantity on Values. You should have the pivot shown below. Note that the total order quantity will change as you click on the slicers.

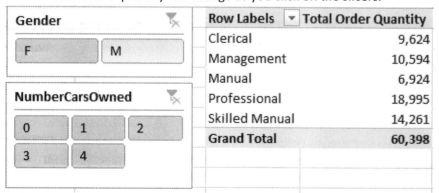

There are a number of steps to get to the end state (which is shown below). The step-by-step instructions are on the following pages, and you should work through each step and write the DAX you need to get to the end state. At each step along the way, check that the results you see in your pivot table make sense. Once again, this is the entire reason we write DAX in the context of a pivot table—it is just easier to get your head around what you are doing.

The following pivot table shows all the calculated fields you need to write (just so you have an overview of what you'll accomplish with the following steps).

Row Labels	Total Order Quantity	Total Orders All Customers	Baseline Orders for All customers with this Occupation	Baseline % this Occupation is of All Customer Orders	Total Orders Selected Customers	Occupation % of Selected Customers	Percentage Point variation to baseline
Clerical	7	60,398	9,624	15.9%	2,199	0.3%	-15.6%
Management	872	60,398	10,594	17.5%	2,199	39.7%	22.1%
Manual	1	60,398	6,924	11.5%	2,199	0.0%	-11.4%
Professional	1,263	60,398	18,995	31.4%	2,199	57.4%	26.0%
Skilled Manual	56	60,398	14,261	23.6%	2,199	2.5%	-21.1%
Grand Total	2,199	60,398	60,398	100.0%	2,199	100.0%	0.0%

And here is the end state you are working toward, with just the final calculated fields included:

Row Labels	Total Order Quantity	Occupation % of Selected Customers	Baseline % this Occupation is of All Customer Orders	Percentage Point variation to baseline
Clerical	7	0.3%	15.9%	-15.6%
Management	872	39.7%	17.5%	22.1%
Manual	1	0.0%	11.5%	-11.4%
Professional	1,263	57.4%	31.4%	26.0%
Skilled Manual	56	2.5%	23.6%	-21.1%
Grand Total	2,199	100.0%	100.0%	0.0%

Gender: F, M

NumberCarsOwned: 0, 1, 2, 3, 4

As you can imagine, with this pivot table, it is possible to select different combinations of gender and number of cars and then compare the variation between the baseline order quantity and the order quantities for the selected filter.

Write the following DAX formulas one at a time, checking to make sure each looks correct before moving to the next one.

Practice Exercises: ALL(), ALLEXCEPT(), and ALLSELECTED(), Cont.

Find the solutions to these practice exercises in "N. ALL(), ALLEXCEPT(), and ALLSELECTED()" on page 178.

53. [Total Orders All Customers]

To check this, click on the slicers and note that `[Total Order Quantity]` should change but `[Total Orders All Customers]` should not change based on slicers.

54. [Baseline Orders for All Customers with This Occupation]

This calculated field should not change when you make changes to the slicers either. However, note that you should get a different value for each occupation—unlike with `[Total Orders All Customers]` above. This will be the baseline for comparison.

Next, turn the baseline above into a percentage of all orders baseline.

55. [Baseline % This Occupation of All Customer Orders]

The description of this calculated field should help you work out how to write the DAX. Test the slicers again and make sure this new baseline percentage doesn't change with the slicers.

56. [Total Orders Selected Customers]

This calculated field should adjust depending on the selections you have in the slicers. *Hint:* Use `ALLSELECTED()`.

57. [Occupation % of Selected Customers]

You can use the interim calculated fields above to create this one. Click on the slicers a few times and see which values change. This new calculated field should change based on the values you select in the slicers.

58. [Percentage Point Variation to Baseline]

This calculated field should take the percentage value from Practice Exercise 56 above and subtract the percentage value from Practice Exercise 54 above (i.e., it is simply the percentage of selected customers minus the baseline).

Now you should have an interactive pivot table where you can drill into customer attributes (gender and number of cars owned) and see the impact on the mix of business vs. the baseline of all customers.

It is also worth pointing out here that sometimes it may be useful to change the descriptions of the final calculated fields as they appear in a pivot table. So while `[Baseline % This Occupation of All Customer Orders]` is a good name for your calculated field because you know what it means, when you use this calculated field in a specific pivot table, it may be a good idea to rename it. You can do this by just clicking on the heading in the pivot table and giving it a new name.

After giving your calculated fields new names, you might end up with something like the pivot table shown below.

Row Labels	Total Orders	Share of Selected Filter	Baseline Share All Customers	Variation to baseline
Clerical	7	0.3%	15.9%	-15.6%
Management	872	39.7%	17.5%	22.1%
Manual	1	0.0%	11.5%	-11.4%
Professional	1,263	57.4%	31.4%	26.0%
Skilled Manual	56	2.5%	23.6%	-21.1%
Grand Total	2,199	100.0%	100.0%	0.0%

Note If you change the description in the pivot, the easiest way to change it back is to right-click on the heading name in the pivot, select Value Field Settings, and then change the Custom Name setting in the Value Field Settings dialog box.

Row Labels	Total Orders	Share of Selected Filter	Baseline Share All Customers	Variation to baseline
Clerical	7	0.3%	15.9%	-15.6%
Management	872	39.7%	17.5%	22.1%
Manual	1	0.0%	11.5%	-11.4%
Professional	1,263	57.4%	31.4%	26.0%
Skilled Manual	56	2.5%	23.6%	-21.1%
Grand Total	2,199	100.0%	100.0%	0.0%

Value Field Settings

Source Name: Baseline % this Occupation is of All Custome...

Custom Name: Baseline Share All Customers

Summarize Values By | Show Values As

Show values as

No Calculation

13: DAX Topic: FILTER()

`FILTER()` is a very powerful function in DAX. When `FILTER()` and `CALCULATE()` are combined, these two functions allow you to alter the filter context in your pivot tables any way you want. However, before we move to using `FILTER()` with `CALCULATE()`, I think it is worth looking at `FILTER()` on its own with a couple of simple examples.

> **Note** These examples demonstrate how the `FILTER()` function works, but you probably would not actually write such formulas in real DAX. These formulas are created here just for demonstration purposes.

The syntax of `FILTER()` is as follows:

```
= FILTER(Table , myFilter)
```

Table is any table (or function that returns a table, such as `ALL()`), and *myFilter* is any expression that evaluates to a `TRUE/FALSE` answer.

The `FILTER()` function returns a table that contains zero or more rows from the original table. Said another way, the table returned by `FILTER()` can contain zero rows, one row, two rows, or any other number of rows up to and including the total number of rows in the original table. The purpose of `FILTER()` therefore is to determine which rows will be returned into the final table result after using the *myFilter* test.

`FILTER()` is an iterator, and as such it can complete granular-level analysis to determine which rows will be included in the final table. But because it is an iterator, it is not always fast (as discussed in Chapter 6), so use `FILTER()` carefully. Generally, it is fine to use `FILTER()` over lookup tables, but it's somewhat more risky to use it over data tables. It does depend on your data and also what you need.

Let's work through an example. Set up a new pivot table with `Customers[Occupation]` on Rows and the calculated field `[Total Number of Customers]` on Values.

Row Labels ▼	Total number of Customers
Clerical	2,928
Management	3,075
Manual	2,384
Professional	5,520
Skilled Manual	4,577
Grand Total	**18,484**

This pivot shows how many customers there are in the entire customer database for each occupation type. But what if you wanted to know how many customers there are in the database that have an income of more than $80,000 per year? Consider the following formula:

```
=FILTER(Customers, Customers[YearlyIncome] >= 80000)
```

The result of this formula is a table of customers (that retains a link to the original table of customers), and this new virtual table of customers includes all the customers that have an income greater than or equal to $80,000 per year. But note that it is a table, and you can't put a table of values into a pivot table. So if you want to see the result (in this case, the total count of rows) inside a pivot table, you have to wrap this table that was returned by `FILTER()` inside a function that returns a value instead of a table of values (such as an aggregator).

It is possible to count the number of rows in this table by wrapping the above formula inside another formula, like this:

```
[Total Customers with Income of $80,000 or above]
    = COUNTROWS (
    FILTER(
        Customers,
        Customers[YearlyIncome]>=80000
      )
    )
```

If you write this formula and put it in the pivot table, it looks as shown below. You should do this now for practice.

Row Labels ▼	Total number of Customers	Total Customers with Income of $80,000 or above
Clerical	2,928	
Management	3,075	1,963
Manual	2,384	
Professional	5,520	1,976
Skilled Manual	4,577	443
Grand Total	**18,484**	**4,382**

You can see from the pivot table that not all occupations have customers that earn this amount of money.

These are the key points to take away from this example:

- `FILTER()` returns a table.

- This table retains a link to the original table and can have an effect on the other tables in the data model. (More on this later in this chapter.)

- You can't put the table returned by `Filter()` into a pivot table as is because you simply can't put a table into a pivot. But you can count how many rows there are in this table and put the answer into the pivot. This is exactly what happens with this calculated field.

So How Does FILTER() Actually Work?

It is essential that you understand how the `FILTER()` function works before moving on. Let's look just at the `FILTER()` portion of the formula above:

```
FILTER(Customers, Customers[YearlyIncome]>=80000)
```

`FILTER()` is an iterator just like `SUMX()`, covered in Chapter 6. As such, `FILTER()` first creates a row context and then iterates through each row in the table to check whether the row passes the test. If an individual row passes the test, it is retained in the final table result. If an individual row fails the test, it is omitted from the final table result.

Let's look at a simple example. Assume that the `Customers` table has five rows, as shown here:

Row	CustomerKey	YearlyIncome
1	11003	$ 70,000
2	11004	$ 80,000
3	11005	$ 70,000
4	11007	$ 60,000
5	11058	$ 80,000

Note The Row column has been added here to assist in the explanation of how filter works; it does not actually exist in the `Customers` table.

Here again is the `FILTER()` portion of the formula from above:

```
FILTER(Customers, Customers[YearlyIncome]>=80000)
```

This is what the `FILTER()` function does:

1. It first creates a new row context over the `Customers` table. The row context allows `FILTER()` to keep track of which row it is looking at, and it also provides the capability to isolate a single row (one at a time) and refer to the single value that is the intersection between the single row and any column in the table.

2. Now that there is a row context, `FILTER()` then goes to row 1 and asks the question (from the *myFilter* portion of the formula) "Is the value in the column `Customers[YearlyIncome]` for the customer in this row greater than or equal to $80,000?" If the answer is yes, then row 1 survives the filter test, and the row is kept in the final table result. If the answer is no, then row 1 is discarded

from the final table result. So in this case (row 1), the yearly income is $70,000, so it fails the test, and row 1 is discarded from the final table result.

3. FILTER() then moves to the second row (using the row context to keep track of where it is) and asks the same question again for this new row: "Is the value in the column Customers[YearlyIncome] for the customer in this row greater than or equal to $80,000?" If the answer is yes, then the row survives the filter test, and the row is kept in the final table result. If the answer is no, then it fails the test, and the row is discarded from the final table result. In the case of row 2, it passes the test and hence row 2 is retained.

4. FILTER() then works down the table one row at a time and tests each row against the filter test. It decides which rows to keep and which rows to discard by checking each row, one at a time, against the filter test.

5. Once the last row has been evaluated, FILTER() returns a table that contains just the rows that passed the test. All rows that failed the test are discarded.

Rows that pass the test			Final result	Rows that fail the test		
Row	CustomerKey	YearlyIncome		Row	CustomerKey	YearlyIncome
2	11004	$ 80,000		1	11003	$ 70,000
5	11058	$ 80,000		3	11005	$ 70,000
				4	11007	$ 60,000

So it is clear from the image above that if you now count the rows of the table on the left (which is the result of FILTER()), you will get the answer 2 (i.e., there are two rows in this table).

If you now refer back to the earlier example, it is clear how the formula gave you the results. Here is the formula, shown again for convenience:

```
[Total Customers with Income of $80,000 or above]
    = COUNTROWS(
    FILTER(
        Customers,
        Customers[YearlyIncome]>=80000
    )
)
```

The formula [Total Customers with Income of $80,000 or Above] iterates through the Customers table, checking the value in the Customers[YearlyIncome] column of each individual customer to see if the value is greater than or equal to $80,000.

Row Labels	Total number of Customers	Total Customers with Income of $80,000 or above
Clerical	2,928	
Management	3,075	1,963
Manual	2,384	
Professional	5,520	1,976
Skilled Manual	4,577	443
Grand Total	18,484	4,382

FILTER() returns a table of all customers that passed this test, and then COUNTROWS() counts them. The formula finds that 1,963 customers have the occupation *management* and also pass this test, and 4,382 customers in total pass the test for all occupations.

Note It is convenient to think of the iteration process being from the top of the table to the bottom. But FILTER() may not necessarily work through each row in order from top to bottom. It is actually irrelevant which order is used in the iteration process as all rows are iterated once and only once, and the order of the iteration has no impact on the final result.

Using FILTER() Inside CALCULATE()

As mentioned earlier, `FILTER()` is most commonly used as an advanced filter inside `CALCULATE()`. `FILTER()` is an iterator, and it therefore allows a very granular level of evaluation of a table and is a very powerful tool for altering the filter context of a pivot table however you want and at a level of detail that is not otherwise possible using a simple filter inside `CALCULATE()`.

Consider the following formula:

```
[Total Customers with Income of $80,000 or above 2]
    = CALCULATE(COUNTROWS(Customers),
    Customers[YearlyIncome]>=80000)
```

This formula returns exactly the same result as the `FILTER()` version above. In this version, the filter portion of the formula uses a simple filter, or raw filter. A simple filter has a column name on one side of the formula (in this case, `Customers[YearlyIncome]`) and a value on the right side (in this case, `80000`).

`CALCULATE()` is quite capable of this type of calculation on its own, without using the `FILTER()` function. In fact, what is much more important is that `CALCULATE()` is actually optimised to do these types of calculations using simple filters with lightning speed (by using the storage engine instead of the formula engine). Wherever possible, you should use these simple filters to take advantage of this optimisation as it will give you the fastest results.

However, there is a limit to what `CALCULATE()` can do with one of these simple filters. It works only if you have a column name on the left side of the filter portion of the equation and a value on the right side of the equation. But what if you want to do something more complex, like check whether another calculated field is greater than a value? Let's look at another example.

Example: Calculating Lifetime Customer Purchases

Say that you want to know how many customers have purchased more than $5,000 of goods from you over all time. You can't use a simple `CALCULATE()` filter in this case because you don't have a column that contains a single value that tells the total sales for each customer (because customers may have purchased from you on many occasions). If you tried to write this formula using a simple filter, it would look like this:

```
[Customers with Sales Greater Than $5,000 Doesn't Work]
    = CALCULATE(Countrows(Customers),[Total Sales Amount] > 5000)
```

In this formula, there is a calculated field on the left side—and that is not allowed as a simple filter! A simple filter *must* have a column on the left side and a value on the right, so a simple filter doesn't work in this scenario.

This is where `FILTER()` comes in. Now take a look at the following formula:

```
[Customers with Sales Greater Than $5,000]
    = CALCULATE (
        COUNTROWS(Customers),
        FILTER(Customers,
            [Total Sales Amount] >= 5000
        )
    )
```

It is worth stepping through how `FILTER()` works again in this example because there is a slight difference from the earlier example.

> **Note** The `FILTER()` portion of the formula is *evaluated first*. This is always the case with `CALCULATE()`. The filter portion is *always* evaluated first (for both simple filters and advanced filters).

Let's start by looking at just the `FILTER()` portion of this formula:

```
FILTER(Customers, [Total Sales Amount] >= 5000)
```

Here's what's happening in this portion of the formula:

1. `FILTER()` creates a row context for the `Customers` table. `FILTER()` then goes to row 1 in the `Customers` table and applies a filter to that single customer.

2. **This is very important:** The filter then propagates down through the relationship with the `Customers` table and filters the `Sales` table so that only sales for this customer are unfiltered. (There is more important information on this filter propagation later in the chapter.)

3. The calculated field `[Total Sales Amount]` is then evaluated after the `Sales` table is filtered for this one single customer.

4. `FILTER()` then asks the question "Is the value of `[Total Sales Amount]` for this one customer in this first row of the `Customers` table greater than or equal to $5,000?" If the answer is yes, then this customer survives the filter test, and the row is kept in the final table result. If the answer is no, the customer is discarded from the final table result.

5. `FILTER()` then moves to the second row in the row context of the `Customers` table, propagates the filter for the second customer from the `Customers` table through to the `Sales` table, evaluates the calculated field `[Total Sales Amount]` against the rows in the `Sales` table that remain, and then checks whether `[Total Sales Amount]` for this second customer is greater than $5,000. Once again, if the answer is yes, the customer survives the filter and remains in the final table results. If the customer fails the test, it is discarded.

6. `FILTER()` proceeds through every customer in the `Customers` table, testing each one to see if the `[Total Sales Amount]` of all the records for that specific customer in the `Sales` table is greater than $5,000. All customers that pass the test are retained in the final table, and the ones that fail the test are discarded from the final table.

When the `FILTER()` portion is finishes its work, `FILTER()` returns a table of customers that passed the test. You can imagine the *myFilter* portion of the original formula looking like this:

```
[Customers with Sales Greater Than $5,000]
    = CALCULATE(
        COUNTROWS(Customers),
        Only_Use_The_Table_of_Customers_Provided_By_FILTER
    )
```

The `FILTER()` formula above determines which customers passed the test and returns this table of customers to `CACLUATE()`. The resulting filtered table of customers is then accepted and applied as a filter by `CALCULATE()` before it evaluates the `COUNTROWS(Customers)` potion of the formula. There are actually 1,732 customers out of a total of 18,484 customers that passed the `FILTER()` test. By the time `COUNTROWS()` is executed, just the 1,732 customers that passed the `FILTER()` test remain, so `COUNTROWS()` returns 1,732.

Practice Exercises: FILTER()

Set up a new pivot table with `Products[Category]` on Rows and `[Total Sales Amount]` on Values and then write the following two formulas. Find the solutions to these practice exercises in "O. FILTER()" on page 180.

59. [Total Sales of Products That Have Some Sales but Less Than $10,000]

What you need to do here is get `FILTER()` to iterate over the `Products` table to determine whether each product has some sales and also whether the total of those sales is less than $10,000.

Note that you can use the double ampersand operator (`&&`) if you need more than one condition in your expression:

```
Condition1 && Condition2
```

60. [Count of Products That Have Some Sales but Less Than $10,000]

You should end up with a pivot table like this:

Row Labels	Total Sales Amount	Total Sales of Products that have some sales but less than $10,000	Count of Products that have some sales but less than $10,000
Accessories	$700,760	$31,431	4
Bikes	$28,318,145		
Clothing	$339,773	$5,106	2
Grand Total	$29,358,677	$36,538	6

A good exercise now is to remove [Total Sales Amount] from the pivot table and add ProductName on Rows. If you don't remove [Total Sales Amount] first, you will get every single product that has sold at least once in your pivot.

You should end up with this:

Row Labels	Total Sales of Products that have some sales but less than $10,000	Count of Products that have some sales but less than $10,000
⊟ Accessories	$31,431	4
Bike Wash - Dissolver	$7,219	1
Patch Kit/8 Patches	$7,307	1
Road Tire Tube	$9,480	1
Touring Tire Tube	$7,425	1
⊟ Clothing	$5,106	2
Racing Socks, L	$2,427	1
Racing Socks, M	$2,679	1
Grand Total	$36,538	6

Revisiting Filter Propagation

Earlier in this chapter, we looked at a FILTER() example with a calculated field on the left side of the filter test and a value on the right side:

```
[Customers with Sales Greater Than $5,000]
    = CALCULATE(COUNTROWS(Customers),
      FILTER(Customers,
          [Total Sales Amount] >= 5000
      )
    )
```

Let's revisit how FILTER() operates in the formula above. (You can't hear this too many times.) The FILTER() portion is evaluated first:

1. FILTER() creates a row context for the Customers table. FILTER() then goes to row 1 in the Customers table and applies a filter to that single customer (context transition from a row context to a filter context).

2. The filter on the first row of the Customers table then propagates down through the relationship with the Customers table and filters the Sales table so that only sales for this customer are unfiltered.

3. The calculated field [Total Sales Amount] is evaluated after the Sales table is first filtered for this one single customer (returning the value $8,249 in this case).

There is something I didn't explain before that is very important. But let me work up to the explanation.

Do you remember what the formula for [Total Sales Amount] is? The formula is as follows:

```
[Total Sales Amount] = SUM(Sales[ExtendedAmount])
```

So given that `[Total Sales Amount]` evaluates to exactly the same result as `SUM(Sales[ExtendedAmount])`, what do you expect will happen if you substitute `SUM(Sales[Ex-tendedAmount])` into the formula above, like this:

```
[Customers with sales greater than $5,000 Version2]
    = CALCULATE(COUNTROWS(Customers),
        FILTER(Customers,
            SUM(Sales[ExtendedAmount]) >= 5000
        )
    )
```

You should go ahead and create this formula and see what happens. When you do this, you see the following:

Row Labels	Total Sales Amount	Customers That Have Purchased	Customers with Total Sales more than $5,000	Customers with sales greater than $5,000 Version2
Australia	$9,061,001	3,591	719	18,484
Canada	$1,977,845	1,571	42	18,484
France	$2,644,018	1,810	163	18,484
Germany	$2,894,312	1,780	158	18,484
United Kingdom	$3,391,712	1,913	280	18,484
United States	$9,389,790	7,819	370	18,484
Grand Total	$29,358,677	18,484	1,732	18,484

The new formula returns the entire table of customers instead of the value you are looking for. Why is this?

Well, there is a very important difference between a calculated field and the formula inside a calculated field.

Technically speaking, when you write the following calculated field:

```
[Total Sales Amount] = SUM(Sales[ExtendedAmount])
```

what is actually happening under the hood in Power Pivot is the following:

```
[Total Sales Amount] = CALCULATE(SUM(Sales[ExtendedAmount]))
```

Power Pivot adds a `CALCULATE()` function and wraps it around your formula. You can't see this `CALCULATE()`, but it is there. We call this "invisible" `CALCULATE()` an "implicit `CALCULATE()`."

Okay, let's get back to the problem at hand. Go back into the new calculated field you just created and wrap the `SUM()` function in `CALCULATE()` as follows:

```
[Customers with Sales Greater Than $5,000 Version2]
    = CALCULATE(COUNTROWS(Customers),
        FILTER(Customers,
            CALCULATE(SUM(Sales[ExtendedAmount])) >= 5000
        )
    )
```

When you manually place `CALCULATE()` like this, it is called an "explicit `CALCULATE()`." Once you make this change, you get the expected result, as shown below.

Row Labels	Total Sales Amount	Customers That Have Purchased	Customers with Total Sales more than $5,000	Customers with sales greater than $5,000 Version2
Australia	$9,061,001	3,591	719	719
Canada	$1,977,845	1,571	42	42
France	$2,644,018	1,810	163	163
Germany	$2,894,312	1,780	158	158
United Kingdom	$3,391,712	1,913	280	280
United States	$9,389,790	7,819	370	370
Grand Total	$29,358,677	18,484	1,732	1,732

The point is that without the CALCULATE () function wrapped around SUM (Sales [ExtendedAmount]), something stops working. It doesn't matter if there is an implicit CALCULATE () that you can't see (inside another calculated field) or if there's an explicit CALCULATE () that you add yourself. You simply must have a CALCULATE () if you want this formula to work. Why is this?

Remember that Chapter 9 said that a row context does not automatically create a filter context. Chapter 9 was talking about the row context in a calculated column, but it is exactly the same in a function that has a row context—in this case, the FILTER () function. The CALCULATE () function tells Power Pivot to "run the filter engine again." If you don't have this extra CALCULATE (), the filter that is first applied to the Customers table *will not* propagate to the Sales table as described above. It is the second CALCULATE () (either implicit or explicit) that causes the filter on the Customers table to propagate through the relationship to the Sales table *before* the rest of the FILTER () expression is evaluated.

So let's step through what happens without the extra CALCULATE () by going back to this version, which didn't work:

```
[Customers with sales greater than $5,000 Version2]
    = CALCULATE (COUNTROWS (Customers),
      FILTER (Customers,
         SUM (Sales [ExtendedAmount]) >= 5000
      )
    )
```

Of course, the FILTER portion is evaluated first, just like before. And then the following happens:

1. FILTER () creates a row context on the Customers table. FILTER () then goes to row 1 in the row context. No filter context currently exists because a row context doesn't automatically create a filter context.

2. Given that there is no filter context, the Customers table *does nothing* to filter the Sales table. The CALCULATE () function (implicit or explicit) tells Power Pivot to propagate filters down through the existing relationships. If this CALCULATE () is omitted, then *nothing happens*, and as a result, the Sales table is completely unfiltered.

3. SUM (Sales [ExtendedAmount]) is then evaluated over the entire Sales table for *all customers* (returning the value $29,358,677). Since $29 million is greater than $5,000, this customer survives the filter test.

4. FILTER () then goes to the next customer, and exactly the same thing happens again. It doesn't matter what customer is selected in the row context in the Customers table; there is no filtering through to the Sales table, and therefore the result of every iteration step is that every customer passes the test. Because they all pass the test, all customers are returned in the answer.

> **Note** This topic can take some time to get your head around. If this is not crystal clear, I recommend that you go back through this chapter and work through the examples again until it is clear in your mind.

The new table is linked to your data model. Let's jump back to the version that works:

```
[Customers with Sales Greater Than $5,000]
    = CALCULATE (COUNTROWS (Customers),
      FILTER (Customers,
         [Total Sales Amount] >= 5000
      )
    )
```

When you think about the new table returned by FILTER () in the above formula, your first inclination may be to think about it as a standalone table, but that's not the case. Any table object returned by a table function in DAX always retains a link to the data model. I find it useful to visualise a temporary table being created above the real table in the data model, as shown below.

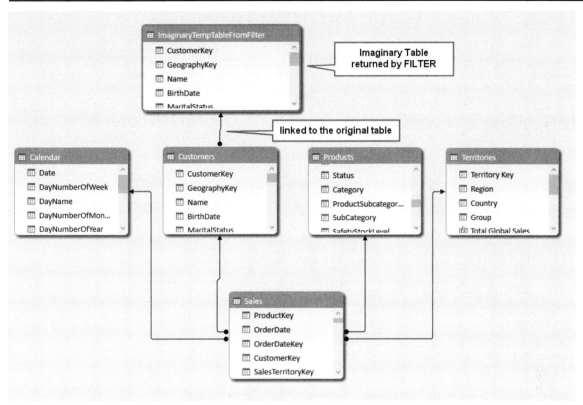

This new temporary table contains a subset of rows as determined by FILTER(), but, importantly, it has the link back to the original table. Therefore, when this new temporary table is used inside CALCULATE() (as is the case here), CALCULATE() tells Power Pivot to run the filter propagation again, and this new table therefore filters the original table and any other tables that are connected downstream to the original table.

14: DAX Topic: Time Intelligence

Time intelligence is a very important and powerful feature in DAX. *Time intelligence* refers to the ability to write formulas that refer to other time periods within a pivot table without needing to change the time filters.

Consider the following pivot table, which shows sales for the year 2003.

CalendarYear	2003	⫟

Row Labels ▼	Total Sales Amount
Accessories	$293,710
Bikes	$9,359,103
Clothing	$138,248
Grand Total	**$9,791,060**

Now what if you wanted to see the sales for the preceding year as well as the change in sales compared to the preceding year? Well, one thing you could do is to toggle the filter between the calendar years 2003 and 2002 to see the results for the preceding year, or you could bring `CalendarYear` and place it on Columns and then filter out the years that you are not interested in. From there you could calculate the change compared to last year in cells next to the pivot table.

> **Bring CalendarYear into columns and then hide the years you don't need.**

	A					F
1						
2						
3	Total Sales Amount	Column Labels				
4	Row Labels ▼	2001	2002	2003	2004	Grand Total
5	Accessories			$293,710	$407,050	$700,760
6	Bikes	$3,266,374	$6,530,344	$9,359,103	$9,162,325	$28,318,145
7	Clothing			$138,248	$201,525	$339,773
8	**Grand Total**	**$3,266,374**	**$6,530,344**	**$9,791,060**	**$9,770,900**	**$29,358,677**

But doing it this way is a bit of a hack, and it isn't reusable in other pivots without doing further hacks.

Here is the original pivot table:

CalendarYear	2003	⫟

Row Labels ▼	Total Sales Amount
Accessories	$293,710
Bikes	$9,359,103
Clothing	$138,248
Grand Total	**$9,791,060**

If you want to look at a different year other than 2003, you have to change the filter settings manually to select the specific year. All this is a bit inconvenient, and indeed there is a better way, discussed next.

Using Time Intelligence Functions

You can use time intelligence functions to create the new calculated fields discussed above without having to change the date selections in the pivot table. This makes everything easier to do, and it also means that you can build pivot tables that would not be possible any other way, like the following:

Row Labels ▼	Total Sales Amount	Change in Sales vs LY
2001	$3,266,374	$3,266,374
2002	$6,530,344	$3,263,970
2003	$9,791,060	$3,260,717
2004	$9,770,900	-$20,161
Grand Total	**$29,358,677**	**$9,770,900**

DAX comes bundled with a number of inbuilt time intelligence functions, and in addition you can write custom time intelligence functions yourself when needed. There are some limitations to the inbuilt time intelligence functions, and they work only under certain circumstances. There are some rules for using inbuilt time intelligence functions:

- You must have a `Calendar` table that contains a contiguous range of dates that covers every day in the period you are analysing. Every date must exist once and only once in the `Calendar` table. You can't skip any dates (e.g., you can't skip weekend dates just because you don't work weekends).

- You must mark your `Calendar` table as the "date table" within Power Pivot. (More on this later in the chapter.)

- Inbuilt time intelligence works only on a standard calendar—that is, a calendar like one that you might hang on a wall, where the start of the year is January 1, the end of the year is December 31, the last day of May is May 31, etc. A standard calendar can also be customised for different financial years (e.g., you can set the end date for a calendar to be June 30 instead of December 31).

If for some reason these rules aren't met, you can't use the inbuilt time intelligence functions. In such a case, you can write your own custom time intelligence functions from scratch, using `FILTER()`. The DAX for this tends to be a bit complex, but don't worry, you can learn it.

Nonstandard Calendars

These are some examples of when you would not use a standard calendar:

- When you are building your data model using weekly or monthly time periods and using a weekly or monthly calendar instead of a daily calendar. (Note that you could load your data weekly or monthly and still use a daily calendar—and this would still work with inbuilt time intelligence, as long as all the other criteria were still met.)

- If you use an ISO or 445 calendar for your accounting periods. This is very common in the retail industry, where businesses want to have regular trading periods. In the case of a 445 calendar, there are 2 months that consist of 4 calendar weeks followed by 1 month with 5 calendar weeks. This helps smooth the months so they all start on a Monday and finish on a Sunday (for example) while also having 91 days in the quarter (91 × 4 quarters = 364 days)

- With a 13 × 4-week periods instead of calendar months.

There are so many variations that it is impossible to mention them all here, and it is also impossible for Power Pivot to cater for them all with inbuilt functions. So the rule is, if you have a standard calendar, you can use the inbuilt functions. If you don't have a standard calendar, then you need to write your own custom time intelligence using `FILTER()`.

Inbuilt Time Intelligence

The first thing to do before using the inbuilt time intelligence functions is to validate that the prerequisite requirements are covered.

Using a Contiguous Date Range

In the sample data that you have been working with, the `Calendar` table already contains all the days of the year for the period that covers the `Sales` table. It is easy to check this. Just create a new pivot table, put `Calendar[CalendarYear]` on Rows, and drop any string-based column (I used `MonthName`) into the Values section. (I did tell you never to do this unless you are just doing a quick test. This is one of those cases where it is fine to do this.)

Row Labels ▾	Count of MonthName
2001	184
2002	365
2003	365
2004	366
Grand Total	1280

As you can see, the default behaviour of putting a string value into the Values section is that the pivot counts the occurrences of the string value. So as you can see above, the `Calendar` table has half a year for 2001 plus a full year for each of the following three years (including a leap year for 2004).

Here's How: Marking the Table as a Date Table

To mark the table as a data table, do the following:

1. Go to the Power Pivot window, navigate to the `Calendar` table (see #1 below), and go to the Data view.

2. In the Design tab (#2), click on Mark as Date Table (#3).

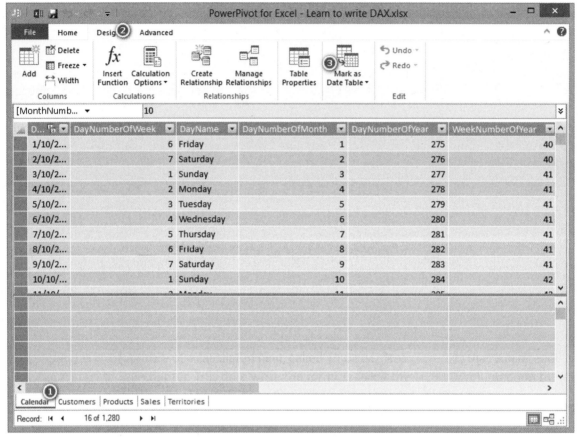

Power Pivot automatically detects the date column in your table and offers this column to you in the Mark as Date Table dialog box. Just click OK to confirm.

Now you'll write some calculated fields using some inbuilt time intelligence functions.

The SAMEPERIODLASTYEAR() Function

With this first time intelligence function you can easily write the `[Total Sales Last Year]` calculated field discussed earlier.

First, set up your pivot table like the one below, with `Calendar[CalendarYear]` on Rows and `[Total Sales Amount]` on Values.

Row Labels ▾	Total Sales Amount
2001	$3,266,374
2002	$6,530,344
2003	$9,791,060
2004	$9,770,900
Grand Total	**$29,358,677**

Click in the pivot table and write the following new calculated field:

```
[Total Sales LY]
    = CALCULATE([Total Sales Amount],
    SAMEPERIODLASTYEAR(Calendar[Date]))
```

If you pause after typing `SAMEPERIODLASTYEAR` and before you type `(`, you see from the IntelliSense that this function will return a list of dates from the current filter context but time shifted back by a year.

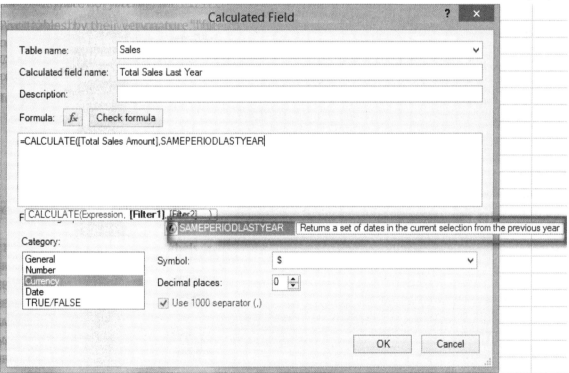

You should recognise that this is a table of values and that `SAMEPERIODLASTYEAR()` is being used inside `CALCULATE()` as an advanced filter.

Pause again after typing the (for SAMEPERIODLASTYEAR() and note that IntelliSense needs a Dates parameter as its only input.

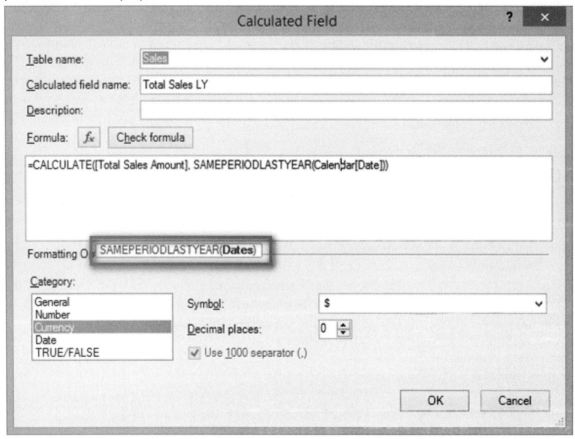

All inbuilt time intelligence functions ask for this Dates parameter, and it always refers to the date column in your Calendar table. This is the same column you indicated in the Power Pivot Mark as Date Table dialog box. Frankly, I think this is a duplication of effort, given that you have already told Power Pivot where the date column is, but this is just the way it works. You have to tell Power Pivot twice where your date column is—once inside the Power Pivot window in the Mark as Date Table dialog box and again inside every inbuilt time intelligence formula you write.

How Does SAMEPERIODLASTYEAR() Work?

In Chapter 13 I explained how CALCULATE() can take a table as an advanced filter input, and you can imagine the new table to be connected to the data model. The new table then filters the rest of the tables in the data model (in this case, the Calendar table and the Sales table) before CALCULATE() completes the calculation. It is exactly the same here:

```
[Total Sales LY]
    = CALCULATE([Total Sales Amount],
    SAMEPERIODLASTYEAR(Calendar[Date]))
```

In this instance, SAMEPERIODLASTYEAR() returns a table of dates that are the same dates coming from the pivot table for the selected year, but these dates are time shifted back by one year.

Take the cell highlighted in the table below.

Row Labels	Total Sales Amount	Total Sales LY
2001	$3,266,374	
2002	$6,530,344	$3,266,374
2003	$9,791,060	$6,530,344
2004	$9,770,900	$9,791,060
Grand Total	$29,358,677	$19,587,777

The function `SAMEPERIODLASTYEAR()` first reads the filter context from the current pivot table to see which dates apply for "this year." In this case, the filter is on `CalendarYear`, and the filter for this cell is 2003. So the dates for "this year" are all dates from January 1, 2003, through to December 31, 2003. The `SAMEPERIODLASTYEAR()` function then takes the dates from the current filter context in the pivot table and time shifts them back one year before returning a table of dates from January 1, 2002, through to December 31, 2002.

The new table created by `SAMEPERIODLASTYEAR()` can be imagined as a temporary table sitting above the `Calendar` table and retaining a relationship to the original `Calendar` table, like this:

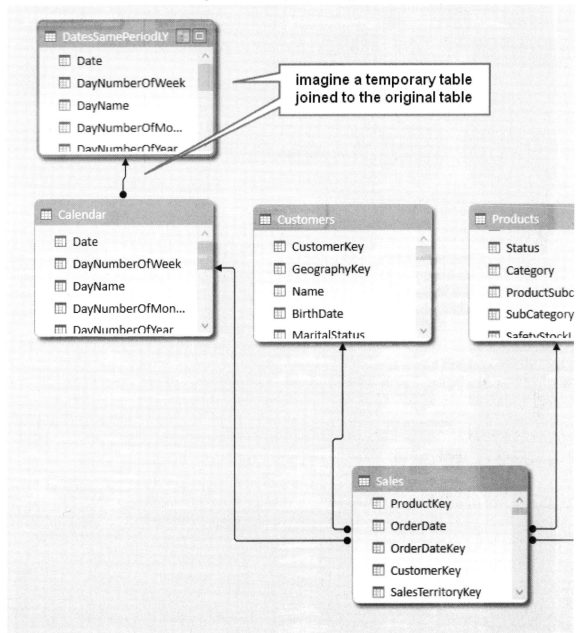

This table is then passed to `CALCULATE()`, and `CALCULATE()` uses this temporary table to rerun the filter propagation. The temporary table (the table of dates from `SAMEPERIODLASTYEAR()`) filters the `Calendar` table, which then filters the `Sales` table before the calculation finally returns the sales for the prior year into the selected cell. (Read this a couple of times if you need to so you have it clearly in your head.)

Calculating Sales Year to Date

A very common business need is to calculate figures on a year-to-date (YTD) basis. Fortunately, there is an inbuilt function for this.

Before you write any YTD formula, it is a good idea to set up a pivot table that will give you immediate feedback if your formula is performing as expected. It is also important to set up your pivot so that you only have a continuous date range. Set up a new pivot table like the one shown below before proceeding. Note the filter on `CalendarYear = 2003`.

Note how the periods in the pivot are contiguous (i.e., the months of the year 2003). If you didn't have a filter on `CalendarYear = 2003` but instead had `CalendarYear = ALL`, the pivot table would show the total sales for January across all years, for February across all years, etc. This would not be a contiguous range, and hence the formula would not work.

Now click in the pivot table and write the following formula:

```
[Total Sales YTD] = TOTALYTD([Total
Sales Amount], Calendar[Date])
```

CalendarYear 2003	
Row Labels ▼	**Total Sales Amount**
January	$438,865
February	$489,090
March	$485,575
April	$506,399
May	$562,773
June	$554,799
July	$886,669
August	$847,414
September	$1,010,258
October	$1,080,450
November	$1,196,981
December	$1,731,788
Grand Total	**$9,791,060**

When you are done, it is very easy to check whether the formula is working correctly. Simply select a contiguous range of cells starting from January in the `Total Sales Amount` column and then check the running total against the result in the `Total Sales YTD` column.

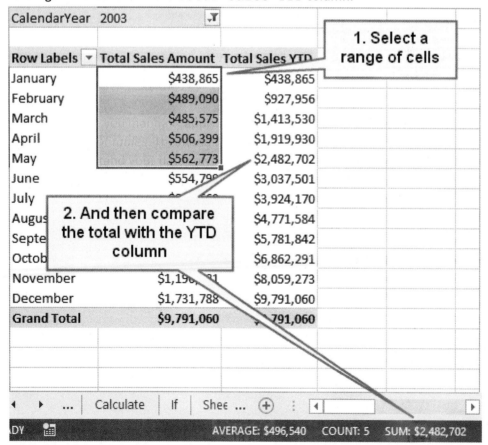

This is a really good example of the benefit of writing calculated fields in the context of a pivot table. The immediate feedback you get to check whether your formula is correct is well worth the effort. As mentioned before, this is not the only way to do it, but it is the best way for Excel users to learn how to write DAX. At some time in the future, when you are a DAX superhero, you may choose to write some of your formulas in the Power Pivot window. Until then, stick with writing them in the context of a suitably configured pivot table.

Once you have written your formula, you can apply some conditional formatting to your table, as shown below, to get another visual clue that all is working well.

CalendarYear	2003		ⵟ

Row Labels	▾	Total Sales Amount	Total Sales YTD
January		$438,865	$438,865
February		$489,090	$927,956
March		$485,575	$1,413,530
April		$506,399	$1,919,930
May		$562,773	$2,482,702
June		$554,799	$3,037,501
July		$886,669	$3,924,170
August		$847,414	$4,771,584
September		$1,010,258	$5,781,842
October		$1,080,450	$6,862,291
November		$1,196,981	$8,059,273
December		$1,731,788	$9,791,060
Grand Total		**$9,791,060**	**$9,791,060**

Practice Exercises: Time Intelligence

When writing the previous formula, you may have noticed from the IntelliSense tooltip that there are two other functions that are very similar: `TOTALMTD()` and `TOTALQTD()`. In this section you'll get some practice using these two functions. Before you do these two exercises, make sure you set up a pivot table that will give you feedback if your formula is correct. Set up a pivot table like this:

1. Place `Year` and `Month` on Filter.
2. Filter for `Year = 2003` and `Month = January`.
3. Put `Calendar[DayNumberOfMonth]` on Rows.

CalendarYear	2003	ⵟ
MonthName	January	ⵟ

Row Labels	▾	Total Sales Amount
1		$12,445
2		$19,703
3		$13,520
4		$18,629
5		$13,497
6		$4,363
7		$14,623

Write formulas for the following calculated columns. Find the solutions to these practice exercises in "P. Time Intelligence" on page 180 A.

61. [Total Sales Month to Date]

62. [Total Sales Quarter to Date]

Changing Financial Year-Ending Dates

Many of the inbuilt time intelligence functions allow you to specify a different end-of-year date. If this applies, there will be an optional parameter where you specify the year end date:

```
[Total Sales FYTD]
= TOTALYTD([Total Sales Amount],
    Calendar[Date],"YearEndDateHere")
```

Here's an example for a financial year ending June 30:

```
[Total Sales FYTD]
    = TOTALYTD([Total Sales Amount],
    Calendar[Date],"30/6")
```

Note that this example uses a non-U.S. date format. If you are using the U.S. date format, then it would be as follows:

```
[Total Sales FYTD USA]
    = TOTALYTD([Total Sales Amount], Calendar[Date],"6/30")
```

You can practice this by changing the year-end date in the [Total Sales YTD] example above and seeing what it does to your pivot table. Try setting the end of the financial year to be June 30 and also try with March 31 and create the following two formulas.

Practice Exercises: Time Intelligence, Cont.

Write formulas for the following calculated columns. Find the solutions to these practice exercises in "P. Time Intelligence" on page 180.

63. [Total Sales FYTD 30 June]

64. [Total Sales FYTD 31 March]

Format your pivot table by selecting Conditional Formatting, Data Bars to make it easier to spot the pattern.

Practicing with Other Time Intelligence Functions

There are a lot of inbuilt time intelligence functions, and for most of them, it's easy to tell what they do. PREVIOUSMONTH(), PREVIOUSQUARTER(), and PREVIOUSDAY(), for example, all return tables of dates referring to the previous period and probably don't need further explanation. To see how they work, set up a pivot table with contiguous months, like this:

CalendarYear 2003	
Row Labels	**Total Sales Amount**
January	$438,865
February	$489,090
March	$485,575
April	$506,399
May	$562,773
June	$554,799
July	$886,669
August	$847,414
September	$1,010,258
October	$1,080,450
November	$1,196,981
December	$1,731,788
Grand Total	**$9,791,060**

Practice Exercises: Time Intelligence, Cont.

Write the following formulas. Find the solutions to these practice exercises in "P. Time Intelligence" on page 180.

65. [Total Sales Previous Month]

Given that the PREVIOUSMONTH() formula will return a table of dates, you need to embed the time intelligence formula inside a CALCULATE().

66. [Total Sales Previous Day]

You need to set up a suitable pivot table that gives you immediate feedback about whether your formula is working. Put Calendar[DayNumberOfMonth] on Rows and make sure you filter for a single month.

67. [Total Sales Previous Quarter]

As with Practice Exercise 66, you need to set up a suitable pivot table for context. You can work out how to do this one yourself.

Writing Your Own Time Intelligence Functions

As mentioned earlier in this chapter, writing your own time intelligence functions is a bit harder than using the inbuilt functions, particularly when you are learning. However, once you get the hang of it, you will find it quite easy, and this will also be a good sign of how much progress you are making in your understanding of DAX.

There are a couple of strange things in the syntax that you need to get your head around before you will get it. The good news is that I explain these things in this chapter, and you will be writing your own custom intelligence in no time at all. These are the two concepts you need to get your head around:

- Concept 1: Thinking "whole of table" when thinking about filter context
- Concept 2: Knowing how to use MIN and MAX

Let me cover these concepts before we get into any examples. That way, when we get into the examples, you will be primed and ready to go.

Concept 1: Thinking "Whole of Table" When Thinking About Filter Context

Consider the single row highlighted in the pivot table below. (This is the same pivot table you were just looking at above.)

CalendarYear	2003	

Row Labels	Total Sales Amount
January	$438,865
February	$489,090
March	$485,575
April	$506,399
May	$562,773
June	$554,799
July	$886,669
August	$847,414
September	$1,010,258
October	$1,080,450
November	$1,196,981
December	$1,731,788
Grand Total	$9,791,060

This pivot table is filtered for Calendar[CalendarYear]= 2003 in the filter. Also, the highlighted row (January) is also filtered—by Calendar[MonthName]="January", which appears in the Rows area of the pivot. When these two filters are combined, the single cell/value for [Total Sales Amount] is filtered for the period January 2003. So there are only 31 days that are used in the Calendar table in the data model for this cell. It is possible to *imagine* this filter applied on the back end. In fact, you can simulate what is happening by going into the Power Pivot window and manually applying these filters, as shown on the next page.

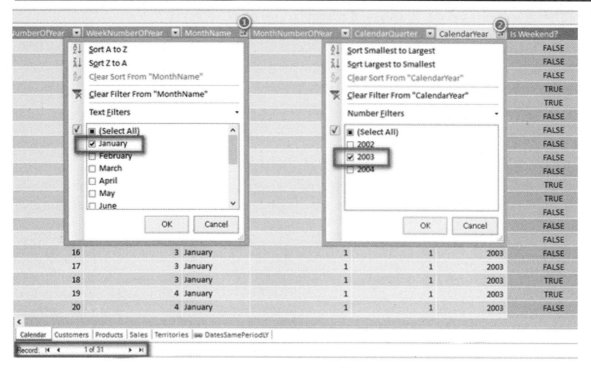

Applying a manual filter like this on a table in the Power Pivot window has no impact on any formula, but it does allow you to see what is happening behind the scenes (albeit a simulation). Once you have done this a few times, you will learn to mentally visualise what is happening behind the scenes, which in turn will increase your understanding of how Power Pivot works.

> **Tip** Always try to think about what these "filtered" tables would look like. (For example, in the above example the `Calendar` table would have only 31 days visible.) This is all happening "in memory," on-the-fly. You can't open up Power Pivot and see this filtering happening (even though you can simulate it as described above), but it is important that you be able to imagine it happening in your mind. Thinking about what is happening behind the scenes like this will make it easier to write custom time intelligence formula.

When thinking about the filtering that is being applied, you should think about *the whole table*, not just the two columns with filters applied. It is clear that there is only one month visible (January) and only one year visible (2003), but it is also true that there are 31 `DayNumberOfMonth` values visible (those from 1 through 31), and there are 4 different `WeekNumberOfYear` values (1 through 4). It is possible to reference any and all of these other columns and values in your DAX formulas after the initial filter context is applied, and this makes it very powerful indeed.

This is one of the main reasons you should also include an ID column in your `Calendar` table if you are going to write custom time intelligence functions. As you can see in the next image, after you filter the `Calendar` table based on January and 2003, there are actually 31 rows in the table, and the ID numbers of those rows run from 550 to 580. You can reference these ID values that remain in the filtered table in your DAX formulas to write very powerful DAX. But you need to be able to think "whole of table" to be able to understand how to do this.

ID	Date	DayNumb...	Da...	DayNumbe...	DayNum...	WeekNum...	Mont...	MonthNum...	Calenda...	Calen...
550	1/01/2003 1...	4	Wedne...	1	1	1	January	1	1	2003
551	2/01/2003 1...	5	Thursd...	2	2	1	January	1	1	2003
552	3/01/2003 1...	6	Friday	3	3	1	January	1	1	2003
553	4/01/2003 1...	7	Saturday	4	4	1	January	1	1	2003
554	5/01/2003 1...	1	Sunday	5	5	2	January	1	1	2003
555	6/01/2003 1...	2	Monday	6	6	2	January	1	1	2003
556	7/01/2003 1...	3	Tuesday	7	7	2	January	1	1	2003
557	8/01/2003 1...	4	Wedne...	8	8	2	January	1	1	2003
558	9/01/2003 1...	5	Thursd...	9	9	2	January	1	1	2003
559	10/01/2003 ...	6	Friday	10	10	2	January	1	1	2003
560	11/01/2003 ...	7	Saturday	11	11	2	January	1	1	2003
561	12/01/2003 ...	1	Sunday	12	12	3	January	1	1	2003
562	13/01/2003 ...	2	Monday	13	13	3	January	1	1	2003
563	14/01/2003 ...	3	Tuesday	14	14	3	January	1	1	2003
564	15/01/2003 ...	4	Wedne...	15	15	3	January	1	1	2003
565	16/01/2003 ...	5	Thursd...	16	16	3	January	1	1	2003
566	17/01/2003 ...	6	Friday	17	17	3	January	1	1	2003
567	18/01/2003 ...	7	Saturday	18	18	3	January	1	1	2003
568	19/01/2003 ...	1	Sunday	19	19	4	January	1	1	2003
569	20/01/2003 ...	2	Monday	20	20	4	January	1	1	2003
570	21/01/2003 ...	3	Tuesday	21	21	4	January	1	1	2003
571	22/01/2003 ...	4	Wedne...	22	22	4	January	1	1	2003
572	23/01/2003 ...	5	Thursd...	23	23	4	January	1	1	2003
573	24/01/2003 ...	6	Friday	24	24	4	January	1	1	2003
574	25/01/2003 ...	7	Saturday	25	25	4	January	1	1	2003
575	26/01/2003 ...	1	Sunday	26	26	5	January	1	1	2003
576	27/01/2003 ...	2	Monday	27	27	5	January	1	1	2003
577	28/01/2003 ...	3	Tuesday	28	28	5	January	1	1	2003
578	29/01/2003 ...	4	Wedne...	29	29	5	January	1	1	2003
579	30/01/2003 ...	5	Thursd...	30	30	5	January	1	1	2003
580	31/01/2003 ...	6	Friday	31	31	5	January	1	1	2003

Concept 2: Knowing How to Use MIN() and MAX()

It is very common to use the MIN() and MAX() functions inside FILTER() when you write custom time intelligence functions. This is covered in more detail in the examples that follow, but for now there is one key concept about MIN() and MAX() that you should understand: Whenever you use an aggregation function around a column in a DAX formula, *it will always respect the initial filter context coming from the pivot table.*

So let's go back to the pivot table from before, shown here again for convenience.

CalendarYear	2003

Row Labels	Total Sales Amount
January	$438,865
February	$489,090
March	$485,575
April	$506,399
May	$562,773
June	$554,799
July	$886,669
August	$847,414
September	$1,010,258
October	$1,080,450
November	$1,196,981
December	$1,731,788
Grand Total	$9,791,060

You know that the pivot table has filtered the Calendar table so that only 31 days remain. Given that MIN() and MAX() always respect the current filter context, what would be the results of the following DAX formulas for the highlighted row in the pivot table above?

1.   = MIN(Calendar[Date])
2.   = MAX(Calendar[Date])
3.   = MIN(Calendar[ID])
4.   = MAX(Calendar[ID])

The answer to question 1 is, of course, January 1, 2003—the first date in the filter context. It's not the first date in the Calendar table but the first date in the current filter context. And the answer to question 2 is January 31, 2003, the last date in the filter context. But, importantly, the answers to questions 3 and 4 are 550 and 580, respectively, even though this ID column was not part of the filter. So you can think of MIN() and MAX() as tools that can "harvest" the value from the current filter context, in any available column across the whole table, and you can use this harvested value in your DAX formulas. Remember this fact about MIN() and MAX() when you get into the examples below.

Writing Custom Time Intelligence Functions

Now you are going to write a custom version of [Total Sales YTD], using CALCULATE() and FILTER(). I strongly encourage you to physically write this formula. There is a lot that can (and will) go wrong when you type your own custom time intelligence functions, and you will need *lots* of practice to get it right. There are square bracket sets, sets of parentheses, new line spacing to make it easier to read, commas to be added in the right places, etc. *So make sure you actually write the following formula on own computer.* Go ahead and do that now before moving on to the explanation. Make sure you set up a pivot table like the one you used earlier so that you can get immediate feedback about whether your formula is correct.

```
[Total Sales YTD Manual] = CALCULATE([Total Sales Amount],
    FILTER(ALL(Calendar),
        Calendar[CalendarYear]=MAX(Calendar[CalendarYear]) &&
        Calendar[Date] <=MAX(Calendar[Date])
    )
)
```

This formula needs a bit of explanation. I have used http://daxformatter.com in the following pages to make it easier to refer to the lines in the formula. I mentioned DAX Formatter earlier in the book, and you can see that it is a great tool to help you read your DAX formulas.

You can see that lines 4 through 8 above are all part of a FILTER() function because you can see that the) on line 8 is left aligned to the F in FILTER() on line 4. Also note the vertical line that is left aligned to lines 5, 6, and 7; this is another visual indicator that all these lines of code are part of the FILTER() function.

This FILTER() function returns a table to the function CALCULATE(). CALCULATE() then adds up the [Total Sales Amount] *only for the dates returned by the* FILTER() *function.*

Let's look more closely at lines 6 and 7 in the FILTER() function. Line 6 reads:

```
Calendar[CalendarYear] = MAX(Calendar[CalendarYear])
```

Okay, I hear you saying "how can calendar year be equal to the MAX() of calendar year?" What is really happening is that there is *a column name* on the left side of the equals sign, and there is *a* MAX() *function* on the right side. Remember from earlier in this chapter that whenever you see MIN() or MAX() in a formula like this, it always respects the current filter context. So the way to read line 6 of this formula is as follows: "Add a filter to the table so that the column Calendar[CalendarYear] is equal to the maximum value in my current filter context coming from my pivot table."

For example, in the pivot table below, the maximum of the highlighted row is March 31, 2003, and hence MAX(Calendar[CalendarYear]) = 2003.

	Total Sales	Total Sales YTD
Row Labels ▾	**Amount**	**Manual**
January	$438,865	$438,865
February	$489,090	$927,956
March	$485,575	$1,413,530
April	$506,399	$1,919,930
May	$562,773	$2,482,702
June	$554,799	$3,037,501
July	$886,669	$3,924,170
August	$847,414	$4,771,584
September	$1,010,258	$5,781,842
October	$1,080,450	$6,862,291
November	$1,196,981	$8,059,273
December	$1,731,788	$9,791,060
Grand Total	**$9,791,060**	**$9,791,060**

CalendarYear 2003

See how you need to think "whole of table" here? The initial filter context is applied over the month of March 2003, but the MAX() formula is working over the year column. When you simulated this filter context in the Power Pivot window (by manually applying the filters), there were 31 rows left in the Calendar table, and for each of these rows, the value in Calendar[CalendarYear] was 2003. As a result (in this case), the MIN() of Calendar[CalendarYear] would also return 2003, as would SUM() and AVERAGE(), for that matter.

So line 6 is really saying "filter my table where Calendar[CalendarYear]=*the current filter context year*," which is 2003 in this case.

Let's move on. Line 7 starts with the double ampersand operator (which means *and* (i.e., do both line 6 *and* line 7) and then says:

```
Calendar[Date] <=MAX(Calendar[Date])
```

The same applies here as with line 6. MAX(Calendar[Date]) reads the initial filter context from the pivot table and hence returns the value March 31, 2003, for the highlighted row in the pivot. Therefore, this part of the formula adds an AND condition so that the underlying table is filtered for Calendar[CalendarYear] = 2003 *and* also for the condition Calendar[Date] is *on or before* March 31, 2003. As you can deduce, this is all the dates year to date.

As you go to the next row in the pivot table, the calendar year stays the same, but the month-end date moves to the end of the next month. So the number of days that are included increases as you work down the rows in the pivot table.

Now it is important to point out that you could not use MIN() in line 7 as you do in line 6; this time it has to be MAX(). If you used MIN(), you would get March 1, 2003, as the last date, and the year-to-date result would be out by almost a full month of sales. It is important to think about what your formulas need and make sure you provide the right formulas to achieve that outcome (of course).

Now let's go back to ALL(Calendar). Line 5 of the formula refers to ALL(Calendar) instead of just the Calendar table (which you have used previously). ALL(), as discussed in Chapter 12, is the "remove filter" function. (If necessary, go back and refresh your memory about it before moving on.)

It is important to use the ALL() function here because you know that the pivot table reads the current filter context before doing the calculation. Probably the easiest way to explain why you need the ALL() function is to consider what would happen if you didn't use ALL().

Consider again the highlighted row in the table below.

CalendarYear	2003		
Row Labels ▼	**Total Sales Amount**	**Total Sales YTD Does Not Work**	
January	$438,865	$438,865	
February	$489,090	$489,090	
March	$485,575	$485,575	
April	$506,399	$506,399	
May	$562,773	$562,773	
June	$554,799	$554,799	
July	$886,669	$886,669	
August	$847,414	$847,414	
September	$1,010,258	$1,010,258	
October	$1,080,450	$1,080,450	
November	$1,196,981	$1,196,981	
December	$1,731,788	$1,731,788	
Grand Total	**$9,791,060**	**$9,791,060**	

You know that the initial filter context for this row of the pivot is for all 31 days in the month of March 2003. You can "imagine" that the Calendar table is filtered behind the scenes so that only these 31 days of March 2003 are visible.

Now consider that the [Total Sales YTD] formula does not work without the ALL() function. You should write this formula and add it to your pivot. (Don't miss the opportunity to practice now!)

```
=
CALCULATE (
    [Total Sales Amount],
    FILTER (
        Calendar,
        Calendar[CalendarYear] = MAX ( Calendar[CalendarYear] )
            && Calendar[Date] <= MAX ( Calendar[Date] )
```

You can see in the pivot table above (and in the one you have done yourself) that this formula is giving the sales *for the current month rather than YTD* in each row of the pivot table. The reason it doesn't work like the first one is related to the initial filter context discussed above. For the highlighted row of March 2003, the initial filter context applied a filter so that only the 31 days of March 2003 were "visible" in the Calendar table (behind the scenes). So how can the formula possibly return sales for all days "year to date," including the sales from January and February? The dates in January and February were already filtered out by the pivot table from the initial filter context, so you can't get the sales for these months to somehow reappear for the new formula if you write it this way.

If you want to include sales from January and February in the row next to the actual sales for March, you must first "remove the filter" created by the pivot table. This is what ALL() does when it is wrapped around the Calendar table in line 5: It removes the filter context that comes from the pivot table that is automatically applied to the Calendar table. You then reapply the filters you want to use in lines 6 and 7 so that you end up with all the dates YTD.

Tip Go back and read this section again if necessary until you understand it well.

Now let me come back to that `ID` column I talked about earlier. A good `ID` column in a `Calendar` table starts at 1 and increments by 1 for every row in the table. So in the case of this `Calendar` table, each day of the year has an `ID` value that increments by 1. But the same applies to 445 calendars and weekly calendars. You should always have an `ID` column that increments by 1 for each row in the table (in chronological order, of course). This gives you a nice clean numeric column to move back and forward inside your formulas. To illustrate this point, the following formula will works for YTD:

```
[Total Sales YTD Manual ID] = CALCULATE([Total Sales Amount],
    FILTER(ALL(Calendar),
        Calendar[CalendarYear]=MAX(Calendar[CalendarYear]) &&
        Calendar[ID] <=MAX(Calendar[ID])
    )
)
```

Notice that here you replace the `Date` column with the `ID` column. Using the `ID` column like this is very powerful and allows you to jump back and forward in time, using your knowledge of the `Calendar` table structure by just doing numeric addition and subtraction on the `ID` column.

For one more example using the `ID` column, you'll write a calculated field that returns the total sales for the same period last year. You did this earlier, using the function `SAMEPERIODLASTYEAR()`, but recall that this inbuilt time intelligence function works only for a standard calendar. You can also write a custom time intelligence function that works with a custom calendar using `FILTER()`. Note in the pivot table below that `[Total Sales LY]` works on both the month level and the year level.

CalendarYear	MonthName	Total Sales Amount	Total Sales LY
2001	July	$473,388	
	August	$506,192	
	September	$473,943	
	October	$513,329	
	November	$543,993	
	December	$755,528	
2001 Total		$3,266,374	
2002	January	$596,747	
	February	$550,817	
	March	$644,135	
	April	$663,692	
	May	$673,556	
	June	$676,764	
	July	$500,365	$473,388
	August	$546,001	$506,192
	September	$350,467	$473,943
	October	$415,390	$513,329
	November	$335,095	$543,993
	December	$577,314	$755,528
2002 Total		$6,530,344	$3,266,374

Here is the formula you need to write for this:

```
[Total Sales LY] = CALCULATE([Total Sales Amount],
    FILTER(ALL(calendar),
        Calendar[ID] >=MIN(Calendar[ID]) -365 &&
        Calendar[ID] <=MAX(Calendar[ID]) - 365
    )
)
```

Note that you can use the `ID` column to your advantage here to move back in time by 365 days. Also note how the first reference inside `FILTER()` is to `MIN(Calendar[ID])`, and the second one is to `MAX(Calendar[ID])`. It's time to think "whole of table" again. Let's take a look at two different areas of the pivot table.

CalendarYear ▾	MonthName ▾	Total Sales Amount	Total Sales LY
⊞ 2001		$3,266,374	
⊞ 2002		$6,530,344	$3,266,374
⊟ 2003	January	$438,865	$596,747
	February	$489,090	$550,817
	March	$485,575	$644,135
	April	$506,399	$663,692
	May	$562,773	$673,556
	June	$554,799	$676,764
	July	$886,669	$500,365
	August	$847,414	$546,001
	September	$1,010,258	$350,467
	October	$1,080,450	❶ $415,390
	November	$1,196,981	$335,095
	December	$1,731,788	$577,314
2003 Total		$9,791,060	❷ $6,530,344
⊟ 2004	January	$1,340,245	$438,865

In the pivot table cell, marked #1 above (October 2003), you need to be able to visualise the `Calendar` table as it is currently filtered. In the case of October 2003, there are 31 rows that remain unfiltered. The first (earliest) of these rows is October 1, 2003, and it has an ID of 823. The last unfiltered row is October 31, 2003, and it has an ID of 853. So "October this year" can be thought of as:

```
Calendar[ID] >=823 && Calendar[ID] <=853
```

And October last year can be thought of as:

```
Calendar[ID] >=823 - 365 && Calendar[ID] <=853 - 365
```

When you write it this way, it is obvious why you use >= MIN for the first filter line and <= MAX for the second one. And the really great thing is that this works regardless of the time period you are looking at. In this first example, you are looking at a month, but if you look at the #2 in the pivot table above, this time the filter context is on an entire year. The formula therefore is filtering for all periods after the first date of the entire year (1/1/2003 – `Calendar[ID]` = 550) and also for less than the last date of the calendar year (31/12/2003 – `Calendar[ID]` = 914). Once you learn to trust this "whole of table" behaviour, you will be able to very quickly write custom time intelligence formulas referencing the ID column alone.

> **What About Leap Years?** Astute readers will already be crying foul about leap years by now. Well, as I said earlier on, every business is different, and different businesses handle these things in different ways. It is beyond the scope of this book to provide solutions to this problem, but you can read about some possible approaches at http://www.daxpatterns.com/time-patterns/.

Practice Exercises: Time Intelligence, Cont.

It's time for some practice. Write the following formulas. First set up an appropriate pivot table so that you will get immediate feedback if your formula is correct. Find the solutions to these practice exercises in "P. Time Intelligence" on page 180.

68. [Total Sales Moving Annual Total]

With this DAX formula, you need to create a rolling 12-month total of sales. It will always show you 12 months' worth of sales, up to the end of the current month. Think about the problem using English words first and then convert that to DAX, using the techniques you have learnt here. A fully worked-through solution is provided later in this chapter, but give it a go yourself first.

69. [Total Sales Rolling 90 Days]

This is the same as the formula above, but instead of delivering a rolling 12-month total, you will instead deliver a rolling 90-day total. Try to do this one from scratch, without referencing the one above. This is good practice to help you think like the DAX engine.

Creating a Moving Annual Total

Start by setting up a new pivot table with `Years` and `Months` on Rows and `Total Sales Amount` on Values.

Row Labels	Total Sales Amount
⊟ 2001	$3,266,374
July	$473,388
August	$506,192
September	$473,943
October	$513,329
November	$543,993
December	$755,528
⊟ 2002	$6,530,344
January	$596,747
February	$550,817
March	$644,135
April	$663,692
May	$673,556
June	$676,764
July	$500,365
August	$546,001
September	$350,467
October	$415,390
November	$335,095
December	$577,314
⊟ 2003	$9,791,060
January	$438,865
February	$489,090
March	$485,575

Then write your formula:

```
[Total Sales Moving Annual Total]
    = CALCULATE([Total Sales Amount],
      FILTER(ALL(Calendar),
          Calendar[ID] > MAX(Calendar[ID]) - 365 &&
          Calendar[ID] <= MAX(Calendar[ID])
      )
    )
```

Note This is not the only way to write this formula. Just like in Excel, there are often multiple ways to write a formula. If you have something different and it works, that's great. Also note that this formula may not work with leap years, depending on how your business handles the extra day. (Some businesses ignore the extra day and actually have 6 × 364-day years followed by 1 × 371-day extraordinary year, so it depends.)

Now check your formulas against the pivot table, as shown below. Select the sales for a period (e.g., #1 and #2 below) and then compare the total of your selection against the running total in your pivot (#3).

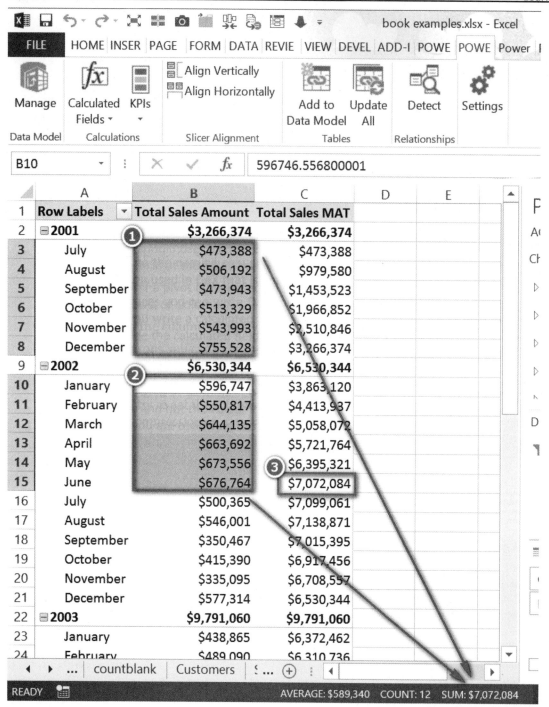

One thing to note is that the first FILTER() line in the formula says *greater than*, and the last FILTER() line says *less than or equal to*. It is easy to get these things wrong when writing formulas, but you should not worry about this. As long as you set up a pivot table so that you can test the formulas you are writing, you can just take a guess and then change it if you need to. Of course, in this example, if you used *greater than or equal to*, you would end up with 366 days, which is incorrect.

But What About the First Year?

Now, if you want to get technical, the [Total Sales Moving Annual Total] result really doesn't make sense in the first 11 months of the sales data because you didn't have a full year of sales until the end of June 2002. There are many ways to solve this problem using the IF() function. Here is one solution:

```
[Total Sales MAT Improved] = if(MAX(Calendar[ID])>=365,
        CALCULATE([Total Sales Amount],
            FILTER(ALL(Calendar),
```

```
                                    Calendar[ID] > MAX(Calendar[ID]) - 365 &&
                                    Calendar[ID] <= MAX(Calendar[ID])
                    )
               )
          )
```

> **Tip** By now you may have realised that it is easier to copy one formula and then edit the copied version for the new formula. Indeed, this is a good idea, but try to keep it to a minimum while you are learning and need the extra DAX writing practice.

Researching DAX Functions

There are a lot of other time intelligence functions that you can use to write time-based DAX formulas. A key piece of advice as you learn how to use these other time intelligence functions (indeed, all other DAX functions) is to do a quick online search and read the relevant information in the documentation.

To do this, do a web search for the function name followed by the word *DAX*. In the example below, I have searched for "DATEADD DAX."

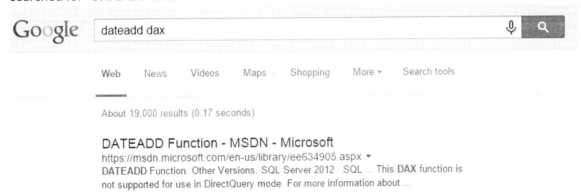

The first result returned is normally the official Microsoft documentation (MSDN) site. When you click on this MSDN link, you see something like the following.

Now I think the official documentation is not as useful as other websites in many cases. But there is some very important information that you can get from MSDN: the syntax, parameters, and return value. You can find the syntax and parameters by typing a formula directly into the Calculated Field dialog in Excel, but sometimes this IntelliSense help doesn't clearly tell you the return value—and this is where doing a web search can help. The return value is a key piece of information that helps you understand how to use the function. In the case of DATEADD() above, the return value is a table, and hence you would use DATEADD() inside CALCULATE() to do a time shift. So you might write something like this:

```
[Total Sales LY DATEADD] = CALCULATE([Total Sales Amount]
    ,DATEADD(Calendar[Date],-1,Year)
)
```

This formula works on various different time horizons, including years and also quarters.

Row Labels ▾	Total Sales Amount	Total Sales LY DATEADD
⊟ 2001	$3,266,374	
3	$1,453,523	
4	$1,812,851	
⊟ 2002	$6,530,344	$3,266,374
1	$1,791,698	
2	$2,014,012	
3	$1,396,834	$1,453,523
4	$1,327,799	$1,812,851
⊟ 2003	$9,791,060	$6,530,344
1	$1,413,530	$1,791,698
2	$1,623,971	$2,014,012
3	$2,744,340	$1,396,834
4	$4,009,218	$1,327,799
⊟ 2004	$9,770,900	$9,791,060
1	$4,283,630	$1,413,530
2	$5,436,429	$1,623,971
3	$50,841	$2,744,340
4		$4,009,218
Grand Total	**$29,358,677**	**$19,587,777**

You may realise by now that this is basically the same as the SAMEPERIODLASTYEAR() example earlier in this chapter.

Let's look at another example. When you search for FIRSTDATE, a quick search finds the MSDN site the first time again.

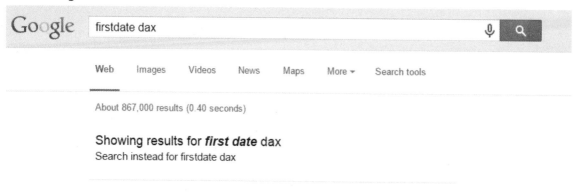

And the returned value is a special table that has a single column and a single row.

FIRSTDATE Function

Other Versions ▾

Topic Status: Some information in this topic is preview and subject to change in future releases. Preview info

Returns the first date in the current context for the specified column of dates.

◢ Syntax

```
FIRSTDATE(<dates>)
```

◢ Parameters

Term	Definition
dates	A column that contains dates.

◢ Return Value

A table containing a single column and single row with a date value.

Because `FIRSTDATE()` returns a single value (in a table), you are able to put this value directly into a cell in a pivot table. So you could write a formula like this:

```
[First Date] = FIRSTDATE(Calendar[Date])
```

Row Labels ▼	Total Sales Amount	Total Sales LY DATEADD	First Date
⊟ 2001	$3,266,374		1/07/2001
3	$1,453,523		1/07/2001
4	$1,812,851		1/10/2001
⊟ 2002	$6,530,344	$3,266,374	1/01/2002
1	$1,791,698		1/01/2002
2	$2,014,012		1/04/2002
3	$1,396,834	$1,453,523	1/07/2002
4	$1,327,799	$1,812,851	1/10/2002
⊟ 2003	$9,791,060	$6,530,344	1/01/2003
1	$1,413,530	$1,791,698	1/01/2003
2	$1,623,971	$2,014,012	1/04/2003
3	$2,744,340	$1,396,834	1/07/2003
4	$4,009,218	$1,327,799	1/10/2003
⊟ 2004	$9,770,900	$9,791,060	1/01/2004
1	$4,283,630	$1,413,530	1/01/2004
2	$5,436,429	$1,623,971	1/04/2004
3	$50,841	$2,744,340	1/07/2004
4		$4,009,218	1/10/2004
Grand Total	**$29,358,677**	**$19,587,777**	**1/07/2001**

Other Time Intelligence Functions

Here is a list of other time intelligence functions that you might want to explore:

```
DATESINPERIOD(date_column, start_date, number_of_intervals, intervals)
DATESBETWEEN(column, start_date, end_date)
DATEADD(date_column, number_of_intervals, interval)
FIRSTDATE (datecolumn)
LASTDATE (datecolumn)
LASTNONBLANKDATE (datecolumn, [expression])
STARTOFMONTH (date_column)
STARTOFQUARTER (date_column)
STARTOFYEAR(date_column [,YE_date])
ENDOFMONTH(date_column)
ENDOFQUARTER(date_column)
ENDOFYEAR(date_column)
PARALLELPERIOD(date_column)
PREVIOUSDAY(date_column)
PREVIOUSMONTH(date_column)
PREVIOUSQUARTER(date_column)
PREVIOUSYEAR(date_column)
NEXTDAY(date_column)
NEXTMONTH(date_column)
NEXTQUARTER (date_column)
NEXTYEAR(date_column [,YE_date])
DATESMTD(date_column)
DATESQTD (date_column)
DATESYTD (date_column [,YE_date])
TOTALMTD(expression, dates, filter)
TOTALQTD(expression, dates, filter)
```

15: DAX Topic: RELATED() and RELATEDTA-BLE()

The functions RELATED() and RELATEDTABLE() are typically used in calculated columns to reference relevant records in other tables, although they can be used in calculated fields, too. They are a bit like VLOOKUP() for tables that have a relationship.

When to Use RELATED() vs. RELATEDTABLE()

To understand when to use each of these functions, you need to understand what each one returns. You can use IntelliSense in the Power Pivot window to find out what each of these functions returns.

You can see below that RELATED() returns a value.

You can see below that RELATEDTABLE() returns a table.

Remember from Chapter 2 that relationships between tables in Power Pivot are always of the type "one to many." Also remember from Chapter 2 that best practice for Excel users is to lay out tables in the Power Pivot window with the lookup table at the top (the "one" side of the relationship) and the data tables to the bottom (the "many" side of the relationship), as shown below.

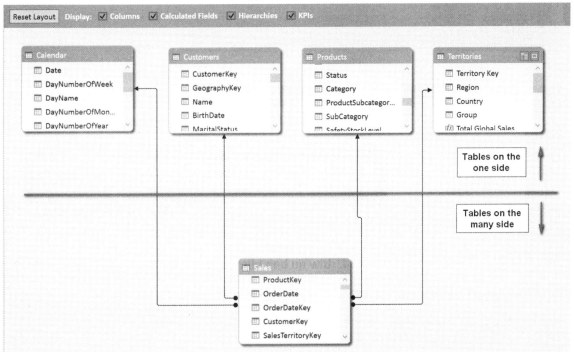

The two RELATED functions allow you to refer to columns in another connected table. So when you think about it, if you are wanting to add a custom column in a table on the "one" side of the relationship—i.e., add a new column in a lookup table (a table above the line in the image above)—then it is highly likely that there will be multiple rows on the "many" side of the relationship. So when writing a formula in a calculated column on a lookup table, you must use the RELATEDTABLE() function *because it will fetch a table of values*, including all the matching values in the data table. Conversely, if you are writing a calculated column in a table on the "many" side of the relationship (i.e., a data table), then there will be only one matching row in the lookup table, and hence you use RELATED() to return that single value.

The RELATED() Function

Next you'll look at an example where you bring a value from a column in a lookup table into a table on the "many" side of the relationship. For the sake of this example, assume that your business has a new management layer, and you want to add a new level of reporting to cover this new management layer. In effect, you need to enhance the `Territories` table to add a new geographic region. To achieve this, you need to do the following:

1. Create a new table that contains the logic of the new management layer.

2. Import the new table into the data model.

3. Join the new table to the existing `Territories` table (in this example).

4. Create a new calculated column in the `Territories` table (on the "many" side of the relationship) and bring in the new management layer from the new table into the `Territories` table as a new column.

This will all make more sense as you work through the example.

Here's How: Adding a New Column to a Table from a New Linked Table

1. Insert a new worksheet in your workbook and add the following data to the sheet. You are going to create a new management level for the Northern and Southern Hemispheres of the world.

Group	Hemisphere
Europe	Northern
NA	NA
North America	Northern
Pacific	Southern

2. Select one of the cells and press Ctrl+L (or press Ctrl+T or select Insert, Table). You need to make sure there is no other data in the surrounding cells to help Excel auto-detect the table.

3. While you still have the new table selected, go to the Table Name box on the File tab and rename the table to something more meaningful, such as `Hemisphere`.

> **Note** You must rename your linked tables inside Excel. Unlike with other imported tables, you can't change linked table names inside Power Pivot.

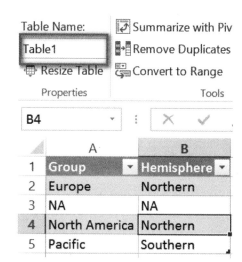

4. From the Power Pivot tab select Add to Data Model. (In Excel 2010, from the Power Pivot tab select Create Linked Table.)

5. Switch to the Power Pivot window and rearrange the new tables so that the new table (which is a lookup table to another lookup table and will be on the "one" side of the relationship) is sitting above the current `Territories` table, as shown on the next page.

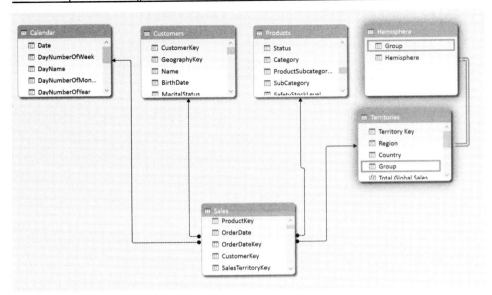

6. Join the tables by dragging the `Group` column from the `Territories` table up and dropping it on top of the `Group` column in the new `Hemisphere` table.

Note The `Territories` table now has two roles. It is now acting as a lookup table to the `Sales` table and as a data table to the new `Hemisphere` table.

7. Bring the data that resides in the `Hemisphere[Hemisphere]` column and make it appear in a new calculated column inside the `Territories` table. Navigate to the `Territories` table, switch to the Data view, and then type in the new formula shown below.

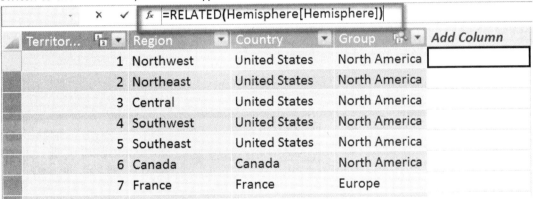

8. After you press Enter, you see all the values appear in the new calculated column. It is a lot like `VLOOKUP()`! You can rename the new column by double-clicking the heading and giving it a new name.

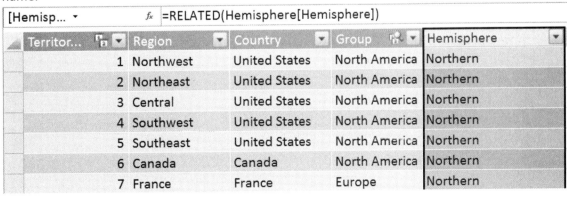

9. Finally, hide the `Hemisphere` table from the client tools by navigating to the Diagram view, right-clicking on the `Hemisphere` table, and selecting Hide from Client Tools, as shown below.

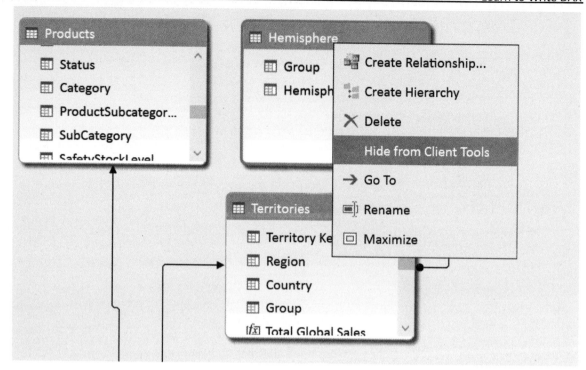

It is good practice to bring data from an "add-on table" like this Hemisphere table into the main Territories table as an additional column. It is possible to leave the Territories table untouched and use the columns from the Hemisphere table in your pivot tables. But the problem is that this can be confusing to users. It doesn't make business sense to have all the geographic information in the Territories table *except* for the hemisphere information, which is in the Hemisphere table. So for consistency and simplicity for the end user, it is better to bring all the "like data" into the same table, as shown here. And, of course, it is better to change the Territories table back at the source to include the new Hemisphere column, but that is not always possible in a timely manner.

The RELATEDTABLE() Function

As discussed earlier, RELATEDTABLE() is used to reference a table on the "many" side of the relationship. A simple example is to add a new calculated column to count how many sales there have been for each product. Once again, I generally don't recommend that you do this, but there may be valid reasons to do it in some cases.

Go ahead now and add the following calculated column in the Products table:

```
= COUNTROWS (RELATEDTABLE (Sales))
```

As you know, RELATEDTABLE() returns a table, and COUNTROWS() counts the rows in that table. This calculated column in the Products table therefore takes the row context in the calculated column and leverages the relationship with the Sales table to count the rows in the Sales table for just the single product. As a result, you end up with a new column that indicates the number of items sold (over all time) for each product in the Products table.

> **Note** You do not need to use CALCULATE() with RELATEDTABLE() to force context transition and convert the row context to a filter context. RELATEDTABLE() will work on its own.

When to Use RELATEDTABLE()

One valid use case for using RELATEDTABLE() would be if you want to create a slicer to filter on slow-, moderate-, and fast-selling products. If you want to use a slicer, you must write your DAX as a calculated column. (You can't place calculated fields in slicers.) You could first create a calculated column and then use the banding technique discussed in Chapter 16 to group products into slow-, moderate-, and fast-moving products. (Park this thought for now and come back after you have read Chapter 16 if you want to try out this technique.)

16: Concept: Disconnected Tables

So far as you have worked through this book, you have always loaded tables into the data model and then connected them to other tables. This is a fundamental technique with Power Pivot that allows you to work across multiple tables without using VLOOKUP(). However, you are not required to join tables together in the data model, and indeed there are some instances when it doesn't make sense to do so. This chapter discusses two techniques that do not involve connecting tables:

- Using harvester calculated fields
- Using banding

Using Harvester Calculated Fields

I learnt this technique from Rob Collie and have borrowed his name for it: *harvester*. As the name suggests, a *harvester calculated field* (or *harvester measure*, as Rob calls it) is used to "harvest" something, such as input from a user. Let's look at an example to demonstrate.

Imagine that in your data, sales is directly proportional to profit. You have sales data and want to see what impact an increase in sales will have on your total profit. You could write a new calculated field hard-coded at a 10% increase, as shown below.

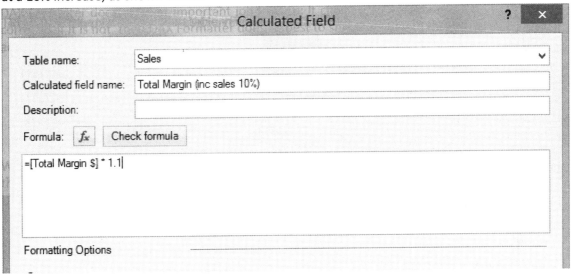

And it would look as follows in a pivot table.

CalendarYear	2003		

Row Labels ▼	Total Sales Amount	Total Margin $	Total Margin (inc sales 10%)
Accessories	$293,710	$183,862	$202,248
Bikes	$9,359,103	$3,833,345	$4,216,680
Clothing	$138,248	$55,526	$61,078
Grand Total	**$9,791,060**	**$4,072,733**	**$4,480,006**

But what if you wanted to see what it looks like for a 5% increase in sales, or 15% or some other percentage? It would not be efficient to create lots of new calculated fields, one for each value. A better approach is to create a table of possible values and then create a harvester calculated field to receive input from the user on which value to use.

Here's How: Creating a Harvester Calculated Field

Follow these steps to create a harvester calculated field:

1. Start with a clean blank worksheet in your workbook and create a list of possible values, like this:

Value
1
2
3
4
5
6
7
8
9
10
11
12
13
14
15

2. Click anywhere in the list and press Ctrl+L to create an Excel table. You get something like this:

Value ▼
1
2
3
4
5
6
7
8
9
10
11
12
13
14
15

3. Click inside the table, make sure the Design tab is selected (it should be automatically) and then in the Table Name box, change the name of the table to In-crease.

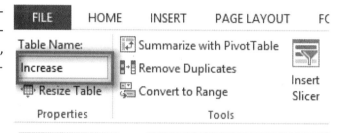

4. Add this table to the data model. To do this, select any cell in the table and then go to the Power Pivot tab and select Add to Data Model (or, in Excel 2010, select Create Linked Table). After you do this, the Data View will open, and you will see the new linked table inside Power Pivot.

5. Switch to the Diagram view so you can see your new table. This time you will not join the table to any other table. Just position it somewhere so it is easy to see on the screen, as shown below.

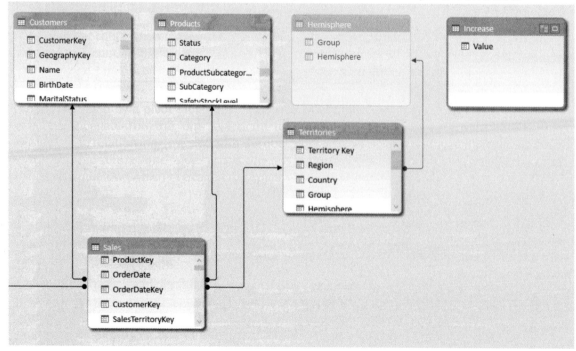

6. Now create a new pivot table and put `Increase[Value]` on Rows (just for this demo). Then add `Increase[Value]` on Slicers as well. You should have a pivot table like the one below.

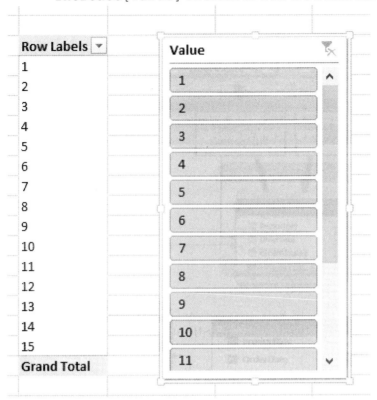

Note what happens when you click on one of the values in the slicer. It filters the pivot table so that only that single value is visible in rows. What you now want to do is "harvest" this selection *into a calculated field*.

7. Click inside the pivot table and write the following calculated field:

   `[Selected Value] = MAX(Increase[Value])`

8. Remove `Value` from Rows and just leave the new calculated field `[Selected Value]` in the Values area. As you can see below, when you select a value in the slicer, the selected value is shown in your harvester calculated field in the pivot table.

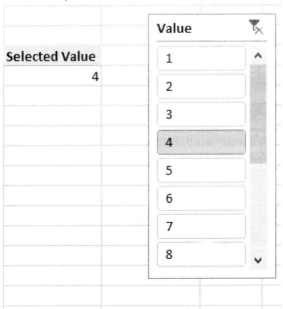

Note This is what is happening here:

- The slicer is connected to the table called `Increase` in the data model.

- When you select a single item in the slicer, the slicer filters the `Increase` table in the data model so that only that single row is left unfiltered. (You can imagine this table filtered this way or you can simulate what is happening by applying a filter to the table inside Power Pivot.)

- The calculated field `[Selected Value]` respects the pivot table filter context. (Remember that the slicer is part of the filter context.) Then the calculated field finds the maximum of `Value` in the current filter context. Given that there is only one value that is unfiltered, the calculated field returns this value.

So it should be obvious that you can use almost any aggregation formula in place of `MAX()`. `MIN()`, `AVERAGE()`, and `SUM()` will all work just as well because the slicer selection has only a single item selected. These other aggregation approaches give you different results if you select more than one item from the slicer, but in this scenario, you are only expecting the user to select a single value.

9. Once you have `Value` selected in the slicer available as a calculated field, you can write a new DAX formula that uses it:

```
[Total Margin with Selected Increase] =
    [Total Margin $] * (100 + [Selected Value])/100
```

CalendarYear 2003

Row Labels	Total Sales Amount	Total Margin $	Total Margin with Selected Increase
Accessories	$293,710	$183,862	$191,216
Bikes	$9,359,103	$3,833,345	$3,986,679
Clothing	$138,248	$55,526	$57,747
Grand Total	$9,791,060	$4,072,733	$4,235,642

Value: 1, 2, 3, **4**, 5

10. To tidy this up a bit, change the description in the slicer. To do this, right-click on the slicer and select Slicer Settings. Then change the caption to read `% Sales Increase`.

CalendarYear 2003

Row Labels	Total Sales Amount	Total Margin $	Total Margin with Selected Increase
Accessories	$293,710	$183,862	$191,216
Bikes	$9,359,103	$3,833,345	$3,986,679
Clothing	$138,248	$55,526	$57,747
Grand Total	$9,791,060	$4,072,733	$4,235,642

% Sales Increase: 1, 2, 3, **4**, 5

Practice Exercise: Harvester Calculated Fields

In Chapter 8, you created the following DAX formula:

```
[Total Customers Born Before 1950] = CALCULATE([Total number of Customers], Customers[BirthDate] <DATE(1950,1,1))
```

Using the technique described above, create a new pivot table report that allows the user to select from a list of years in a slicer. Write the following new DAX formula. Find the solution to this practice exercise in "Q. Harvester Calculated Fields" on page 181.

70. [Total Customers Born Before Selected Year]

This is quite a difficult problem. You should try to do this yourself, and if you get stuck, read the hint below and then try to solve the problem again. There is a worked-through example later in this chapter.

> **Hint** There is a trick to this practice example problem. The original calculated field you created used a "simple filter" in `CALCULATE()`. If you simply replace the "year value" from the first formula with the calculated field `[Selected Year]`, you get the following error message.

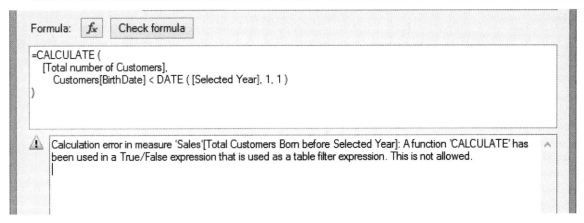

The problem is that you cannot use calculated fields in a "simple" `CALCULATE()` formula. Remember this! If you want to use calculated fields (as you do in this case), you must use the `FILTER()` function inside `CALCULATE()`. So instead of writing this: `Customers[BirthDate] < DATE ( [Selected Year], 1, 1 )` you need to write a `FILTER()` function that filters the **Customers** table to replace the above line. Go back and give it a go; see if you can write the correct formula using `FILTER()` instead of a simple filter in that uses the format `TableName[ColumnName]`=*some value*. If you still need more help, then read on to see the correct formula.

Here's How: Solving Exercise 70

Here is the worked-through solution for Practice Exercise 70. Follow these steps:

1. Create a list of values in Excel for years (say 1900 through 2000). Give the column a header such as `Years`.

2. Convert the list to an Excel table and give it a name like `YearTable`, then and add it to the data model. Do not connect the table to any other tables.

3. Insert a slicer for the new table. Find the new table in the Pivot Table Fields list, right click on the column, and select Add as Slicer.

4. Create a new pivot table and put `Customer[Occupation]` on Rows.

5. Click inside the new pivot table and then write a new calculated field to harvest the selected value from the slicer:

        [Selected Year] = MAX(YearTable[Years])

6. Write the following calculated field to put into your pivot table:

        [Total Customers Born Before Selected Year]
           = CALCULATE (
             [Total number of Customers],
             FILTER (
                 Customers,
                 Customers[BirthDate] < DATE ([Selected Year], 1, 1)
)
)

You should end up with something that looks as shown below. When you click on a year in the slicer, the [Selected Year] calculated field updates in the pivot table, and the results for [Total Customers Born before Selected Year] updates to show the value for [Selected Year].

Row Labels	Selected Year	Total Customers Born before Selected Year
Clerical	1965	1,567
Management	1965	2,229
Manual	1965	860
Professional	1965	3,382
Skilled Manual	1965	2,071
Grand Total	1965	10,109

Year slicer values: 1963, 1964, 1965, 1966, 1967, 1968, 1969, 1970

The [Selected Year] calculated field is not required to be in the pivot table, and you can and should remove it once you know it is working.

Using Banding

Another disconnected table technique is banding; I learnt this technique from Marco Russo and Alberto Ferrari at http://sqlbi.com.

To understand banding, think about the earlier example in which you created a slicer based on the year the customer was born. A more common and practical need is to be able to analyse customers based on their age group rather than their actual age, like this:

- Under 20
- 20 but less than 30
- 30 to less than 40
- 40 to less than 50
- 50 to less than 60
- 60 and over

It is possible to write a calculated column in the Customers table that creates these age group bands. But it would be a very complex formula, and it would be hard to edit.

For the sake of the exercise, I will use January 1, 2003, as the "current date" from which to work out the age of each customer. Of course, in reality, each customer's age band will change over time, but I have ignored this fact for this example.

A hard-coded calculated column formula for age group might look like this:

```
=if(((date(2003,1,1) - Customers[BirthDate])/365)<20,"Less than 20",if
(((date(2003,1,1) - Customers[BirthDate])/365)<30,"20 to less than
30",if(((date(2003,1,1) - Customers[BirthDate])/365)<40,"30 to less
than 40",if(((date(2003,1,1) - Customers[BirthDate])/365)<50,"40 to
less than 50",if(((date(2003,1,1) - Customers[BirthDate])/365)<60,"50
to less than 60","Greater than 60")))))
```

This DAX works, but it is not very user friendly, it is hard to write, and it is even harder to read and maintain.

A better approach is to use banding.

Here's How: Banding

The first step in banding is to create a linked table in Excel that contains the upper and lower values for each band, as well as a text description. Follow these steps:

1. Create a list of values in Excel and convert it to a table (by pressing Ctrl+L). You should have something that looks like the table below.

2. Inside Excel, go to the Table Design tab and rename the table AgeBands. (You can't change a linked table name inside Power Pivot, so you need to change it from Excel.)

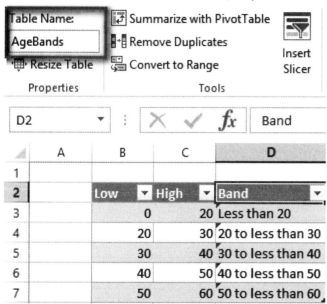

Note It is important to set up the banding table so there is no crossover of ages between the Low and High ranges. The table above covers all possible ages between 0 and 999, without any duplication. Of course, the 999 value is any arbitrarily large value to catch everyone.

3. To add your table to the data model, go to the Power Pivot tab and select Add to Data Model. (In Excel 2010, select Create Linked Table.)

Note There is no need to join this table to any other table in the data model. In fact, there is no workable way you can do this anyway. Even if there were an age column in the Customers table, you still couldn't join this table to the age column. This banding table doesn't contain all the possible ages for customers; it just has the age bands. So if you first create a customer age column and then joined the Low column to this new column, the data will only match for customers who are 20, 30, 40, etc. There will be no match for customers with an age that doesn't end in a zero (e.g., 21, 22, 23, etc.). So that is not going to work.

4. Go to the Customers table in Data view and scroll all the way to the right of the table until you see Add Column as the next column name.

5. Click in the first cell in this blank column and type in the following formula:

        =(DATE(2003,1,1) - Customers[BirthDate])/365

Press Enter, and Power Pivot automatically renames the column Calculated Column 1. Just double-click that column name and give rename it something like Age.

Note Although it is not required to make this banding technique work, you could enhance this formula with some rounding, as follows:

    = ROUNDDOWN((date(2003,1,1) - Customers[BirthDate])/365,0)

Custome...	GeographyKey	Name	BirthDate	Age
13152	348	Gabrielle Butler	16/02/1978 ...	24
14095	343	Paige Griffin	10/09/1976 ...	26
14349	546	Nicole Griffin	11/05/1976 ...	26
15252	547	Jada Murphy	14/02/1980 ...	22
15258	607	Chloe Reed	7/05/1978 1...	24
15816	50	Victoria Miller	20/05/1976 ...	26
17338	62	Jordyn Long	17/02/1976 ...	26
17359	637	María Flores	8/03/1975 1...	27
18345	53	Samantha Bryant	19/09/1975 ...	27
18762	345	Arthur Wilson	22/05/1978 ...	24
18775	546	Andrea Bell	18/05/1975 ...	27
18790	635	Julia Martin	26/09/1979 ...	23
18915	316	Sydney Gonzalez	5/01/1975 1...	28
19636	536	Jessica Lee	17/11/1976 ...	26

Now that you have this new calculated column, you can write some DAX to create the banding column.

6.   Move to the right of the `Customers` table until you see Add Column, click in the first cell of this empty column, and enter the following formula:

```
= CALCULATE (VALUES (AgeBands [Band]),
        FILTER (AgeBands,
            Customers [Age]  >= AgeBands [Low] &&
            Customers [Age] < AgeBands [High]
        )
    )
```

7.   Double-click the column heading and name this column `Age Group`.

The key to this formula is the `FILTER ()` function. The `FILTER ()` function iterates over the `AgeBands` table and checks the customer's age against the low and high values for each band. There is only ever one single row in the `AgeBands` table that matches the age of the customer. The `FILTER ()` function inside `CALCULATE ()` first filters the `AgeBands` table so that only the one row that matches the age band is left visible. Then `CALCULATE ()` evaluates the expression `VALUES (AgeBands [Band])`, and because there is only one row visible, `VALUES ()` returns the name of the band as a text value into the column.

> **Note** There are two main benefits of taking this approach to the banding:
> - The DAX formula is easier to read and understand. Once you get used to the concept, it is easier to write, too.
> - It is easy to make changes in the future. So if you want to add another age band to your analysis (e.g., a new "Greater than 70" age band, all you need to do is add another row to your `AgeBands` table and then click Refresh—that's it.

8.   Add a new row to the table, like this:

Low	High	Band
0	20	Less than 20
20	30	20 to 30
30	40	30 to 40
40	50	40 to 50
50	60	50 to 60
60	70	60 to 70
70	999	Greater than 70

9. Click inside the table, navigate to the Power Pivot tab, and click Update All.

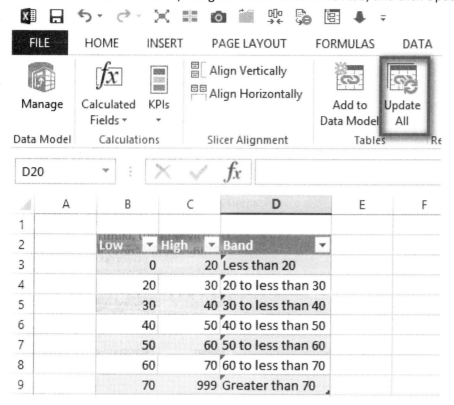

> **Note** In Excel 2013, all you need to do is open the Power Pivot window, and it should update automatically.

It's time to use this new calculated column in a pivot table. Create a new pivot table on a new sheet. Put Age Group on Rows and then add a couple of the calculated fields you wrote earlier:

```
[Customers That Have Purchased]
[Total Sales Amount]
```

You can also add some conditional formatting so that the pivot table is easier to read. You should end up with something like this:

Row Labels	Customers That Have Purchased	Total Sales Amount
20 to 30	3,319	$4,356,580
30 to 40	6,301	$11,537,347
40 to 50	4,937	$8,585,476
50 to 60	2,727	$3,685,270
60 to 70	1,076	$1,117,530
Greater than 70	124	$76,475
Grand Total	**18,484**	**$29,358,677**

It is easy to see the power of banding. It is unlikely that you will ever want to analyse a business based on sales to customers who are 20, 21, 22, etc. Grouping customers into age brackets is more practical, and this disconnected table banding technique makes it a snap.

A Final Word About Interim Calculated Columns

In the banding example, you first created an Age calculated column and then created an Age Group calculated column. Breaking the problem into parts like this makes the DAX easier to read, write, and debug. However, you should be aware that it is generally not considered good practice to leave interim calculated columns in your data model as they inefficiently take up extra space. What you really should do after you get the final column working as expected is combine all the interim columns into a single column and then delete the interim column.

Here's How: Deleting Interim Calculated Columns

Follow these steps to combine all the interim columns into a single column and then delete the interim column:

1. Navigate to the interim calculated column in the table (Age in this example).

2. Press Ctrl+C to copy the formula from the interim column, taking care to exclude the equals sign.

3. Navigate to the final calculated column (Age Group in this example). You can enlarge the editing window by using the mouse as shown below.

```
= CALCULATE(VALUES(AgeBands[Band]),
      FILTER(AgeBands,
         (Customers[Age]) >= AgeBands[Low] &&
         (Customers[Age]) < AgeBands[High]
      )
  )
```

> **Hover mouse and then click and drag down to create a larger editing window.**

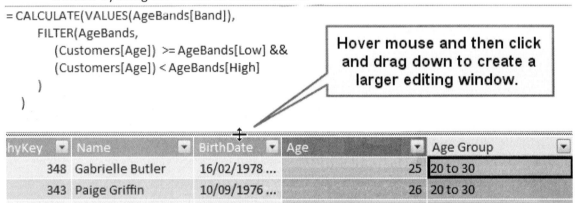

4. For each occurrence of the interim column in the DAX formula, replace the column name with the formula copied in step 2—from this:

```
= CALCULATE(VALUES(AgeBands[Band]),
      FILTER(AgeBands,
         (Customers[Age]) >= AgeBands[Low] &&
         (Customers[Age]) < AgeBands[High]
      )
  )
```

> **Replace these with the formula from the column**

to this:

```
= CALCULATE(VALUES(AgeBands[Band]),
      FILTER(AgeBands,
         (DATE(2003,1,1) - Customers[BirthDate])/365 >= AgeBands[Low] &&
         (DATE(2003,1,1) - Customers[BirthDate])/365 < AgeBands[High]
      )
  )
```

5. Finally, delete the interim column (Age in this example).

Of course, if you need the interim column in your table, you should keep it. But if you don't need it, you should delete it.

17: Concept: KPIs and Multiple Data Tables

Power Pivot has a feature called *KPIs*, which is basically a visualisation tool that uses graphical icons to indicate how well a value compares to some target value. (KPI stands for *key performance indicator*.) You can use KPIs to add interesting visualisations to your pivot tables so the reader can instantly see if things are on track. To see how it works, let's look at an example.

In the following pivot table, I have created a KPI against the `[Margin %]` calculated field. Note that the icons visually indicate the status.

Row Labels ▼	Total Sales Amount	Margin %	Margin % Status
Bike Racks	$39,360	62.6%	⚪
Bike Stands	$39,591	62.6%	⚪
Bottles and Cages	$56,798	62.6%	⚪
Caps	$19,688	23.0%	⚪
Cleaners	$7,219	62.6%	⚪
Fenders	$46,620	62.6%	⚪
Gloves	$35,021	62.6%	⚪
Helmets	$225,336	62.6%	⚪
Hydration Packs	$40,308	62.6%	⚪

> **Note** Excel 2013 seems to have a bug with KPIs. The only visualisation that works in Excel 2013 is the "round dot" icon shown above. Best practice with visualisations like this is to use an icon that makes sense in colour as well as black and white (so it can be understood for people who are colour-blind, too). If you are reading a black-and-white printed copy of this book, you will see the problem immediately: When you can't see the colour, the round dots above are pretty much useless.

When you set up a KPI, you are given a choice of icon sets, and many of the icon sets are great—including the set shown below that provides a tick, an exclamation point, and an x.

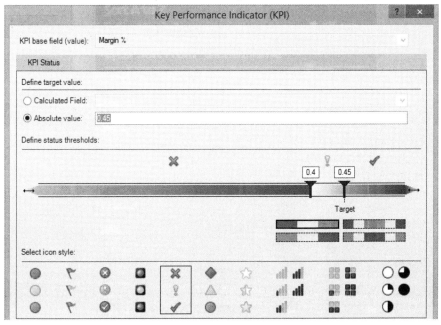

But in Excel 2013, it doesn't matter what icon set you select in the above dialog; you will always get those annoying round coloured circles. Selecting a different icon set simply doesn't work. (It does work with Power View but not inside Excel pivot tables.) This is not the case in Excel 2010, though, and the other icon sets work just fine, as you can see in the next screenshot of a pivot table created using Excel 2010.

Row Labels	▼	Total Sales Amount	Total Margin % Value	Total Margin % Status
Bike Racks		$39,360	62.6%	✓
Bike Stands		$39,591	62.6%	✓
Bottles and Cages		$56,798	62.6%	✓
Caps		$19,688	23.0%	✗
Cleaners		$7,219	62.6%	✓
Fenders		$46,620	62.6%	✓
Gloves		$35,021	62.6%	✓

With the icon set in this pivot table, it doesn't matter if you are reading a black-and-white copy of this book (or if you are colour-blind); it is clear what these icons mean.

Despite this bug in Excel 2013, KPIs can be useful, so let's look at them a bit more.

Here's How: Creating a KPI

Follow these steps to create a KPI:

1. Set up a new pivot table with `Products[SubCategory]` on Rows and then add `[Total Sales Amount]` and `[Total Margin %]` on Values.

2. Click inside the pivot table, navigate to the Power Pivot tab, and select KPIs, New KPI.

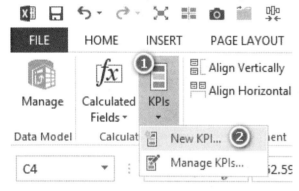

3. Select Margin % from the KPI Base Field (Value) drop-down (shown below).

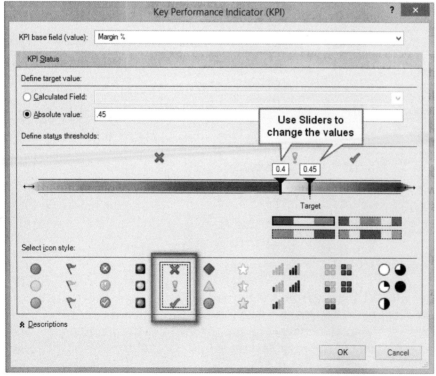

4. In the section Define Target Value, where you have two choices, select Absolute Value and set it to 0.45. (Note that 45% is actually 0.45; if you type 45 instead, it won't work.)

5. As shown in the figure above, set the lower slider to 0.40 and the upper slider to 0.45.

6. Select an icon set that works for people who are colour-blind.

At this point, you come to another bug in Excel 2013. When you finish writing this KPI, the pivot table looks like this:

Row Labels ▼	Total Sales Amount	Margin %	Margin % Status
Bike Racks	$39,360	62.6%	1
Bike Stands	$39,591	62.6%	1
Bottles and Cages	$56,798	62.6%	1
Caps	$19,688	23.0%	-1
Cleaners	$7,219	62.6%	1
Fenders	$46,620	62.6%	1
Gloves	$35,021	62.6%	1
Helmets	$225,336	62.6%	1
Hydration Packs	$40,308	62.6%	1
Jerseys	$172,951	23.0%	-1
Mountain Bikes	$9,952,760	45.4%	1
Road Bikes	$14,520,584	38.1%	-1

In Excel 2013, you need to remove `[Margin % Status]` from the pivot table and then put it back in again in order to see the icon. And, of course, after you do that, you are only going to get that round icon and not the one you selected. Here's what you end up with:

Row Labels ▼	Total Sales Amount	Margin %	Margin % Status
Bike Racks	$39,360	62.6%	⬤
Bike Stands	$39,591	62.6%	⬤
Bottles and Ca,	$56,798	62.6%	⬤
Caps	$19,688	23.0%	⬤
Cleaners	$7,219	62.6%	⬤
Fenders	$46,620	62.6%	⬤
Gloves	$35,021	62.6%	⬤
Helmets	$225,336	62.6%	⬤
Hydration Pack	$40,308	62.6%	⬤
Jerseys	$172,951	23.0%	⬤
Mountain Bike	$9,952,760	45.4%	⬤
Road Bikes	$14,520,584	38.1%	⬤
Shorts	$71,320	62.6%	⬤
Socks	$5,106	62.6%	⬤
Tires and Tube	$245,529	62.6%	⬤
Touring Bikes	$3,844,801	37.8%	⬤
Vests	$35,687	62.6%	⬤
Grand Total	$29,358,677	41.1%	◯

Again, there's no problem in Excel 2010, and you'll see the icon set you selected.

Here's How: Adding a Budget Table

A common business scenario is to have a budget at a different level of granularity than sales. For example, sales may be captured and reported every day for every individual product, but budgets may be set only for each month and for each product category. The following steps walk you through the process of importing a budget table and creating a calculated field for the budget:

1. To bring in the budget data and a new `BudgetPeriod` table, in the Power Pivot window, select Home, Existing Connections.

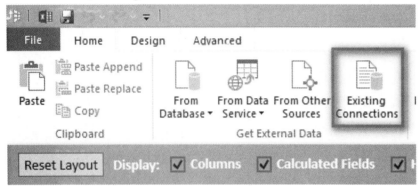

2. Select the Access database you have been using (see #1 below) and then click Open (#2).

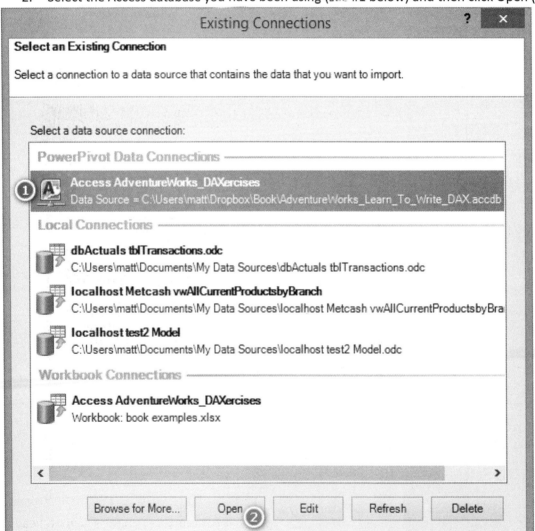

3. Select the first option, Select from a List of Tables, and click Next.

4. Select the `Budget` table, the `BudgetPeriod` table, and the `dimProductCategory` table. Rename the `dimProductCategory` table to `ProductCategory`, as shown below and click the Preview & Filter button.

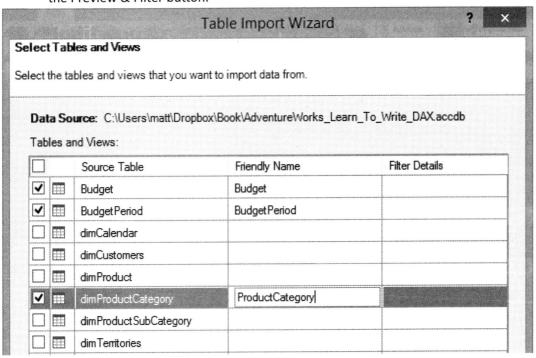

5. Deselect all the columns (see #1 below) and then just select the `EnglishProductCategoryName` column (#2) and click Save.

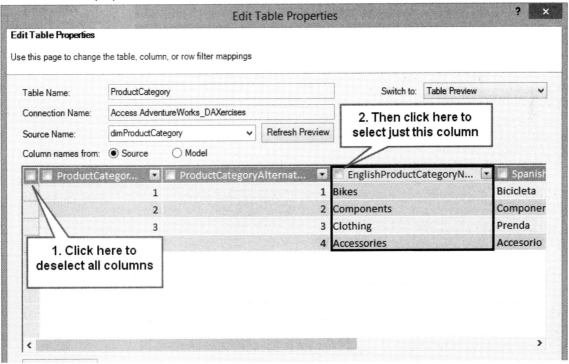

6. Click Save and then click Finish to complete the import.

7. Click Close.

8. To tidy things up a bit, go to the `ProductCategory` table, double-click on the column heading `EnglishProductCategoryName`, and rename it `Category`. Then take some time to look at the data in these three tables:

- **Budget table**—The `Budget` table has a monthly sales budget for each category. The `Period` column is in the format YYYYMM for year and month, as shown below.

Category	Budget	Period
Accessories	16000	200307
Accessories	53000	200308
Accessories	56000	200309
Accessories	56000	200310

- **BudgetPeriod table**—The `BudgetPeriod` table is a type of calendar table and is different from what you have used so far. Like the `Budget` table, it contains a `Period` column in the format YYYYMM, as shown below.

CalendarYear	MonthName	Month Number	Period
2003	July	7	200307
2003	August	8	200308
2003	September	9	200309
2003	October	10	200310
2003	November	11	200311
2003	December	12	200312
2004	January	1	200401

- **ProductCategory table**—The `ProductCategory` table has a list of the four possible product categories, as shown below.

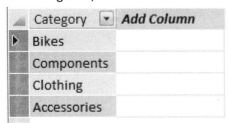

Category	Add Column
▶ Bikes	
Components	
Clothing	
Accessories	

The reason you need all these new tables will make sense shortly.

9. Switch to Diagram view. If necessary, you should click the Fit to Screen button (see the following figure) so that you can see all of the tables on the screen.

10. Rearrange your tables as shown below. Place the `BudgetPeriod` table (#1) above the `Calendar` table and place the `Budget` table (#2) next to the `Sales` table. You may already have the `SubProductCategory` table in your data model from one of the earlier practice exercises. If so, just move it over so you can put the `ProductCategory` table (#3) above the `Products` table, as shown.

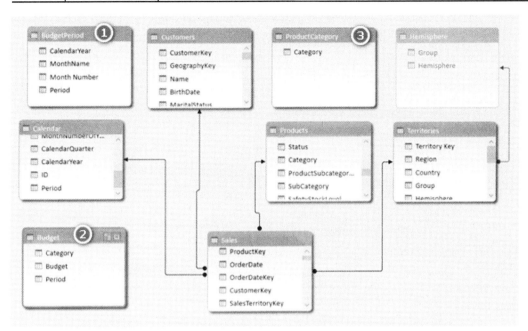

Note Now let me explain why you need the `BudgetPeriod` table. Go ahead and try to join the `Budget` table to the `Calendar` table. Click on the `Period` column in the `Budget` table and drag and drop it on the `Period` column in the `Calendar` table.

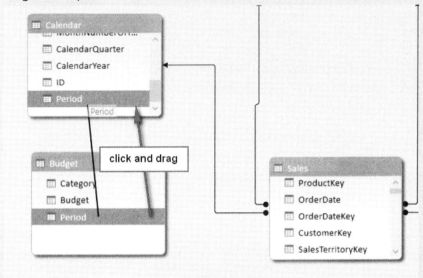

When you do this, you get the following error:

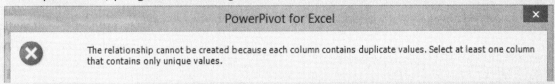

Do you see the issue? The `Calendar` table is a daily calendar, but the `Budget` table is a monthly budget (a very common business scenario). There are between 28 and 31 entries for each month in the `Period` column in the `Calendar` table. *But Power Pivot supports only one-to-many relationships.* The lookup table (`Calendar`) at the top simply must have a single value for `Period` if you are to make the join, so this is not going to work. This is why you need the `BudgetPeriod` table. There is only one value for each `Period` in the `BudgetPeriod` table, and hence you are able to join the `Budget` table to the `BudgetPeriod` table.

11. Click and hold on `Period` in the `Budget` table, drag it up to the `Period` column in the `BudgetPeriod` table, and release to create the relationship (see #1 below).

12. Join the `Calendar` table to the `BudgetPeriod` table by dragging the `Period` column from the `Calendar` table to the `Period` column in the `BudgetPeriod` table (#2).

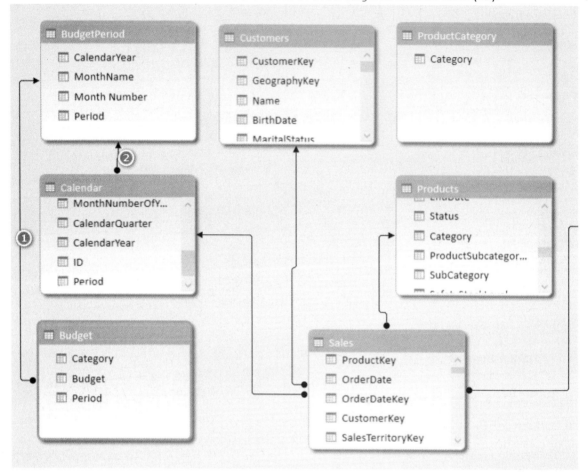

Now you need to do the same again and this time join the `ProductCategory` table to the `Budget` table. If you try to join the `Budget[Category]` column to the `Products` table, you will get the same error as before.

13. To join the `Budget` table to the `ProductCategory` table, click and drag the column `Budget[Category]` to `ProductCategory[Category]`.

14. To join the `Products` table to the `ProductCategory` table, click and drag the column `Products[Category]` to the `ProductCategory[Category]` column.

When you are finished, it will look something like the layout shown below. Notice that it becomes difficult to keep track of all the relationships when you have lots of tables in your data model. This is one reason it is best practice for Excel users to lay out the tables as shown below.

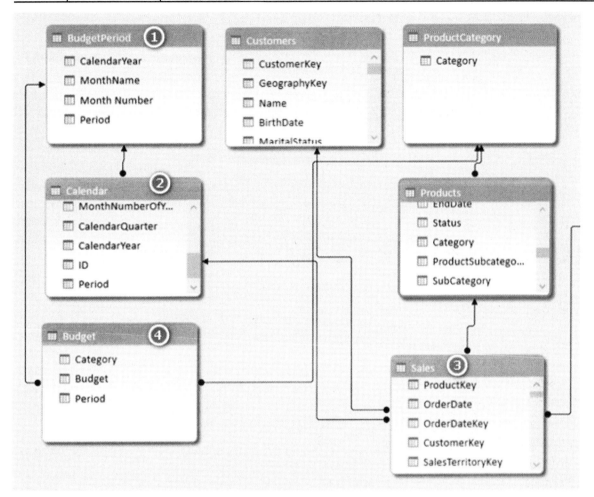

The tables on the "many" side of the relationship are down below, and the tables on the "one" side of the relationship are up high. The filters always flow downhill, and this layout makes it much easier to understand how the filters flow. So if you filter on the BudgetPeriod table (see #1 above), this table directly filters the Budget table (#4) via the direct relationship. In addition, the BudgetPeriod table (#1) directly filters the Calendar table (#2), and the Calendar table (#2) filters the Sales table (#3). So the net result is that any filter you apply to the BudgetPeriod table (#1) filters both the Sales table (#3) and the Budget table (#4). The same applies to the ProductCategory table.

When working with data tables of differing granularities, as in this case, it is important to use the correct tables and columns in your pivot table filters. So when working with both the Sales table and the Budget table, you must use the columns from the BudgetPeriod table in your pivots; columns from *the* Calendar *table will not work.*

Practice Exercises: KPIs

It's time to get some practice writing some new DAX formulas across the two data tables: `Budget` and `Sales`. First create a new pivot table. Then put `ProductCategory[Category]` on Rows, `BudgetPeriod[Period]` on Rows, and `[Total Sales Amount]` on Values. Make sure you select the correct columns from the two new tables (`ProductCategory` and `BudgetPeriod`).

Once your pivot is set up, click in the pivot table and then write the following new calculated fields. Find the solutions to these practice exercises in "R. KPIs" on page 181.

71. [Total Budget]

72. [Change in Sales vs. Budget]

Row Labels ▼	Total Sales Amount
⊟ Accessories	$700,760
200307	$14,468
200308	$52,057
200309	$52,150
200310	$54,595
200311	$54,832
200312	$65,608
200401	$56,457
200402	$56,996
200403	$60,098
200404	$62,674
200405	$71,880
200406	$65,201
200407	$33,745
⊟ Bikes	$28,318,145
200107	$473,388
200108	$506,192
200109	$473,943

73. [% Change in Sales vs. Budget]

Here is what the pivot table looks like with these formulas and the addition of conditional formatting.

Row Labels ▼	Total Sales Amount	Total Budget	Change in Sales vs Budget	% Change in Sales vs Budget
⊟ Accessories	$700,760	$739,000	-$38,240	-5.2%
200307	$14,468	$16,000	-$1,532	-9.6%
200308	$52,057	$53,000	-$943	-1.8%
200309	$52,150	$56,000	-$3,850	-6.9%
200310	$54,595	$56,000	-$1,405	-2.5%
200311	$54,832	$54,000	$832	1.5%
200312	$65,608	$72,000	-$6,392	-8.9%
200401	$56,457	$61,000	-$4,543	-7.4%
200402	$56,996	$63,000	-$6,004	-9.5%
200403	$60,098	$63,000	-$2,902	-4.6%
200404	$62,674	$68,000	-$5,326	-7.8%
200405	$71,880	$78,000	-$6,120	-7.8%
200406	$65,201	$63,000	$2,201	3.5%

Here's How: Creating a Budget KPI

Here is how you can use this new budget table to create a KPI:

1. Click in the pivot table you created for Practice Exercises 70–72 and select Pivot Table, KPI, New KPI.
2. Select Total Sales Amount for the KPI Base Field.
3. Select Total Budget in the Define Target Value section as the calculated field.
4. Adjust the sliders so that they are set to 95% and 100%.
5. Click OK.

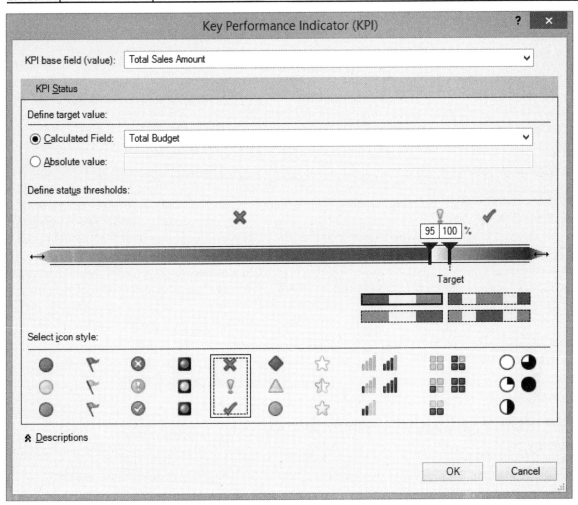

6. If you are using Excel 2013, remove this new KPI from your pivot table and then add it back. Once you have done that, you see the following.

Row Labels	Total Sales Amount	Total Budget	Change in Sales vs Budget	% Change in Sales vs Budget	Total Sales Amount Status
⊟ Accessories	$700,760	$739,000	-$38,240	-5.2%	●
200307	$14,468	$16,000	-$1,532	-9.6%	●
200308	$52,057	$53,000	-$943	-1.8%	○
200309	$52,150	$56,000	-$3,850	-6.9%	●
200310	$54,595	$56,000	-$1,405	-2.5%	○
200311	$54,832	$54,000	$832	1.5%	●
200312	$65,608	$72,000	-$6,392	-8.9%	●
200401	$56,457	$61,000	-$4,543	-7.4%	●
200402	$56,996	$63,000	-$6,004	-9.5%	●
200403	$60,098	$63,000	-$2,902	-4.6%	○
200404	$62,674	$68,000	-$5,326	-7.8%	●
200405	$71,880	$78,000	-$6,120	-7.8%	●
200406	$65,201	$63,000	$2,201	3.5%	●
200407	$33,745	$36,000	-$2,255	-6.3%	●
⊟ Bikes	$28,318,145	$28,750,000	-$431,855	-1.5%	○
200107	$473,388	$483,000	-$9,612	-2.0%	○
200108	$506,192	$516,000	-$9,808	-1.9%	○
200109	$473,943	$502,000	-$28,057	-5.6%	●

The new KPI shows red, yellow, and green to indicate how close the actual sales were to the budget.

18: Concept: Cube Formulas

The final topic in this book is one of my favourites: cube formulas. Cube formulas have been around for many years. But before Power Pivot was launched, the only way you could use cube formulas was to connect to a SQL Server Analysis Services (SSAS) multidimensional cube. Some large companies have SSAS set up, and some of those companies may connect directly to SSAS from Excel, and some of those that do may have discovered cube formulas. But given how rare the above scenario is, most people have never come across cube formulas prior to discovering Power Pivot.

What Is a Cube Formula?

Well, so far in this book, you have always consumed and visualised the information from the data model in a pivot table. Pivot tables are great, and I use them all the time, but they do have some limitations. The biggest limitation is that you are locked in to the format that the pivot table gives you. But what if you want to put a single value in a single cell in a workbook? In that case, you could create a pivot table and then point the cell in question to the pivot table, but that involves a lot of overhead. In addition, if the pivot table changes shape at any time (e.g., on refresh), then chances are the cell positions will change, and your formula may point to the wrong cell. The best-case scenario is that you realise there is a problem. The worst-case scenario is that your formula points to another similar cell in the pivot table, and you don't even notice!

"What about `GETPIVOTDATA()`?" I hear some of you say. Well, yes, you can use `GETPIVOTDATA()`, but you still have the overhead of the pivot table, and the bottom line is that cube formulas are much better.

The easiest way to get started with cube formulas is to convert an existing pivot table to cube formulas. The following pages walk you through how to do that.

Here's How: Converting a Pivot Table to Cube Formulas

Follow these steps to convert a pivot table to cube formulas:

1. Create a new blank sheet in your workbook and insert a pivot table like the one shown below.

2. Put `Calendar[CalendarYear]` on Rows, `Products[Category]` on Columns, and `[Total Sales Amount]` on Values. Also add a slicer for `Customers[Occupation]`. Click on the slicer and make sure it works before proceeding.

Occupation 🔽	Total Sales Amount	Column Labels 🔽		
	Row Labels 🔽	Accessories	Bikes	Clothing	Grand Total
Clerical	2001		$3,266,374		$3,266,374
Management	2002		$6,530,344		$6,530,344
Manual	2003	$293,710	$9,359,103	$138,248	$9,791,060
Professional	2004	$407,050	$9,162,325	$201,525	$9,770,900
Skilled Manual	Grand Total	$700,760	$28,318,145	$339,773	$29,358,677

3. To convert the pivot table to cube formulas, click inside the pivot table and then select Analyze (see #1 below), OLAP Tools (#2), Convert to Formulas (#3).

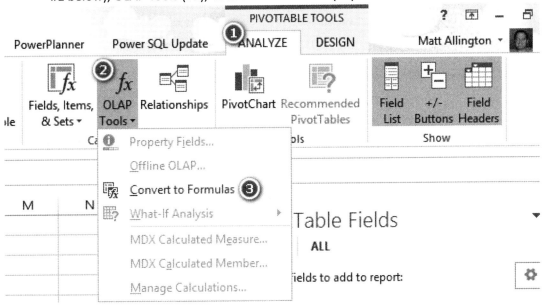

And then BAM! Your pivot table is converted to a stack of standalone formulas that you can move around as you want on the spreadsheet.

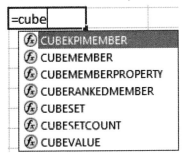

Total Sales Amount	Column Labels			
Row Labels	Accessories	Bikes	Clothing	Grand Total
2001		$3,266,374		$3,266,374
2002		$6,530,344		$6,530,344
2003	$293,710	$9,359,103	$138,248	$9,791,060
2004	$407,050	$9,162,325	$201,525	$9,770,900
Grand Total	$700,760	$28,318,145	$339,773	$29,358,677

What's more, the slicer still works! Go ahead and drag the formulas around to a new location in your spreadsheet and then click on the slicer to verify that it works.

Writing Your Own Cube Formulas

There are seven cube formulas in total, and they all start with the word CUBE. You can see the list by typing =CUBE into a cell in your workbook.

=cube

- CUBEKPIMEMBER
- CUBEMEMBER
- CUBEMEMBERPROPERTY
- CUBERANKEDMEMBER
- CUBESET
- CUBESETCOUNT
- CUBEVALUE

This book covers the two most-used formulas, CUBEVALUE() and CUBEMEMBER(). Once you have mastered these two formulas, you can do some research to learn about the other five.

CUBEVALUE() vs. CUBEMEMBER()

Go back to the pivot table that you just converted and click inside the grand total cell (see #1 below) so that Excel is in Edit mode. Notice in the formula bar (#2) that this grand total cell is a CUBEVALUE() formula, and it points to a number of other cells (#3). The formulas inside each of these other cells are CUBEMEMBER() formulas.

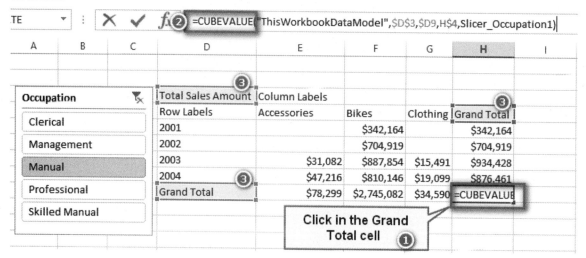

CUBEVALUE() is used to extract the value of a calculated field from the data model, and CUBEMEMBER() is used to extract a value from a column/lookup table. When they are used together, CUBEMEMBER() filters the data model before calculating the CUBEVALUE() expression.

Now that you know about cube formulas, you can build a pivot table that contains the cube formulas you want in your spreadsheet and then simply select Analyze, OLAP Tools, Convert to Formulas. Once you have done this, you can copy and paste the resulting formulas wherever you want. But it actually isn't very hard to write cube formulas from scratch, so let's do that together now.

Here's How: Writing CUBEVALUE() from Scratch

The important keyboard keys when writing cube formulas are the double quote, the square brackets, and the full stop (period in the USA). This information will make sense as you work through these steps. Be sure to follow these steps exactly:

1. Click in an empty cell in your workbook and type **=CUBEVALUE(**. Notice the tooltip that pops up. It is asking for a connection and one or more member expressions. The member expressions can be either calculated fields or table columns from your data model.

2. Type " (a double quote). You are presented with a list of connections available to the workbook. Normally there is only one for a Power Pivot workbook. In Excel 2013 it is called ThisWorkbookDataModel, and in Excel 2010 it is called PowerPivot Data.

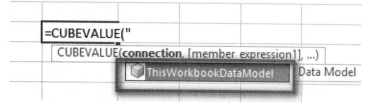

3. Press the Tab key to select the connection and then type " again.

4. Type **,** (a comma).

5. Type **"** (a double quote) again to start the next parameter. This time notice that the tooltip shows you a list of all the tables in the data model (see below). There is also one additional item in the list, [Measures]. All of your DAX formulas are stored in [Measures].

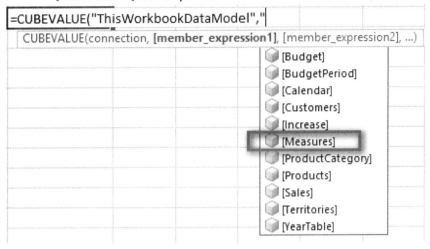

6. Type **[** and then M and press Tab to select [Measures].

7. Type **.** (a period), and you see a list of all the calculated fields that exist in the data model. From here you can either keep typing **[** followed by the name of the calculated field or use the up and down arrow keys on the keyboard to navigate to the calculated field you want to select.

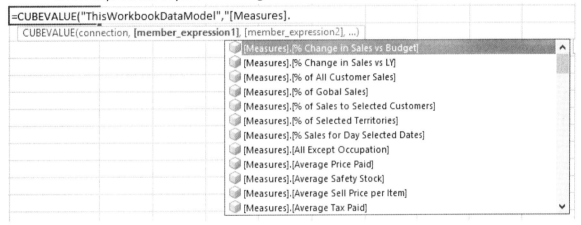

8. Type **[** and then type Total S. This brings the [Total Sales Amount] calculated field to the top.

9. Press Tab, type **")**, and press Enter

If you follow these instructions exactly, you end up with a value in a cell, as shown below. This is your first hand-written cube formula:

```
= CUBEVALUE("ThisWorkbookDataModel","[Measures].[Total Sales Amount]")
```

You probably noticed that the value you end up with after writing this cube formula is the grand total for all the data in the data model. It should therefore be clear that the data model is completely unfiltered. It is possible to filter this formula just like in a pivot table by adding some CUBEMEMBER() functions into the formula (sort of like adding a column to Rows in a pivot).

> **Note** Before moving on, you should rewrite the formula above a couple of times for practice. Remember that the most important keys on your keyboard in this process are double quotes, square brackets, and the period, along with Tab to select the highlighted selection. Practice the rhythm of writing these formulas using these keys on the keyboard.

Here's How: Applying Filters to Cube Formulas

To filter an existing formula, follow these steps:

1. Select one of the formulas you have already written and start to edit it.
2. Delete the last **)** and then type **,** (a comma). The tooltip asks for `member_expression2`.
3. Type **"[**.
4. Use the down arrow key to select `[Calendar]` then press Tab.
5. Type **.** (full stop/period) and use the down arrow to select `[CalendarYear]`. Then press Tab.
6. Type **.** (full stop/period) and notice that the tooltip offers only a single choice, `[All]`. Selecting `[All]` leaves the data model unfiltered. Instead of selecting `[All]`, type `&[2003]`. Notice that the tooltip doesn't prompt you here.
7. Finish the formula by typing **")** and pressing Enter.

This is the final formula:

```
= CUBEVALUE("ThisWorkbookDataModel","[Measures].[Total Sales Amount]",
  "[Calendar].[CalendarYear].&[2003]")
```

The `&` character tells Power Pivot that you are about to enter a value that exists in the column (also known as one of the _member children_). You must enter the value exactly as it appears in your table, or it won't work.

Go back into this formula again and delete the **)**, add another **,** (a comma), and then follow the same process as above to add another cube member, this time for `Products[Category] = "Clothing"`. This is the formula you need:

```
= CUBEVALUE("ThisWorkbookDataModel",
    "[Measures].[Total Sales Amount]",
    "[Calendar].[CalendarYear].&[2003]",
    "[Products].[Category].&[Clothing]"
  )
```

You can add any calculated field from your data model into your spreadsheet by writing a cube formula like this. You can further filter the calculated field in your cube formula by adding additional `CUBEMEMBER()` expressions inside the cube formula you are writing.

Here's How: Adding a Slicer Without a Pivot Table

Connecting your formulas to slicers is easy. You should have a slicer for `Customers[Occupation]` on the sheet. If you don't have this slicer, then go ahead and add it now. Here are the steps to add a slicer when there is no pivot table:

1. Select Insert, Slicer.

    Note In this case you can't right-click on a column in the Pivot Table Fields list because there is no pivot table.

2. In the Existing Connections dialog that appears, select the Data Model tab (see #1 below), select Tables in This Workbook (#2), and click Open (#3).

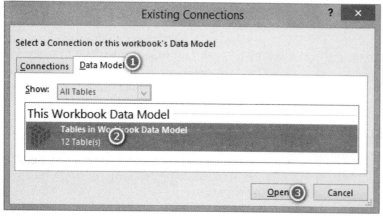

3.   Find the `Customers[Occupation]` slicer in the list, select the correct check box, and click OK.

You now have a slicer on your sheet, but it is not connected to your formula.

Here's How: Connecting a Slicer to a Cube Formula

Follow these steps to connect a slicer to a cube formula:

1.   Check the unique name for this slicer by right-clicking on the slicer and selecting Slicer Settings.

2.   In the Slicer Settings dialog that appears, note and memorise the value that appears in the second line in the dialog box, Name to Use in Formulas. You will need the name of the slicer in the next step. In my case it is called `Slicer_Occupation1`. In your case it may be called something different. Click Cancel.

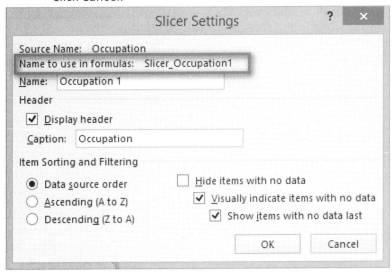

3.   Go back into the cube formula you were working on earlier and delete the last **)** and add **,** (a comma) followed by the slicer name from step 2 above and then type **)**.

Your formula should now look something like this (though your slicer may have a slightly different name):

```
= CUBEVALUE("ThisWorkbookDataModel",
    "[Measures].[Total Sales Amount]",
    "[Calendar].[CalendarYear].&[2003]",
    "[Products].[Category].&[Clothing]",
     Slicer_Occupation1
)
```

Note You do not use double quotes around slicer names. This is an unfortunate inconsistency, but it is just how it works.

Now test it out: Click on your slicer and watch your cube formula update.

Take a deep breath and be amazed. How cool are cube formulas?!

Writing CUBEMEMBER() Formulas

In addition to referencing a column name inside a `CUBEVALUE()` formula, it is possible to write a `CUBEMEMBER()` formula directly in a cell in your workbook. Here is an example of a `CUBEMEMBER()` formula:

```
= CUBEMEMBER("ThisWorkbookDataModel",
    "[Customers].[Occupation].&[Manual]"
)
```

You can see a lot more of these formulas if you go back to the original pivot table that you converted and click in the column and row headings. If you write a `CUBEMEMBER()` formula as a standalone formula in a cell, you can reference that cell from within your `CUBEVALUE()` formula by using cell references. Once again, you can see this by examining the formula in your converted pivot table.

19: Moving from Excel to Power BI

PowerBI.com is a relatively new service from Microsoft. If first became generally available in July 2015, after the first draft of this book was already completed. In just its first few monthly updates, the changes have been astonishing. There is no doubt that Excel users will increasingly want to use PowerBI.com as a tool to share workbooks and leverage the modern visualisations that are quickly becoming available.

This chapter provides the information you need to get started with Power BI. The good news is that all the skills you have learnt in this book are fully transferable to Power BI. Even better, writing DAX will help you get value from Power BI, and you already have skills in that area.

There are three tools that you need to know about to take advantage of Power BI: PowerBI.com, Power BI Desktop, and Power BI Mobile.

PowerBI.com

PowerBI.com is Microsoft's cloud-hosted solution. A free version allows you to upload 1 GB of workbooks and reports to the cloud and to share reports and dashboards with other people. There are some limitations to the free version, though, the main one being that you can only share individual reports with single visualisations via a dashboard. If you want to have anything more sophisticated, such as multiple visualisations on the same page that interact together, you need to purchase the subscription service.

At this writing, the PowerBI.com subscription costs US$9.99 per user per month. With this paid service, each user has access to 10 GB of online storage. At this price, the service is a bargain compared to the alternatives that exist.

> **Note** At this writing, even with the subscription, it is only possible to share reports and dashboards with other people in your organisation (i.e., those with the same email address domain). It is likely that Microsoft will loosen this requirement over time.

Power BI Desktop

Power BI Desktop is a free tool that you can download from PowerBI.com and use to author your own data models and reports locally on your PC. It is an incredible piece of software. It offers all the capabilities of Power Pivot and Power Query (Excel version) as well as all the visualisation capability of PowerBI.com, bundled up in a desktop tool that is completely free to download and use. You can import the data models from your Excel workbooks and create new reports, or you can create standalone data models and reporting tools from scratch. When you are done, you can simply keep using the reports natively on your PC, or you can upload the reports to PowerBI.com and share them with others from there.

Power BI Mobile

Power BI Mobile, as its name suggests, is a mobile app. It is available for Microsoft tablets and phones, Apple iPads and iPhones, and Android tablets and phones. The app is native to each individual device, which means the end user gets the best possible experience when looking at reports published at PowerBI.com. Power BI Mobile is used only to consume reports; at this time it cannot be used to author reports.

Differences Between Power BI and Excel 2010/2013

There are a couple of important differences between Power Pivot for Excel (2010/2013) and the Power BI version of Power Pivot:

- More than 20 new functions further enhance the DAX language. You can find out more about them by searching the web for "new DAX functions for Power BI."

- There is no longer a limitation requiring all relationships to be of the type "one to many." It is possible to edit relationships and change them to "one to one" or "many to many."

- It is possible to change the cross-filtering behaviour of relationships so that filters propagate from the "many" side of the relationship to the "one" side of the relationship. Put another way, with Power BI (and Excel 2016), it is possible to have filters propagate "uphill."

- Calculated fields have been renamed "measures" (as in Excel 2010 and 2016). Thankfully, only Excel 2013 used the term calculated fields.

The Power BI Desktop Relationships View

If you know how to use Power Pivot for Excel, using Power BI will be easy for you. As you can see in the image below, the Relationships view in Power BI is very similar to the Diagram view in Power Pivot.

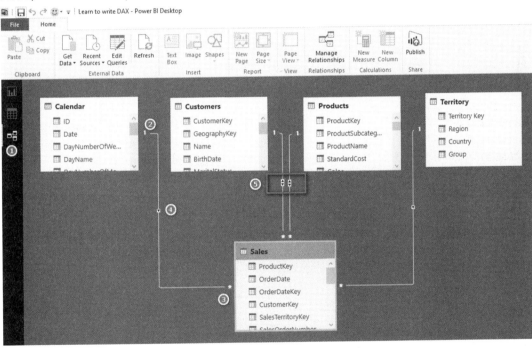

A few things are worth noting here:

- There is a menu on the left-hand side (see #1 above) that switches between Report, Data, and Relationship views.

- The relationship visualisations have been improved. For example, the "one" side of relationships is now indicated by a number 1 (#2), and the "many" side is indicated with an * (#3).

- The direction of filter propagation is now indicated with arrows (#4).

- When a filter is configured to work in both directions, there are arrows pointing in both directions (#5).

Here's How: Installing Power BI Desktop

To download Power BI Desktop, follow these steps:

1. Go to http://powerbi.com.

2. Select Products, Power BI Desktop.

3. Download and install Power BI Desktop on your PC.

Here's How: Importing Data to Power BI Desktop

Once you have Power BI Desktop installed on your PC, you're ready to import data into it. This process is very similar to importing data into Excel, and you can see in these steps:

1. Open Power BI Desktop.

2. If the startup page appears, dismiss it by clicking the x in the top-right corner.

3. Select Home, Get Data, More, Access Database.

4. Navigate to the AdventureWorks database you have been using throughout this book.

5. Import the first five items in the Navigator list (shown below).

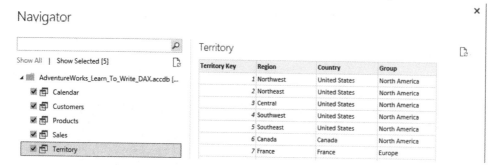

Here's How: Creating Relationships

The process for creating relationships in Power BI is the same as the process of creating relationships in Excel:

1. Switch to the Relationships view by clicking the Relationships icon on the left side of the screen.

2. Move the tables so they are laid out using the Collie layout methodology discussed in Chapter 2. Notice that two relationships have been automatically created, and they are both set to cross-filter in both directions. (You know this because of the double arrows pointing up and down.)

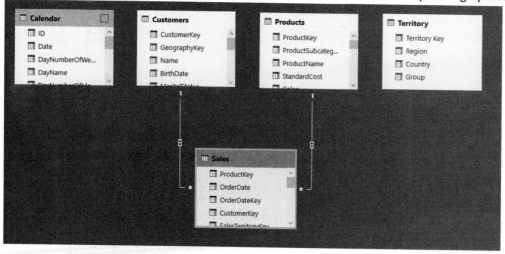

3. Double-click the relationship between the Customers table and the Sales table. The Edit Relationship dialog appears.

4. Click Advanced Options, and from the Cross Filter Direction drop-down, select Single.

Note You can change the relationship type (cardinality) and also the cross-filter direction in the Advanced Options dialog.

5.   Click OK to close the dialog.

6.   Create the relationships between the Sales table and the other two tables as you would do in Excel.

Here's How: Creating New Measures

The process of creating a new measure in Power BI Desktop is almost identical to the process of creating calculated fields in Power Pivot for Excel 2013. You can write measures from either the Report view or the Data view, just as in Excel. Follow these steps to create a new measure (and notice that it's the same approach you have used elsewhere in this book):

1.   Navigate to the Report view.

2.   On the right side of the screen, go to the Visualizations section (see #1 below) and click the Matrix icon (#2). Power BI adds a new matrix visualisation object on the report canvas on the left (#3). A matrix is similar to a pivot table.

3.   Select the matrix on the report canvas (#3 above).

4.   On the right side of the screen, open the Products table (see #1 below) and place a check mark in Category from the list of columns (#2). Power BI adds the Product[Category] column to the Matrix, just as would happen in Excel.

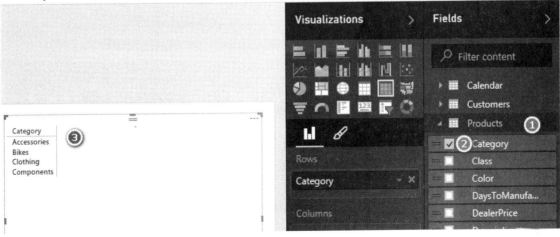

5.   From the Fields list on the right side, select the Sales table to ensure that the new measure you are about to write is placed in the Sales table.

6.   On the ribbon at the top of the page, click New Measure.

7. Write the [Total Sales] measure as shown below and press Enter. (Note that with Power BI, you need to specify the name of the measure and the formula in the formula bar as shown below.)

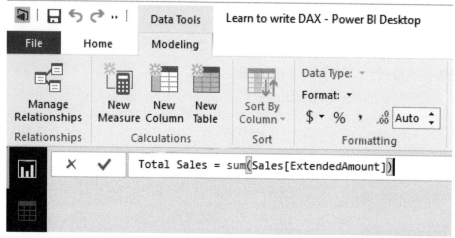

Note There are some significant improvements in the Power BI user interface over the Excel interface, including the following:

- You do not have to place a colon before the equal sign as you do if you write the formula in the Power Pivot widow in Excel 2013.

- You can type the name of a column, and Power BI automatically prepends the table name to the front of column name.

- There is improved IntelliSense, including formula highlighting and bracket matching.

8. After you have finished writing the measure, select the matrix on the canvas and then place a check mark next to the new measure called [Total Sales] that appears in the Sales table on the right. Power BI places the measure into the matrix.

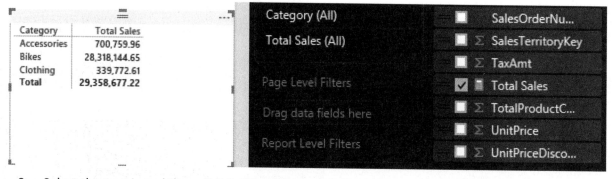

9. Select the matrix and then click the Tree Map visualisation from the visualisations list.

10. Open the Products table in the Fields list on the right side.

11. Remove the check mark from Category and place a check mark next to SubCategory.

12. On the Report Canvas, resize the tree map so that it takes up the full screen, as shown below.

Note The tree map is one of many new visualisations that are available in Power BI. The items in a tree map are sorted from largest to smallest, left to right. The boxes are proportional to the relative size of each item.

Here's How: Publish Your Report to PowerBI.com

Follow these steps to publish a report to PowerBI.com:

1. Save the Power BI workbook. Note that it is saved with a PBIX extension.
2. Click the Publish button in the menu at the top of the page. The first time you use PowerBI.com, you are prompted to create an account.

3. If you don't yet have an account, click Need a Power BI Account? and follow the instructions to set up the account. If you do have an account, just sign in with your credentials. You will get a success message once the file has been loaded to PowerBI.com.
4. In a browser, navigate to http://powerbi.com and click the sign-in link in the top-right corner of the website.
5. Sign in with the same credentials you used in step 3. You will find your data model under Datasets and the tree map in the Reports section.

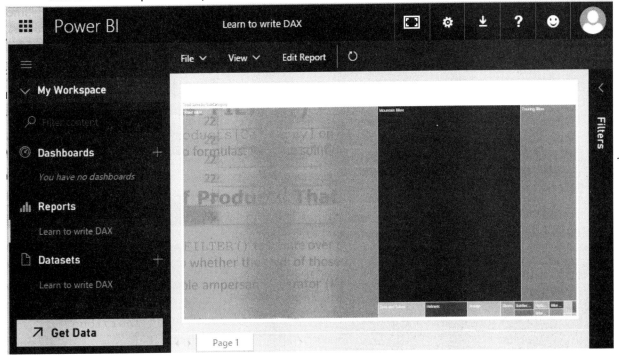

Here's How: Importing Excel Power Pivot Workbooks to Power BI Desktop

It is possible to import a Power Pivot workbook from Excel into Power BI Desktop, along with all the data connections, relationships, and measures. Unfortunately, any reports you have created in Excel will not be migrated and will need to be re-created in Power BI.

> **Note** It is possible to load an Excel Power Pivot workbook into Microsoft OneDrive for Business, synchronise the workbook to Power BI, and display the Excel workbook. You can read about this at http://xbi.com.au/XLPBI.

Follow these steps to import a Power Pivot workbook from Excel into Power BI Desktop:

1. In Power BI Desktop, select File, New.
2. In the new blank Power BI file, click File, Import, Excel Workbook Contents.

3. Navigate to the workbook you have created, click OK, and then select Import.
4. When you get the choice to copy the data from your queries or keep the connection (shown below), select Keep Connection.

✕

Import Excel Workbook Contents

There are queries and Data Model tables that depend on the following worksheet tables in the original workbook:

- Hemisphere

- Increase

- YearTable

Do you want to copy the data from those tables to your Power BI Desktop file or keep a connection to the original Excel workbook for this data?

| Copy Data | Keep Connection | Cancel |

The Excel workbook is then imported into Power BI Desktop. From there you can proceed to use Power BI Desktop instead of Excel and build your own visualisations on top of the Power Pivot data model.

> **Note** Power BI Desktop doesn't include the concept of linked tables. When you import into Power BI Desktop an Excel workbook that contains linked tables, you can either bring the data in as a one-off migration or retain the link to the original linked table in the original Excel workbook.

20: Next Steps on Your DAX Journey

Okay, so you have almost finished reading all the chapters of this book. Now what? First of all, let me assure you that this is just the start, not the end, of your journey to learning to write DAX. As I have been saying all through the book, the most important thing is to practice, practice, practice. Start using your new skills at work and at play so that you build your depth of skill and knowledge. It will take you many months of using your new skills before you become an expert, but you are well on your way already. Now that you have a basic understanding of Power Pivot, you can incrementally learn and improve over time. But there are some things that will help you learn more and faster.

Third-Person Learning

I am a big believer in "third-person learning." I first heard of this term from Stephen Covey, at one of his seminars. The basic idea is that you learn more when you learn with the intent to teach others, and you learn more from the process of teaching others. For this reason, I really believe in the benefits of participating in user forums. As I mentioned at the start of the book, I have set up a forum at http://powerpivotforum.com. au, and it is free for anyone and everyone to ask questions and also to help others. If you want to really cement your new skills and knowledge, then sign up and ask for help, and, more importantly, answer questions and help others on the forum. When you help others, you cement your knowledge and become better and stronger with your DAX.

Blogs

There are a number of Power Pivot blogs that I recommend you subscribe to. Reading blogs is a great way to keep in touch with the latest thinking from people who spend their life working with Power Pivot. Here are some that I think are especially useful:

My blog:	http://xbi.com.au/blog
Rob Collie's blog:	http://powerpivotpro.com
Scott Senkeresty's blog:	http://tinylizard.com
Marco Russo and Alberto Ferrari's blog:	http://sqlbi.com

Books

There are a few really good DAX books that I recommend (and have mentioned previously). These are my favourites:

Rob Collie's DAX Formulas for Power Pivot: The Excel Pro's Guide to Mastering DAX

From Amazon	http://xbi.com.au/DAXFormulas
Australian customers	http://xbi.com.au/books

Alberto Ferrari and Marco Russo's Microsoft Excel 2013: Building Data Models with PowerPivot

From Amazon	http://xbi.com.au/TheItalians
Australian customers	http://xbi.com.au/books

Other Books

I keep a list of books I recommend on my website and update it over time. You can always find an updated list at http://xbi.com.au/books.

Live Training

Some people learn best in a class environment. If this sounds like you, you can attend a live training event in a location suitable for you. My company, Excelerator BI, offers live training courses in Australia. For details about upcoming events, see http://xbi.com.au/training.

If you are in the United States, I recommend that you take a look at Rob Collie's live offerings. For information, see http://powerpivotpro.com.

There are many great things about these training courses, but one super benefit is that both Rob and I teach Power Pivot using the same techniques I have used in this book. By attending one of our live training courses, you will continue to learn using the same methodology you have used in this book.

Other Great "Power" Tools

At this writing, there are three other great "Power" tools that I simply love. If you don't know about these already, you should take a look at the links below.

Power Query

Power Query is a desktop ETL (extract, transform, and load) tool for Excel users. It allows you to connect to data from anywhere, change the shape of that data, and then load it into your workbooks. Once the data is loaded with Power Query, you can easily refresh the link at any time and bring in the latest updated data.

I often blog about Power Query at http://xbi.com.au/blog, and you can also get great information from these websites and books:

- Ken Puls' blog: http://www.excelguru.ca/blog/
- Chris Webb's blog: http://blog.crossjoin.co.uk/
- Chris Webb's book *Power Query for Power BI and Excel*: http://xbi.com.au/ChrisWebbBook
- Power Query Online Training: http://xbi.com.au/PQOT
- Power Query Live Training: http://xbi.com.au/PQLT
- Ken Puls & Miguel Escobar's book *M is for Data Monkey*: http://xbi.com.au/DataMonkey

Power Update

Power Update is a third-party application available for purchase that significantly enhances the process of refreshing Power Pivot workbooks. Power Update allows you to:

- Schedule a single workbook (or a folder of workbooks) to refresh at the optimum time of day.
- Automatically deploy the updated workbooks to anywhere after they are refreshed.
- Run any VBA code before and/or after auto refresh to complete any unique task.

In addition, Power Update works with Power Query, unlike SharePoint.

You can find more information about Power Update at http://xbi.com.au/update.

Power Planner

Power Planner is a third-party add-in for Excel that does something truly amazing: It allows you to directly edit the values inside a pivot table and then save those values back to your data model. This is a very powerful concept that can be used for any number of purposes and is particularly helpful with budgeting, forecasting, and what-if analysis. You can simply load your actual data into your data model, make a copy and name it Budget, and then tweak the values directly in the pivot table to modify the budget or forecast. These changes are stored back to your database, and then you can compare the actuals with the budget and/or forecast.

You have to see it to believe it. See a demo at http://xbi.com.au/planner.

That's All, Folks

I hope you have enjoyed this book and that it has successfully started you on your journey to becoming a DAX superstar. If you liked this book, please tell your Excel friends and colleagues so they, too, can become DAX superstars.

Appendix A: Answers to Practice Exercises

This appendix provides the answers to the practice exercises scattered throughout the book. The answers are in the same order the exercises appear in the book and are numbered so you can easily match up the exercises and the answers.

A. SUM()

These practice exercises appear in Chapter 4. Did you remember to put your calculated fields in the correct table? Did you put the calculated field in the table where the data comes from? Did you format with an appropriate number format?

1. `[Total Sales Amount] = SUM(Sales[ExtendedAmount])`
   or `[Total Sales Amount] = SUM(Sales[SalesAmount])`
2. `[Total Cost Value] = SUM(Sales[TotalProductCost])`
   or `[Total Cost Value] = SUM(Sales[ProductStandardCost])`
3. `[Total Margin $]`
   `    = [Total Sales Value] – [Total Cost Value]`
4. `[Total Margin %] = [Total Margin $] / [Total Sales Value]` **or** `[Total Margin %]`
   `    = DIVIDE([Total Margin $] , [Total Sales Value])`
5. `[Total Sales Tax Paid] = SUM(Sales[SalesTax])`
6. `[Total Sales Including Tax]`
   `    = [Total Sales Value] + [Total Sales Tax]`
7. `[Total Order Quantity] = SUM(Sales[OrderQuantity])`

B. COUNT()

These practice exercises appear in Chapter 4.

8. `[Total Number of Products] = COUNT(Products[ProductKey])`
9. `[Total Number of Customers]`
   `    = COUNT(Customers[CustomerKey])`

Note Counting the "key" columns is generally pretty safe because, by definition, each one must have a value. Technically, you can count any column that has a numeric value in each cell, and you will get the same answer. Just be careful if you are counting a numeric column that may have blank values: COUNT () will not count blanks.

C. COUNTROWS()

These practice exercises appear in Chapter 4.

Note Remember that COUNTROWS () takes a table, not a column, as input.

10. `[Total Number of Products COUNTROWS Version]`
    `    = COUNTROWS(Products)`
11. `[Total Number of Customers COUNTROWS Version]`
    `    = COUNTROWS(Customers)`

D. DISTINCTCOUNT()

These practice exercises appear in Chapter 4.

12. `[Total Customers in Database Distinctcount Version]`
    `    = DISTINCTCOUNT(Customers[CustomerKey])`

13. [Count of Occupation]
        = DISTINCTCOUNT(Customers[Occupation])
14. [Count of Country] = DISTINCTCOUNT(Territories[Country])
15. [Customers That Have Purchased]
        = DISTINCTCOUNT(Sales[CustomerKey])

E.   MAX(), MIN(), and AVERAGE()

These practice exercises appear in Chapter 4.

16. [Maximum Tax Paid on a Product] = MAX(Sales[TaxAmt])
17. [Minimum Price Paid for a Product]
        = MIN(Sales[ExtendedAmount])
18. [Average Price Paid for a Product]
        = AVERAGE(Sales[ExtendedAmount])

F.   COUNTBLANK()

These practice exercises appear in Chapter 4.

19. [Customers Without Address Line 2]
        = COUNTBLANK(Customers[AddressLine2])
20. [Products Without Weight Values]
        = COUNTBLANK(Products[Weight])

G.   DIVIDE()

These practice exercises appear in Chapter 4.

21. [Margin %]
        = DIVIDE([Total Margin $] , [Total Sales Amount])
22. [Markup %]
        = DIVIDE([Total Margin $] ,
        [Total Cost Value])
23. [Tax %]
        = DIVIDE(SUM(Sales[TaxAmt]) ,
        [Total Sales Amount])

H.   SUMX()

These practice exercises appear in Chapter 6.

24. [Total Sales SUMX Version]
        = SUMX(Sales, Sales[OrderQuantity] * Sales[UnitPrice])

Note In this sample database, the order quantity is always 1.

25. [Total Sales Including Tax SUMX Version]
        = SUMX(Sales,Sales[ExtendedAmount] + Sales[TaxAmt])
26. [Total Sales Including Freight]
        = SUMX(Sales,Sales[ExtendedAmount] + Sales[Freight])
27. [Dealer Margin]
        = SUMX (Products,Products[ListPrice] -
        Products[DealerPrice])

I.   AVERAGEX()

These practice exercises appear in Chapter 6.

28. ```
    [Average Sell Price per Item]
       = AVERAGEX(Sales, Sales[OrderQuantity]
       * Sales[UnitPrice])
    ```

29. `[Average Tax Paid] = AVERAGEX(Sales, Sales[TaxAmt])`

   Note how the expression can be a single column. It doesn't have to be an equation using multiple columns.

30. ```
    [Average Safety Stock] =
          AVERAGEX(Products,
          Products[SafetyStockLevel])
    ```

J.   Calculated Columns

This practice exercise appears in Chapter 7.

31. ```
    = IF(OR(Calendar[CalendarQuarter]=1,
          Calendar[CalendarQuarter]=2),"H1","H2")
    ```

   Note There are a number of ways to write this calculated column. If yours is different but works, then all is well and good.

K.   CALCULATE() with a Single Table

These practice exercises appear in Chapter 8.

32. ```
    [Total Male Customers]
       = CALCULATE([Total number of Customers],
       Customers[Gender] = "M")
    ```

33. ```
    [Total Customers Born Before 1950]
       = CALCULATE([Total number of Customers],
       Customers[BirthDate] <DATE(1950,1,1))
    ```

34. ```
    [Total Customers Born in January]
       = CALCULATE([Total number of Customers],
       MONTH(Customers[BirthDate])=1)
    ```

35. ```
    [Customers Earning at Least $100,000 per Year]
       = CALCULATE([Total number of Customers],
       Customers[YearlyIncome]>=100000)
    ```

L.   CALCULATE() with Multiple Tables

These practice exercises appear in Chapter 8.

36. ```
    [Total Sales of Clothing]
       = CALCULATE([Total Sales Amount],
       Products[Category]="Clothing")
    ```

37. ```
    [Sales to Female Customers]
       = CALCULATE([Total Sales Amount],
       Customers[Gender]="F")
    ```
    ```

38. [Sales of Bikes to Married Men]
    = CALCULATE([Total Sales Amount],
    Customers[MaritalStatus]="M",
    Customers[Gender]="M",
    Products[Category]="Bikes")

M. VALUES()

These practice exercises appear in Chapter 11.

39. [Number of Color Variants]
    = COUNTROWS(VALUES(Products[Color]))

40. [Number of Sub Categories]
    = COUNTROWS(VALUES(Products[SubCategory]))

41. [Number of Size Ranges]
    = COUNTROWS(VALUES(Products[SizeRange]))

42. [Product Category (Values)]
    = IF(HASONEVALUE(Products[Category]),
    VALUES(Products[Category])
)

43. [Product Subcategory (Values)]
    = IF(HASONEVALUE(Products[SubCategory]),
    VALUES(Products[SubCategory])
)

44. [Product Color (Values)]
    = IF(HASONEVALUE(Products[color]),
    VALUES(Products[color])
)

45. [Product Subcategory (Values) edited]
    = IF(HASONEVALUE(Products[SubCategory]),
    VALUES(Products[SubCategory]),"More than 1 Sub Cat"
)

46. [Product Color (Values) edited]
    = IF(HASONEVALUE(Products[color]),
    VALUES(Products[color]),"More than 1 Color"
)

N. ALL(), ALLEXCEPT(), and ALLSELECTED()

These practice exercises appear in Chapter 12.

47. [Total Sales to All Customers]
    = CALCULATE([Total Sales Amount] , All(Customers))

Note This calculated field belongs in the Sales table, not the Customers table.

48. [% of All Customer Sales]
    = DIVIDE([Total Sales Amount] ,
    [Total Sales to All Customers])

49. [Total Sales to Selected Customers]
    = CALCULATE([Total Sales Amount] ,
    ALLSELECTED(Customers))

50. [% of Sales to Selected Customers]
      = DIVIDE([Total Sales Amount] ,
      [Total Sales to Selected Customers])

51. [Total Sales for All Days Selected Dates]
      = CALCULATE([Total Sales Amount] ,
      ALLSELECTED(Calendar))

Note Did you know to use ALLSELECTED() and not ALLEXCEPT()?

52. [% Sales for All Days Selected Dates] =
      DIVIDE([Total Sales Amount] ,
      [Total Sales for All Days Selected Dates])

This is what your pivot table should look like:

MonthName

January	February	March	April
May	June	July	August
September	October	November	December

CalendarYear

2001
2002
2003
2004

Row Labels	Total Sales Amount	Total Sales for Day Selected Dates	% Sales for Day Selected Dates
Sunday	$2,321,342	$16,321,404	14.2%
Monday	$2,279,220	$16,321,404	14.0%
Tuesday	$2,315,978	$16,321,404	14.2%
Wednesday	$2,391,460	$16,321,404	14.7%
Thursday	$2,349,082	$16,321,404	14.4%
Friday	$2,307,355	$16,321,404	14.1%
Saturday	$2,356,967	$16,321,404	14.4%
Grand Total	**$16,321,404**	**$16,321,404**	**100.0%**

53. [Total Orders All Customers]
      = CALCULATE([Total Order Quantity] , ALL(Customers))

54. [Baseline Orders for All Customers with This Occupation]
      = CALCULATE([Total Order Quantity] ,
      ALLEXCEPT(Customers, Customers[Occupation]))

55. [Baseline % This Occupation of All Customer Orders]
      = DIVIDE([Baseline Orders for All customers with this
      Occupation] , [Total Orders All Customers])

56. [Total Orders Selected Customers]
      = CALCULATE([Total Order Quantity] ,
      ALLSELECTED(Customers))

57. [Occupation % of Selected Customers]
      = DIVIDE([Total Order Quantity] ,
      [Total Orders Selected Customers])

58. [Percentage Point Variation to Baseline]
      = [Occupation % of Selected Customers] -
      [Baseline % this Occupation is of All Customer Orders]

O. FILTER()

These practice exercises appear in Chapter 13.

59. ```
    [Total Sales of Products That Have Some Sales
         but Less Than $10,000]
         = CALCULATE([Total Sales Amount],
         FILTER(Products, [Total Sales Amount]
         <=10000 && [Total Sales Amount] >0))
    ```

60. ```
    [Count of Products That Have Some Sales
         but Less Than $10,000]
         = CALCULATE(COUNTROWS(Products),
         FILTER(Products, [Total Sales Amount]
         <=10000 && [Total Sales Amount] >0))
    ```

P. Time Intelligence

These practice exercises appear in Chapter 14.

61. ```
    [Total Sales Month to Date]
         = TOTALMTD([Total Sales Amount], Calendar[Date])
    ```

62. ```
    [Total Sales Quarter to Date]
         = TOTALQTD([Total Sales Amount], Calendar[Date])
    ```

Note Did you set up your pivot table correctly? Something like this would be appropriate for QTD:

CalendarYear	2003	
Row Labels	Total Sales Amount	Total Sales QTD
January	$438,865	$438,865
February	$489,090	$927,956
March	$485,575	$1,413,530
April	$506,399	$506,399
May	$562,773	$1,069,172
June	$554,799	$1,623,971
July	$886,669	$886,669
August	$847,414	$1,734,082
September	$1,010,258	$2,744,340
October	$1,080,450	$1,080,450
November	$1,196,981	$2,277,431
December	$1,731,788	$4,009,218
Grand Total	$9,791,060	$4,009,218

Conditional formatting is good because it gives immediate feedback about whether things are working as expected.

63. ```
    [Total Sales FYTD 30 June]
         = TOTALYTD([Total Sales Amount],Calendar[Date],"30/6")
    ```

64. ```
    [Total Sales FYTD 31 March]
         = TOTALYTD([Total Sales Amount],Calendar[Date],"31/3")[Total
    Sales Previous Month]
         = CALCULATE([Total Sales Amount],
         PREVIOUSMONTH(Calendar[Date])
    )
    ```

65. [Total Sales Previous Day]
```
    = CALCULATE([Total Sales Amount],
      PREVIOUSDAY(Calendar[Date])
)
```

66. [Total Sales Previous Quarter]
```
    = CALCULATE([Total Sales Amount],
      PREVIOUSQUARTER(Calendar[Date])
)
```

[Total Sales Moving Annual Total]
```
    = CALCULATE([Total Sales Amount],
      FILTER(ALL(Calendar),
        Calendar[ID] > MAX(Calendar[ID]) - 365 &&
        Calendar[ID] <= MAX(Calendar[ID])
      )
)
```

[Total Sales Rolling 90 Days]
```
    = if(MAX(Calendar[ID])>=90,
        CALCULATE([Total Sales Amount],
          FILTER(ALL(Calendar),
            Calendar[ID] > MAX(Calendar[ID]) - 90 &&
            Calendar[ID] <= MAX(Calendar[ID])
          )
        )
)
```

Q. Harvester Calculated Fields

This practice exercise appears in Chapter 16.

1. [Total Customers Born Before Selected Year]
```
    = CALCULATE (
    [Total number of Customers],
    FILTER (
        Customers,
        Customers[BirthDate] < DATE ( [Selected Year], 1, 1 )
    )
)
```

R. KPIs

These practice exercises appear in Chapter 17.

1. [Total Budget] = SUM(Budget[Budget])

This calculated field should be placed in the Budget table.

2. [Change in Sales vs. Budget]
```
    = [Total Sales Amount] - [Total Budget]
```
This calculated field could be placed in either the Sales table or the Budget table. I normally place it in the Sales table because the name of the calculated field is [Change in Sales vs. Budget].

3. [% Change in Sales vs. Budget]
```
    = DIVIDE([Change in Sales vs Budget] , [Total Budget])
```
Also place this calculate field in the Sales table.

Index

Symbols

445 Calendar 113
% of Grand Total 92
&& operator 107

A

Active learning vi
Add-ins manager 5
AdventureWorks 1
  Loading 5
Aggregation functions 34
Aggregators
  versus X-functions 59
ALL 90
  Passing column 95
  with CALCULATE 91
ALLEXCEPT 95
ALLSELECTED 96
Anchovies 69
Answers 175
Avoiding redundant data 62

B

Banding 144
BLANK
  Result of IF 86
Blogs 173
Budget vs actuals 152

C

Caesar salad 69
CALCULATE 69
  Invisible 109
  using FILTER 106
  with ALL 91
  with multiple tables 72
  With no filters 79
Calculated columns 62, 66
  For filtering 66
  Row context 78
Calculated field
  Moving to other table 48
Calculated field dialog 25
Calculated fields 24
  added automatically 48
  Reusing 35
  Versus columns 62
Calculation area 25
Calendars, Non-standard 113
Calendar table 113
Changing file location 19
Changing load properties 15
Choosing a schema 13
Collie layout methodology 14
Collie, Rob v, 41, 69, 139
COM Add-ins dialog 6

Compression due to unique values
  60
CONCATENATEX 86
Concepts
  Calculated Fields 24
  Cube formulas 160
  Disconnected tables 139
  Evaluation context 76
  Filter propagation 51
  Filter propogation 51
  KPIs 149
  Loading data 5
  Multiple data tables 149
  Pivot tables versus Power Pivot 3
Conditional formatting 42
Context transition 79
Contiguous date range 113
COUNT 37
COUNTROWS 39
Covey, Stephen 173
Creating relationships 11
Cube formulas 160
CUBEMEMBER 165
CUBEVALUE 162
Custom name 41

D

Data Cube 3
Data Modelling 3
Data tables 15
Data view 9
DATE 70
DATEADD 131
Date table 114
DAX
  Researching 131
  Troubleshooting 32
DAX Formatter 74
DAX Topic
  All 90
  AllExcept 90
  AllSelected 90
  AVERAGEX 57
  Calculate 69
  Calculated columns 66
  Count 34
  CountBlank 34
  Countrows 34
  Divide 34
  Filter 103
  Find 80
  HasOneValue 83
  If 80
  Max, Min 34
  RELATED 135
  RELATEDTABLE 135
  Sum 34
  SUMX 57
  Switch 80

Time intelligence 112
  Values 83
Debugging filters 54
Deleting interim columns 148
Dimension is lookup 8
Disconnected tables 139
Display name 40
DISTINCTCOUNT 41
DIVIDE 50
Double ampersand operator 107

E

Easy to read 73
Editing calculated fields 31
Errors
  preventing DIV/0 50
Exercise data 1
Exercises
  ALL 97
  ALLEXCEPT 97
  ALLSELECTED 97
  Answers 175
  AVERAGE 47
  AVERAGEX 65
  Calculated columns 68
  CALCULATE w/ multiple tables 72
  CALCULATE w/ single table 70
  COUNT 38
  COUNTBLANK 48
  COUNTROWS 39
  DISTINCTCOUNT 41, 45
  DIVIDE 50
  FILTER 107
  Harvester field 142
  MAX 47
  MIN 47
  SUM 36
  SUMX 58
  Time intelligence 119
  VALUES 88
Existing connection
  Adding tables 17
External data source 22

F

Fact is data 8
Ferrari, Alberto 60, 74
File location, changing 19
Filter context 52
  ignoring 91
  Whole table 121
FILTER function 103
Filter propagation 51
  Downhill only 55
  with FILTER and CALCULATE
    108
Filters
  Advanced 73
  Advanced with ALL 91

Simple 69
  With cube formulas 164
Financial year 120
FIND 80
FIRSTDATE 132
Fiscal year 120
Flow of filter 52
Formatting DAX 73
Forum 1, 173
Friendly name for views 8

G

GETPIVOTDATA 160
Granularity, different 152

H

Half year 68
Harvester fields 139
HASONEVALUE 61
Hide from client 137

I

Icons
  tables versus views 8
Icon sets 149
ID column
  for custom calendars 122
IF 80
  defaults to BLANK() 86
Implicit CALCULATE 109
Implicit calculated fields 28
Importing
  from existing connection 17
Incremental learning v
Initial filter context 51
  Ignoring 91
Inserting new pivot table 21
IntelliSense 28
Interim calculated fields 94
Invisible CALCULATE 109
Iterators 57
  to fix totals 60

J

Jelen, Bill v
Joining tables 11

K

Key performance indicators 149
KPI's 149

L

Lifetime customer purchases 106
Linked table 136
Loading data 5
Lookup tables 14

M

Manage calculated fields 31
Manually adding field 48

Mark as Date Table 114
MAX 123
MIN 123
More readable pivots 41
Moving annual total 129
MSDN 131

N

Naked columns 34
  in X-functions 57
Naming convention 40
Naming conventions 2

O

OR 67

P

Percentage of total
  Using ALL 92
Pivot Table
  Defined 3
  Inserting new 21
  Setting up viii
  ugly format 160
Power BI 166
  Desktop 166
  Importing data 168
  Measures 169
  Mobile 166
  Relationships 167
Power Pivot
  downloading for 2010 6
Powerpivotforum.com.au 1
PREVIOUSDAY 120
Previously loaded data
  Changing properties 15
PREVIOUSMONTH 120
PREVIOUSYEAR 120
Prior year sales 115

R

Reading filter context 52
Redundant data 62
RELATED 135
RELATEDTABLE 135, 138
Relationships
  Creating 11
  May be needed 56
Remove filters 90
Retail calendar 113
Returning single value 86
Reusing calculated fields 35
Rolling total 129
ROUNDDOWN 145
Row context 57
  versus Filter context 78
  with FILTER 104
Russo, Marco 60, 74

S

SAMEPERIODLASTYEAR 115
Sample data 1
Save icon 12
Schema
  Choosing 13
Select Case 80
Shaping data 12
Single Value
  Returning 86
Slicers 98
  With cube formulas 165
Snowflake schema 13
Sort by column 87
SQLBI.com 62
SQL Server Analysis Services 3
Star schema 13
SUM 28
  versus SUMX 60
SUMX 57
SWITCH 80
Switching to Power Pivot 7

T

Table Properties 15
Taskbar 6
Territories 136
Time intelligence 112
  Custom example 124
  Write your own 121
TOTALMTD 119
TOTALQTD 119
Totals don't add up 60

U

Unique values and compression 60

V

VALUES 83
  Returning single value 86
VBA
  How to use 41
Views
  Friendly name 8
Virtual tables 83
VLOOKUP
  versus relationships 10

W

Weekend calculation 66
Writing calculated fields 26

X

X-functions 57
  versus Aggregators 59

Y

Year-ending date 120
Year-over-year sales 116

Continue the Journey

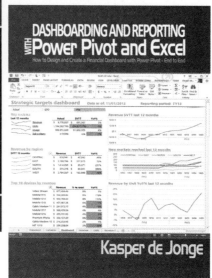

Sharpen your
Power Pivot, Power Map,
Power Map, and Excel
skills with books from
leading authors.